Australia's Money Mandarins

For most of its life the Reserve Bank of Australia (RBA) has led a fairly conservative existence. However, since the early 1980s the economy has experienced financial and market deregulation and general economic liberalisation. The RBA has been caught up with the turbulent policy debates that have ensued.

Australia's Money Mandarins tells the story of the RBA over the past two decades. It discusses how the Bank operated in the new political environment created by deregulation and the fight against inflation. It describes the conflicts with the government and the Department of Treasury, and how the Bank dealt with the rough and tumble of politics and managed to assert a level of independence in the 1990s. Including frank interviews with key figures like Bob Johnston, Bernie Fraser, Ian Macfarlane and Paul Keating, this book will appeal to anyone with an interest in the politics of money.

Stephen Bell is an Associate Professor in the School of Political Science and International Studies, University of Queensland.

T0345619

Australia's Money Mandarins

The Reserve Bank
and the Politics of Money

STEPHEN BELL

CAMBRIDGE
UNIVERSITY PRESS

CAMBRIDGE UNIVERSITY PRESS
Cambridge, New York, Melbourne, Madrid, Cape Town,
Singapore, São Paulo, Delhi, Tokyo, Mexico City

Cambridge University Press
The Edinburgh Building, Cambridge CB2 8RU, UK

Published in the United States of America by Cambridge University Press, New York

www.cambridge.org
Information on this title: www.cambridge.org/9780521839907

First published 2004

A catalogue record for this publication is available from the British Library

National Library of Australia Cataloguing in Publication Data

Bell, Stephen, 1954– .
    Australia's money mandarins: the Reserve Bank and the politics of money.
    Bibliography.
    Includes index.
    ISBN 0 521 83990 4.
    1. Reserve Bank of Australia. 2. Australia – Economic policy – 1965– .
    3. Australia – Economic conditions – 1965– . I. Title.
330.994

ISBN 978-0-521-83990-7 Hardback
ISBN 978-0-521-68989-2 Paperback

Contents

Illustrations

Preface

This book has emerged from my earlier work on the politics of economic policy in Australia, in which I learnt that the Reserve Bank of Australia, especially since financial market deregulation in the 1980s, had become one of the most powerful and significant policy institutions in the country. Yet it had received surprisingly little attention from researchers, and there were few studies of the politics of central banking and monetary policy in Australia.

Central banks now have a great deal of clout in macroeconomic policy. They essentially control monetary policy, which, these days, means controlling the price of money in short-term markets. They also stand at a critical interface between states and financial markets, and between governments and voters. The ways in which central banks operate and manoeuvre in these settings offer rich pickings for political analysis.

There are two main stories in this book. One is about the politics of monetary policy since financial deregulation in the early 1980s – the period in which the Reserve Bank rose to prominence, crunched inflation in the early 1990s recession, and has since presided over an economy featuring low inflation and relatively strong growth. How and why did this pattern of policy emerge? The second story is about the increasing independence of Australia's central bank. How and why did governments pass so much authority to the RBA, and how can such an outcome be justified in a democracy?

Books on the RBA (or its forerunner the Commonwealth Bank of Australia) describe the early history of central banking and the post-war rise of the RBA. The main contribution, especially for the post-war period, is Boris Schedvin's official economic history of the Bank, which covers the period 1945–75. Joan Linklater's *Inside the Bank* mainly deals with the RBA's internal policy and administrative practices. From a political perspective, the main work is Chris Eichbaum's PhD thesis, which provides a useful comparative analysis of

Australian and New Zealand central banking, although only three and a half chapters are devoted to the RBA.

Central banking has traditionally been a secretive world, and it is still the case that most practices, policy-making and power plays occur behind closed doors and are only scantily documented. It was only in the 1990s that the Bank became more forthcoming about its policies, but still most of the politics behind policy, the Bank's relations with the government, and certainly, the deliberations of the Bank's Board, are either secret or difficult to scrutinise directly. Indeed, the Board does not release minutes and the Bank's archives have a 15-year limit on access. I established, by examining the material available in the Bank's archives, that there was not much documentation of the policy machinations and relationships between the Bank and the government.

Hence, the best way to answer the questions posed in this book was to talk to the insiders. I have relied heavily on detailed interviews and correspondence with the major players – all of the Bank's Governors during the relevant period and key respondents in government, including Treasurer (later Prime Minister) Paul Keating. I warmly thank those who agreed to be interviewed. Their names appear in the pages that follow.

One final reason for the writing of this book was my repeated encounters with the abstract formal models of central bank behaviour and relations with government found in economics and economics-inspired 'political economy' literature. This lifeless mode of deductive analysis starts with *a priori* assumptions about preferences, motivations and institutional settings and derives formal models of central banking politics.

Generally speaking, the assumptions about preferences and the institutional analysis in the models are simplistic. The models also say little about the changing historical context in which central banks operate, especially in relation to the discipline that financial markets now exert on policy.

Rather than making assumptions, a better way to understand the politics of central banking is to observe a central bank through time. Given the closed nature of most of the proceedings and interactions, the best way to do this is again to talk to the key players and analyse insider accounts of events.

I would also like to warmly thank those who took the time to read and comment on parts, or in some cases all, of the manuscript: Chris Eichbaum, Bernie Fraser, Simon Guttmann, Ian Macfarlane, Peter Jonson, Bob Johnston, Ross Gittins, John Quiggin, David Emanuel, Fred Argy, Warwick McKibbin, John Edwards, and Michael Keating. Any remaining errors or inaccuracies remain my responsibility.

Chapter 9 draws on a paper that I wrote jointly with John Quiggin, entitled 'Asset Bubbles, Financial Instability and Policy Responses: The Legacy of Liberalisation'.

Thanks also to the Australian Research Council for generous funding support for this project, and to Peter Debus at Cambridge University Press for his support in publishing this work. I would like to thank the School of Political Science and International Studies at the University of Queensland for providing a supportive research environment. I especially thank Jill McTaggart for her patience and unstinting efforts as a research assistant. Thanks also, as always, to Jo and Hillary for their love and support.

Stephen Bell
December 2003

Abbreviations

ACTU	Australian Council of Trade Unions
APRA	Australian Prudential Regulation Authority
BIS	Bank of International Settlements
CAD	current account deficit
CBA	Commonwealth Bank of Australia
CBI	central bank independence
CPI	consumer price index
GDP	gross domestic product
GST	goods and services tax
IMF	International Monetary Fund
NAIRU	non-accelerating inflation rate of unemployment
OECD	Organization for Economic Cooperation and Development
OPEC	Organisation of Petroleum Exporting Countries
RBA	Reserve Bank of Australia
SRDs	Statutory Reserve Deposits

Introduction

Central banks must be among the least well understood institutions in the entire world.

Alan Blinder, former Deputy Chair, US Federal Reserve[1]

Central banking is a strange profession little understood by the members of the public.

H. C. 'Nugget'' Coombs, former RBA Governor[2]

Central banks stand at a fascinating interface between the economy and politics. These days their primary role is to conduct monetary policy, typically by regulating the supply or price of money in the economy. Central banks also have responsibility for the stability of the financial system, act as a lender of last resort in financial calamities, act as a banker to other banks and to governments, and perform a range of other functions in banking and financial systems. In recent decades, in a world of burgeoning financial markets, major assaults on inflation, and a proliferation of financial calamities, central banks have risen to unprecedented prominence. They also face unprecedented challenges.

Central banks became critical institutions in modern capitalism in the latter part of the twentieth century. Standing at the centre of an inflation-prone, traumatised monetary system and at the interface between nation states and newly deregulated and increasingly powerful financial markets, central banks broke out of their cloistered existence and became powerful, aggressive inflation-fighting machines. So pivotal did they become in the fight against inflation that governments worldwide handed them substantial control over monetary policy – these days, the most important weapon of short-term macroeconomic policy. The fight against inflation was a hard-won victory. The early 1980s and early 1990s saw major policy-induced recessions with huge collateral damage in various countries, including Australia, as high unemployment was used to battle inflation. Central banks emerged victorious from this struggle. By the mid-1990s, they had gained new credibility in the financial markets and an unprecedented public profile.

Yet severe challenges confront central banks. In a world simultaneously confronting surging debt and asset prices, it is not clear what role central banks should play, or even if monetary policy – the instrument of choice in the late twentieth century – will retain its former clout.

This book decribes how the Reserve Bank of Australia (RBA) has operated in this testing context. It explains the politics of central banking in Australia, the Bank's changing relationship with the federal government and how and why it emerged from relative obscurity to become one of the most powerful policy institutions in the country.

In the early 1990s the Bank asserted its policy independence from the government, even though the powerful Treasurer (and later Prime Minister), Paul Keating, opposed central bank independence. Why did the RBA adopt a more aggressive stance towards fighting inflation during the early 1990s recession, a strategy which Keating had explicitly rejected in a public showdown with the Bank in 1990? And why did the government come to sanction central bank independence and pass control over monetary policy to the RBA, a strategy at odds with claims by Keating when he said he would not 'abrogate responsibility for the stance of monetary policy from the elected government to unelected and unrepresentative public officials in the name of fighting inflation first'?[3]

In recent decades, monetary policy has primarily involved manipulating short-term interest rates in attempts to control aggregate or CPI inflation. Policy deliberations within the RBA now command attention – especially in the financial markets and the press – because the RBA's interest rate policies directly impact on the fortunes of individuals, businesses, and those within the markets. Interest rates are a blunt instrument. As Australia found out, especially in the early 1990s recession, high interest rates can flatten an entire economy. The steep increase in debt levels in recent years has also exposed more Australians to the potentially punitive impact of interest rate rises.

Things were not always like this, as chapter 1 explains. Only in the last few decades has a relatively powerful and independent RBA emerged. This happened in the context of several factors: the turn towards neo-liberal orthodoxy in economic policy; global financial deregulation and the associated rise (or return) of powerful financial markets; the inflationary capitalism of the 1970s and 1980s, and the attendant policy shift away from the policy of full employment to one focused on low inflation. With the increasingly passive use of fiscal policy, monetary policy has become the 'swing instrument' in dealing with inflation and attempting to guide the macroeconomy.

These changes have restructured power relations within the state and placed central banks in the macroeconomic policy cockpit; a distinct departure from the earlier centrality of fiscal authorities under the post-war (Keynesian), full employment policy paradigm. This book argues that central banks have become so important, particularly in the face of demands by financial markets for policy 'discipline' and 'credibility' on inflation, that their 'independence' from government is now a key indicator of policy 'soundness'. This reflects concerns that monetary policy is now too important to be left to the vagaries of partisan politics or government 'meddling'. It also underscores the new policy authority of central banks and the firm grip they now have on the instruments of monetary policy.

These changes have constituted a world-wide trend as a wide range of economies confronted the common challenge of high inflation in the 1970s and 1980s. The changes reflect the shared experiences of institutional innovation in central banking and in monetary policy. The changes are a response to the impacts of domestic and global financial deregulation since the 1970s and the rise of financial markets as a powerful anti-inflationary constituency.

Much of this book is about the exercise of power in the monetary policy arena. The main protagonists are financial markets, governments and central banks, although wider business interests and an increasingly debt-exposed community are also important. There has been a shift in power towards financial markets and central banks. Ultimately, governments still hold the whip hand, because they set the regulatory and statutory rules for financial markets and central banking. Nevertheless, the processes of domestic and global financial deregulation have created powerful financial market forces that regularly constrain the choices of governments and central banks. Although central banks have become more powerful domestically, their power in relation to financial markets is more limited.

This book is also about the institutional dynamics of the RBA. The RBA has experienced an institutional revolution, but the key changes have been informal rather than statutory. What has mattered most have been *elite* interaction and accommodation behind the scenes. Indeed, decisions and operations in the upper reaches of the Bank and at the level of the Reserve Bank Board still occur in secret, and it is part of the purpose of this book to peer into this closed world.

We will also see how the RBA has operated to achieve two important institutional imperatives: the search for market credibility, and the search for wider institutional legitimacy. The former is the judgement of the markets and other economic players on the Bank's performance (especially on the inflation front but also increasingly on financial stability). The latter is the justification for an *independent* central bank (essentially a technocracy) in a democratic setting. Much of the work of the Bank and most of the institutional innovations, especially in the 1990s, have aimed at these two imperatives.

This is not the kind of story told by mainstream theories of central banking politics. These generally argue that governments are selfish and myopic, likely to 'interfere' with monetary policy and to influence interest rates for short-term electoral advantage. Central bankers are likely to resist this, so the argument goes, and thus conflict arises between governments and central banks. Nor, according to this view, are governments likely to grant central bank independence because this will weaken government control and the options to manipulate monetary policy for electoral ends. Typically, central bankers are depicted as credibility-driven hawks and politicians as vote-calculus doves. The politics is said to involve opportunism by politicians in attempts to manipulate monetary policy for electoral ends and a degree of tension, if not conflict, between the central bank and the government. But reality speaks differently. There has been a large measure of common purpose as governments too have battled inflation. Moreover, governments almost everywhere have not been averse to granting policy independence to their central banks. Even when the RBA asserted more control over the policy agenda in the early 1990s, the government and Treasurer Paul Keating mostly acquiesced.

Politics will always matter, but financial forces and economic outcomes will most likely shape the future of central banking and determine whether monetary policy and central banks will retain their present clout and especially their independence. We have arrived at a new political economy of inflation where the major structural drivers of CPI inflation seem to have been substantially neutralised. Some now worry about deflation. Financial deregulation has helped produce a world of infinite credit, periodic bouts of severe asset inflation and subsequent crashes. Japan has gone through a shocking cycle of an asset bubble, financial collapse and deflation over the last decade. Other large economies, especially the United States, are also of concern. What can monetary policy and central banks do in such a world? As interest rates disappear towards zero in some countries, monetary policy loses its clout. And no one is sure what central banks and monetary policy should do about surging credit and asset inflation. The future looks uncertain for central banks.

CHAPTER 1

Slowly Building the Reserve Bank

The creation of a central bank in Australia was part of a general wave of central bank formation in a range of countries during the early twentieth century. This chapter briefly recounts the political history of central banking in Australia and provides further historical context to the current operations and especially the institutional underpinnings of the RBA. The role and institutional design of the Reserve Bank of Australia and its forerunner, the Commonwealth Bank of Australia, were established during bouts of political conflict in the first half of the twentieth century.[1] In Australia the central bank occupied a zone of conflict between Labor interests and the private banking and financial community. The main contest was over the banks' private prerogatives and their control of the financial and credit system, with Labor interests being especially keen to regulate them. The independent powers conferred on the central bank created tensions with various governments. Generally, the major shifts in central banking have occurred under Labor governments: this is true of the origins of central banking and also of the major changes of the 1940s and the 1980s, the two watersheds of Australian central banking.

ORIGINS OF CENTRAL BANKING

Walter Bagehot, the third editor of *The Economist*, coined the term 'central bank' in 1873. Although some central banks emerged in the seventeenth century (in Sweden and England), and a few were created in the early nineteenth century (in France, Austria, Norway, Spain, Netherlands, Denmark, Finland), there was no clearly defined concept of central banking at this time. Central banks have only become widespread and firmly established since the late nineteenth century.[2] At the turn of the twentieth century there were only eighteen central banks; by its end there were 173.

Central banks first emerged for a range of reasons, often unrelated to what we now take to be the modern functions of central banking.[3] The Bank of England, for example, was founded in 1694 as a private corporation to mobilise funds to help King William III wage war against the French;[4] it did not really develop central banking functions until the nineteenth century. Wars and the mobilisation of finance to help fight them were the prime rationales behind early central bank formation. Indeed, the first twelve central banks established up to 1850 were created in a war context.[5] Central banks were also increasingly given monopoly rights over note issue, and this, combined with their growing role as the government's banker, enhanced their privileged status in the financial system.[6]

Subsequently, depressions, financial crises, banking collapses, the growth of financial markets and government policy ambitions in the economy have shaped central banks. For example, the US central bank, the Federal Reserve, was finally established (after several attempts) mainly for the purposes of bank supervision and as lender of last resort in the wake of the financial crisis and bank runs of 1907.

Central banks often engaged in commercial banking functions. Their privileged and specialised position assisted them to slowly diversify their functions by holding the deposit reserves of other banks and by settling the balances between banks through the use of these deposits. Additional functions tended to be mutually reinforcing. The role of central banks in general liquidity management for the banking sector placed them in a prime position to manage total reserves within the system. The logical extension was for central banks to act as lender of last resort in periods of financial crisis. Because of the high levels of trust and confidence that are required to underpin a banking system, and because banks tend to have long-term assets but short-term, on-call liabilities, there is a strong argument for a 'lender of last resort' function in case major banks face liquidity crises or a creditor panic. This responsibility implied that central banks should have access to information about, and a degree of control over, the banking and financial sector. This kind of access and control was also implied by the need for the central bank to manage foreign reserves.

SLOWLY CREATING AN AUSTRALIAN CENTRAL BANK

The tradition of animus towards the 'money power' and the banks, particularly in Labor circles, goes back a long way in Australia.[7] Government involvement in monetary management was first proposed by Governor Macquarie in 1810, but it was frustration with the performance of essentially unregulated financial markets and the private banking sector which produced the first substantial proposals for a state bank from the aptly named Select Committee on Monetary Confusion, a body established by the New South Wales Legislative Council in the 1840s.[8] By the 1890s, with severe boom and bust and a series of banking collapses, a state bank was on the parliamentary agenda in four colonies.[9] But it was not until the aftermath of the banking crises of the 1890s, the formation of the state and federal Labor parties, federation, and the need for national note issue, that Labor interests successfully mobilised to create a national, central bank. The thrust of Labor's critique of the private banks and of free financial markets was that they were too vulnerable to collapse, that the banks were profiteering, and that their lending practices tended to be pro-cyclical (excessive in an upswing and too restrictionist in a slump, driven by rapid shifts in sentiment from excessive optimism to deep pessimism). The Fisher Labor government created the Commonwealth Bank of Australia (CBA), which commenced operations in 1912.

King O'Malley, the Minister for Home Affairs in the Fisher government, had been a strong proponent for such a bank (having given a five-hour speech on the topic to the House of Representatives in 1909). Generally speaking, however, there was little real understanding of central banking. H. C. 'Nugget' Coombs, the long-serving Governor of the Commonwealth Bank and later the RBA, describes the 'rare confusion of ideals and intentions' that gave rise to the Bank.[10] The elaborate and lofty ideals of many Labor proponents saw the Bank as a weapon in the war against the private banks, a precursor to full nationalisation of the banking system, a mobiliser of finance for the Commonwealth, a provider of financial services to governments, a source of funds for developmental schemes, and a regulator of the banking system.[11] In fact, the Commonwealth Bank emerged as none of these. O'Malley's scheme for a central bank had been 'pasteurised'.[12] The Bank was the product of contest and compromise between radical Labor hopes and the political and institutional conservatism of the financial community. The latter largely won. As Gollan's history of the Commonwealth Bank argues:

> A bank was on the fighting platform of the Labor Party and the government and was under two types of pressure: one from the left wing of the labour movement demanding a bank which would lead an attack on the Money Power; at the other extreme were those who were opposed to any form of government intervention. Fisher's bank was a compromise. [13]

The Bank emerged essentially as a conventional bank, albeit publicly owned. Historian Brian Fitzpatrick notes that the 'Commonwealth bank seemed at length to amount to nothing more than to obtain a share of what new banking business might be forthcoming as the national economy moved forward, so that out of the hypothetical profits some amounts might be set aside for the redemption of public debt'.[14] The Bank was also created to act as the government's banker, 'a plain business-like and practical measure', according to Billy Hughes on the Labor side.[15] Indeed, the Bank's first Governor, Dennison Miller, merely wanted the Bank to be a 'quiet bank', one that would provide support for the country's private banking system.[16] The Commonwealth Bank did not even control national note issue – Treasury did. Nor under its first Governor was the Bank especially keen to compete for business with the private banks. Boris Schedvin, the major historian of the Bank in the post-war era, writes that Dennison Miller 'recognised that a central bank needed to win and maintain the confidence and trust of the commercial banks, and that this could not be achieved if these two levels were in active competition'.[17] This search for trust and some form of accord became a central motif of relations between the Bank and the private banks; it was a long search, not completed until the 1950s.

The CBA was controlled by a Governor appointed for seven years, responsible for the management and direction of the Bank. Although the issue was a source of debate in the federal parliament prior to enactment,[18] under the *Commonwealth Bank Act* the Bank's Governor was not answerable to a Board of Directors (there was no Board) and had almost complete independence from direct government control. There is a suggestion in the literature that independent central banks are created to enhance creditworthiness in the eyes of foreign lenders and investors.[19] Although Australia was heavily exposed to the London markets, there is little evidence that this consideration was important. Instead, independence mainly reflected a desire to reduce local perceptions of the CBA as an instrument of the government amidst the cross-fire of partisan conflict.[20] Independence also reflected the well-established tradition in Australia of creating relatively independent statutory authorities. Prime Minister Fisher thought that the CBA was more likely to be independent if control was vested in one person. As he told the parliament, 'the Governor of the Bank is to be given absolute authority'.[21]

In World War I the Commonwealth Bank played a role in mobilising war finance and, over time, the Bank took on more government banking business. As Nugget Coombs reflected in his 1931 master's thesis on the development of the CBA, the war strengthened the Bank's role.

It emerged a national institution with a distinctive character and a definite place in the Australian economy. It had been the government financial agent in its dealings with the trading banks, the Bank of England and with the Imperial government; it had raised and administered government loans; it had acted as a representative of the trading banks and adjusted bank differences ... These were central bank functions ... Even though the Bank had not proved the restraining influence on government finance that a fully developed central bank might have been ... [22]

This 'restraining influence' on government finance was to be asserted later, in the Depression – an episode that was to embroil the Bank in controversy and bitterness throughout the 1930s and 1940s.

Following World War I the CBA continued to make little effort to compete with the private banks and by the 1920s it was clear that the future of the Bank lay in the further gradual accretion of central banking functions. In 1920, for example, following CBA lobbying, note issue was transferred from the Treasury to an independent Note Issue Board (located within the Bank), and then in 1924 to the Commonwealth Bank proper.[23] Because the CBA posed little in the way of a competitive threat to the private banks, the latter were more inclined to place their reserves with it, a shift supported by the 1924 *Commonwealth Bank Act* which required the private banks to settle their accounts through the CBA.

'One-man central banking' did not last long. In 1924, amidst criticism in various quarters of the Governor's autocratic power and the restrictionist approach to note issue after 1920, the conservative Bruce–Page government, via the new *Commonwealth Bank Act*, installed an eight-member Board (including the Governor and the Treasury Secretary) to dilute the power of the Governor. The Labor Opposition criticised the move as an 'attempt to kill the Bank' by installing a Board that was not sympathetic to the broad aims of a truly national or central bank.[24] Even so, the government barred members of the private banking industry from sitting on the Board and appointed Board members with experience that reflected the economic and geographical diversity of the Commonwealth (a practice which still continues). Giblin, another historian of the Bank, writes that it was a 'Board of amateurs', playing less than a robust role, because its members were inexperienced and had little knowledge of central banking.[25]

The next major accretions of central banking functions were partly a product of the exigencies of the Depression and World War II and partly the product of Labor's unfinished agenda for central banking and banking more generally. During the early phase of the Depression, in 1929, the CBA was given control over gold in a context of rapidly diminishing foreign reserves. In 1930, the Scullin Labor government, in a bid to strengthen central banking powers, introduced two Bills into the federal parliament that were designed to separate the central and commercial banking functions of the CBA. The *Central Reserve*

Bank Bill established a separate central bank with extended powers. The *Commonwealth Bank Amendment Bill* abolished the CBA Board and placed the Bank back under the control of a single Governor. Both Bills, however, were defeated by an anti-Labor majority in the Senate, backed by the private banks.

In 1931, after the abandonment of the gold standard, the Bank was given control over the management of the exchange rate. In that year an event occurred that was to cause ongoing bitterness in Labor ranks and shape the future of Australian banking. Conflict erupted between the Commonwealth Bank and the private banks on the one hand, and the Scullin government on the other, when the Bank refused to extend finances to aid the government's plans for economic stimulation. Labor supporters saw this as an act of treachery and an attack by the financial establishment on an elected government. The refusal challenged the right of the government to determine its own budgetary policy. Coombs later wrote that the 'Commonwealth Bank had not behaved as a central bank should', and that the 'Bank Board had been politically motivated' in its unwillingness to accommodate the Scullin government.[26] The events of 1931 were to cast a long shadow over subsequent developments and, certainly, banking reform and the strengthening of central bank controls moved to the top of Labor's reform agenda.

In a re-run of the 1890s, though on a smaller scale, the excessive lending during the economic boom of the late 1920s, followed by the conservative and restrictionist attitude of the Commonwealth Bank and the private banks during the Depression, were widely thought to have contributed to the economic calamity and created considerable momentum behind banking system reform. Indeed, sentiments were increasingly critical of free financial markets. The issue was central to the 1934 federal election. Egged on by agrarian interests in the Country Party, the anti-Labor coalition government led by Lyons established the Royal Commission on the Monetary and Banking Systems of Australia in 1935. The commission's 1937 report recommended major new regulatory interventions. It was highly critical of the CBA's restrictionist approach to the Depression. It recommended a substantial strengthening of central banking powers and more control over the private banking system, including the requirement for the banks to lodge specified reserves with the CBA in order to help regulate credit, as well as government licensing of the private banks (thus giving the government a major sanction over their operation). It also recommended steps to coordinate CBA and government policy and, in the light of the events of 1931, that the government (not the CBA) should have ultimate authority over monetary policy: as Coombs puts it, this 'shook the doctrinal foundations of the Bank'.[27]

But no effective legislative response to the commission's findings was undertaken in 1938–39. The delay was due largely to the private and public campaigns waged by the private banks. It was clear that no serious banking reform was possible through voluntary cooperation with the banks. Events were soon overtaken by the outbreak of World War II in 1939, and this and its aftermath were to prove a watershed in the development of Australian central banking.

The war context forced a resolution of earlier disputes. A series of emergency National Security Regulations in late 1941 and 1942 drastically increased the power and functions of the Commonwealth Bank and imposed licensing of private banks. To mobilise and control financial resources to aid the war effort, the CBA was given the task of managing foreign reserves as well as control over domestic banking, including powers over investment, lending and interest rates. As Schedvin puts it, 'the pressures of total war completed the transformation of the Commonwealth Bank into a central bank ... The degree of control was such as to gladden the heart of the staunchest opponent of the private banks.'[28]

A CENTRAL BANK EMERGES: 1945

The Labor government was aware that war-time controls could not be maintained indefinitely in peace time, and that the release of pent-up demand was likely to create inflation. At the close of the war, in March 1945, the Chifley Labor government passed two major pieces of banking legislation: the *Commonwealth Bank Bill* and the *Banking Bill*. The former contained the first explicit legislative recognition of the CBA as a central bank, and its main provisions still provide the statutory basis of the Reserve Bank. The Bills reflected the practical experiences of the Depression and the war, and the intellectual substance of the proposals of the 1936–37 Royal Commission. The Bills also reflected the government's new agenda for Keynesian-inspired macroeconomic management and its commitment to full employment and hence an expansionist and accommodating monetary policy.

The *Banking Bill* clipped the wings of the private banks. It tightened the regulations applying to them and licensed their activities, and it included measures regarding prudential supervision of banking, the regulation of bank lending through special accounts (held with the CBA), and through credit and lending controls and controls over interest rates. Suddenly banking had become a highly regulated industry, with the power of the private bankers diminished. It was a Labor triumph. The *Banking Bill* also required all government bodies to conduct their business through the CBA, but this measure was challenged by the banks and later overturned by the High Court. By 1947 Chifley had embarked on all-out war with the banks in the ill-fated attempt to nationalise the banking system.[29]

The *Commonwealth Bank Bill* had four main provisions. First, Labor
ignored the Royal Commission and the advice of Coombs[30] and abolished the
Bank Board, vesting control once again in the Governor. The Governor was to be
assisted by a six-member Advisory Council of Bank officials and public servants, including the Secretary to the Treasury. The Council was to deal with matters referred to it by the Governor. This arrangement reflected Labor's view that
the Bank, but especially the Board, had become too powerful and too reflective
of conservative business sentiment. Love describes it as Labor's 'ideological
revenge' for 1931.[31] Chifley told the parliament:

> In 1931, in the depths of the Depression, the Commonwealth Bank and the private
> banks refused to assist the rehabilitation plan of the commonwealth and State
> governments designed to relieve acute unemployment and to revive industry. The
> present government is determined to ensure ... that this will never be repeated.[32]

Second, following a recommendation of the Royal Commission, the government
clarified its policy relationship with the CBA. The *Commonwealth Bank Bill*
required the Bank and the Secretary of the Treasury to establish a 'close liaison'
and to keep each other fully informed of relevant developments. Section 9 stated
that the Bank was required from time to time to 'inform the Treasurer of its
monetary and banking policy'. The Bill also vested ultimate authority for monetary policy in the government. Reflecting the lessons of 1931, the government
would prevail in any policy dispute with the Commonwealth Bank. This provision diluted the former principle of central bank independence. Needless to say,
it was attacked by the Opposition as an attempt to control the Bank. Later, in
1951, the conservative Menzies government modified the dispute resolution
procedure to ensure that any dispute between the government and the Bank be
aired *publicly*: both the government and the Bank had to provide relevant statements to each house of the federal parliament. This 'disputes provision' was
partly designed to encourage cooperation and dialogue between the government
and the Bank. But policy transparency, via public disclosure, was also partly
designed to help strengthen the Bank: disputes would be damaging for the government, which would be publicly defying the best advice of the Bank. Not surprisingly, the mechanism has never been used, although Coombs apparently did
consider its use during tensions with Treasury amidst the difficult macroeconomic conditions of the early 1960s.[33] As Bean argues, the disputes power 'is the
nuclear button of monetary policy, destined never to be pushed because its
implications are just too awful to contemplate'.[34]

Third, the Act endorsed the Royal Commission's proposal to give greater
central banking powers to the CBA. The Act required the private banks to lodge

minimum reserve deposits with the Bank to help in managing liquidity. It also embodied the central banking powers of the war-time National Security Regulations. The Act sought to extend the Bank's commercial banking activities in areas of industrial and housing finance, partly to fill perceived gaps in credit markets and partly to overcome the Bank's long-standing reluctance to compete actively with the private banks.[35]

Fourth, even more ambitiously, the Act was Keynesian. The post-war era was a receptive period for Keynesian ideas in Australia, although debates continue about the extent to which Keynesian policy was actually pursued during this period.[36] The Depression had undermined faith in untrammelled markets, and the experience of successful war-time economic planning had emboldened policy-makers. Hence, the Act's fundamental assumption (in tandem with the government's 1945 White Paper on Full Employment) was that 'the Government must accept responsibility for the economic condition of the nation'.[37] This macroeconomic responsibility was a new interpretation of the state's role in a capitalist economy. Also, given Labor's long-held view that the banks and gyrations within the monetary system were at the heart of wider economic instability, this implied, at the very least, extensive regulatory powers over banking and credit, a task in which the central bank was pivotal. Schedvin writes, 'the central bank had been elevated … to become the central agency of economic control … it was therefore incumbent on the central bank to steer the ship of capitalism through stormy seas'.[38]

Hence, the Act radically and ambitiously extended the traditional purview of central banking. The commitment to Keynesian or related policies of expansionary macroeconomic policy aimed at low interest rates and employment growth necessitated further regulatory powers for central banks to help regulate credit and interest rates. The Act gave the Bank the dual responsibility of pursuing not only the 'stability of the currency', but also, and more ambitiously, 'the maintenance of full employment in Australia'. Internationally, the newly established Bretton Woods system aimed to stabilise exchange rates and prevent a return to the gyrations of the 1930s. The system was Keynesian in inspiration, seeking to promote economic stability and expansion at the international level to aid the pursuit of domestic goals such as full employment. The new system would see more activism from central banks and governments in managing the exchange rate, which was broadly pegged to the US dollar. In Australia, however, exchange rate management was given not to the Bank but to the Treasury. The government may have institutionalised central banking, but as argued below, it was not about to give the Bank much power.

Chifley's biographer, L. F. Crisp, points out that parliament spent little time debating whether the Bank's dual goals would prove meaningful or compatible.[39]

Coombs, an influential Keynesian contributor to the government's thinking on central banking who became the Governor of the CBA in January 1949, has pointed to the potential conflicts between these dual goals.

> From the Keynesian stronghold of the Ministry of Post-war Reconstruction, I and my colleagues were urging that the Bank legislation should record the commitment to the objective of full employment. Treasury and the Bank argued that the concern of the Bank was essentially financial and that its primary objectives should be the stability of the value of the currency … In the event it was finally agreed that there was no profit to be gained from exploring legislatively the compatibility of these objectives or the nature of the trade-offs between them … [40]

Both Bills were greeted by strong criticism from the banks and the financial community because they clearly reflected Labor's long-held desire to give the government greater control over banking.[41] *The Economist* commented, 'there is no concealing the animus against the trading banks which inspired this legisla-tion'.[42] Nor was Chifley under any illusions about the ongoing resistance the legislation was likely to attract from conservatives and from the banking estab-lishment. In early 1945 the press also attacked the legislation, with the *Bulletin* claiming 'totalitarian control' and 'the seizure by the government of the whole economic life of the nation'.[43] The Opposition claimed the Bills amounted not to 'honest nationalisation' but to 'strangulation by stealth'.[44] Nevertheless, Labor controlled both houses of parliament and enacted the Bills. The public was gen-erally more concerned about the immediate issues of the war and its aftermath than with the complaints of bankers and financiers.[45] Many Labor supporters considered the legislation pragmatic, even conservative. The passage of the leg-islation illustrates the greater autonomy and policy scope that major calamities, such as depression or war, often give to reforming governments.[46]

The Chifley government was emboldened by 1945. After further conflict with the banks (there were High Court challenges to aspects of the 1945 legisla-tion, particularly over the requirement for government bodies to hold accounts only with the Bank),[47] it upped the ante in its long struggle with the banks by attempting to nationalise the banking system in the late 1940s. This failed in the face of a massive fear campaign and political mobilisation led by the private banks.[48] The campaign for nationalisation, driven as it was by credal passions within the labour movement, cost Labor office. This was a triumph for the forces of 'free enterprise', but the resulting tensions were to linger for almost a decade, furthering the wary and suspicious relationship between the Bank and the private banking sector.

A conservative coalition government under Menzies was swept to office in 1949. Significantly, Menzies endorsed Coombs as Governor of the CBA, and, despite earlier protestations, was not perturbed by most of the contents of the 1945 legislation. Clearly, as far as the major parties were concerned, the legitimacy of central banking and the principle of oversight and regulation of the banking system had arrived in Australia.

Even armed with its new powers, however, the Bank was still a fledgling and junior partner. Its relationship with both the Treasury and the private banks augured a difficult path ahead. Coombs, ever the conciliator, steered the Bank away from direct confrontation, but this had its costs, especially the need for the Bank to tread cautiously on policy and in wider public debates. In the difficult inflationary surge of 1951 resulting from the Korean War, for example, the Bank felt restricted in commenting publicly on policy options, lest it antagonise the government, the Treasury or the private banks. The Bank was also reluctant to press the government to aggressively tighten monetary policy for fear of antagonising the banks via the restriction of credit.[49] It was constrained by ongoing difficulties in managing liquidity and by the government's post-war commitment to run a 'cheap money' economy with low interest rates. Coombs privately pressed the government, along with Treasury, to tighten fiscal policy. The 1951 'horror budget' was the outcome: by default, given the limits of monetary policy, the burden of restraint had fallen onto a hurriedly tightened fiscal policy.[50]

Throughout his term as Governor, Coombs remained convinced that governments were too reluctant to use activist, discretionary policy to manage demand, except in the most pressing circumstances. A pattern of stop-go macroeconomic management was the resulting feature of post-war macroeconomic policy: a pattern highlighted again in the policy-induced recession of 1961. The government waited too long and then jammed on the brakes too hard. Although credit was tightened substantially, fiscal policy again took much of the burden of restraint. This policy helped create the creeping inflation of the post-war years, and Coombs lamented that Australians had developed a tolerance of inflation.[51] The stop-go of the post-war era showed that the government's quest for economic expansion sat uneasily with ad hoc and emergency attempts to deal with the inevitable inflationary pressures.

On the question of the Bank's management, partly in response to Coombs's continuing advice, the Menzies government determined to reinstate the Commonwealth Bank Board. When the Labor-controlled Senate sought to block the proposed legislation, Menzies won a double dissolution election in April 1951, repeating the long-standing pattern of partisan conflict over the management of the Bank. Upon winning control over both houses of parliament,

Menzies passed legislation that reinstalled a Board (of ten members, including the Governor, Deputy Governor and the Secretary of the Treasury).[52] This was the last of such partisan moves. Up to this point it was clear that Labor governments favoured a relatively direct relationship with the Bank via the Governor; it preferred a Bank managed by experts, not by a lay Board of potentially partisan business leaders. As Eichbaum points out, the danger for the left lay in arrangements (such as a powerful or activist Board) that provided points of entry or influence for representatives of capital, especially from the financial community. The conservatives, by contrast, favoured relations between the Bank and government to be mediated by an 'independent' Board. For conservatives, potential 'danger lay in arrangements which would permit the conduct of monetary policy to be more responsive to the preferences of government, and much less to the requirements of "sound finance"'.[53]

The other substantial statutory changes to central banking in the post-war period stemmed from the private banks' ongoing campaign to separate the commercial and central banking functions of the Commonwealth Bank. The 1945 legislation had explicitly signalled an end to the informal agreement between the central and the private banks that had limited competition. Coombs acted on this policy and had made substantial progress in expanding the CBA's commercial banking activities in the early 1950s.[54] The private banks claimed that the CBA had an unfair competitive advantage, in part because of the reserve deposits the private banks were obliged to lodge with it. Members of the Liberal Party also complained about the structure of the Bank, and the press also became vocal. The *Sydney Morning Herald* summed up the complaints:

> The fundamental problem in Australian banking is that the Central Bank, the legislator of credit policy, not only has trading functions and trading associations of its own, competing directly or indirectly with the private banks; but it also has the power to commandeer a very substantial part of their assets in the form of Special Accounts and other compulsory deposits – and to use these assets partly to the advantage of the Central Bank's trading interests.[55]

For Coombs, the struggle over the separation of the commercial and central banking functions of the Commonwealth Bank was a key issue of his governorship during the 1950s.[56] He argued before the government that the criticisms lacked substance and that the CBA needed a period of legislative stability. Direct control of a major commercial bank would help to smooth the economic cycle, Coombs said, especially if the Bank confronted a major economic downturn, and the commercial activities of the CBA provided it with key sources of economic and banking information, and also helped with staff development and training.[57] The government was not unsympathetic to these claims, and the Country Party largely supported Coombs (because of their own concerns about the private banks). Nevertheless, the pressure on the government, especially from the banks and sections of the Liberal Party, was intense. The Menzies government sought to hose down the conflict, and in 1953 introduced changes to the structure of the Bank, setting up the Commonwealth Trading Bank as a separate division of the Bank, with its own general manager and functions. But the critics were not appeased: the commercial arm was still operating under the Bank's auspices.

Finally, after parliamentary conflict in 1958 and 1959, the government passed legislation that separated the CBA's commercial and central banking functions. The government hoped to appease the private banks and put an end to the tensions. The institutional remodelling of the Bank thus did not aim to remove or dilute the Bank's central banking powers, but instead to restore greater trust and cooperation between the central bank and the private banks. The changes, plus Coombs's conciliatory approach to the banks, did eventually bring about the desired improvement in relations.

THE RBA

The contemporary statutory form of Australian central banking was achieved with the passage of the *Reserve Bank Act* in 1959. Except on the separation of central banking powers, the Act in content and spirit resembled the 1945 legislation and subsequent revisions. Finally, it seemed, the political heat that had for decades surrounded the question of central banking and banking regulation in Australia had subsided. Coombs's great hope throughout his term as Governor was for the 'professionalisation' of central banking, 'its liberation from politics through the assertion of expertise', as his biographer Rowse puts it.[58] The removal of politics from central banking is never likely to succeed, but the 1959 Act did signal an end to the earlier hostilities. As S. J. Butlin writes in his early post-war review of central banking in Australia:

> As the dust settled in the early 1960s it could be said that for the first time this century the principle of a sustained degree of control and restraint over the trading banks, of the existence of an effective instrument for the exercise of monetary policy, in short of central banking, had been taken out of politics.[59]

The 1959 Act supported price stability, but also the Keynesian-inspired goals of the 1945 Act. These are proudly printed in brass letters on the black marble of the foyer of the Bank's headquarters in Martin Place, Sydney.

> It is the duty of the Board, within the limits of its powers, to ensure that the
> monetary and banking policy of the bank is directed to the greatest advantage of the
> people of Australia: to the stability of the currency, the maintenance of full
> employment, and the economic prosperity of the people of Australia.

The Act also reiterated the 1945 provisions for policy disagreement between the RBA and the government. It endorsed control by a Board, Section 10.1 giving the Bank Board 'the power to determine the policy of the Bank'. The Board was to consist of the Governor (as chair), the Deputy Governor, the Secretary of the Treasury, and seven part-time members (the latter serving five-year terms). The Board, especially the part-time members, was appointed to reflect a diversity of views across the economy. Typically, the Board comprised business leaders from different sectors who were able to inform the Bank of developments. The part-time members usually had no particular monetary policy expertise; they were valued (and still are) mainly for their provision of anecdotal information about the economy and because they lend wider legitimacy to the Board's deliberations.

The post-war era saw the first watershed in Australian central banking. The regulation of the banking and financial system was defined by a generalised mistrust of the banking and financial community. The four decades between the Royal Commission in 1937 and the late 1970s (when the first steps towards market deregulation were taken) was a period of developing and then attempting to manage a complex raft of regulatory controls over the banking and financial system.

A second feature of the post-war watershed was the repudiation of the concept of central bank autonomy. Although the 1959 RBA legislation appeared to support the notion of independence because it charged the Bank Board with control over policy, in fact discretionary control of the main monetary policy instruments was under the direct statutory control of the Treasurer. As a former Deputy Governor of the Bank, John Phillips, puts it:

> The reality was there was no central banking or monetary policy in an independent
> sense … because virtually every weapon that was available for the central bank to
> use, by law, required the specific approval of the Treasurer … So to talk about
> independence of the central bank, other than independence in reaching a view and
> providing advice, well it just didn't exist … I mean, central banking independence
> wasn't an issue that was much discussed.[60]

The *Banking Act* of 1945 had set out most of the relevant provisions in this regard and required the Treasurer's approval for changes in setting statutory reserves, the exchange rate, and interest rates. Hence, despite a notionally increased role, the RBA was largely cast as an agency of policy advice, and especially of routine policy implementation: the increased armoury of regulatory powers was, in fact, not handed to an independent agency. The Bank found itself operating in the shadow of the government and the Treasurer. As Schedvin writes, the Bank was kept on a short leash by Treasury.

> If the central bank was to retain its enlarged wartime power after the hostilities had ceased, the corollary was that the monetary authority must be tied to the government as closely as possible. 'With the approval of the Treasurer' became a crucial phrase in the 1945 legislation. Formally, a powerful central bank was created, but one that was an extension of the executive arm of government.[61]

Beyond this, Coombs, as the Bank's Governor, adhered to the Westminster convention that the final responsibility for policy lay with the government. As John Phillips recalls, 'There was also a view which Coombs enunciated, which I think [subsequent Governors] Jock Phillips and certainly Harry Knight agreed with, that you, the central Bank couldn't on the one hand be a private adviser, and on the other hand, a public critic of the government.'[62] The Bank's role was also subordinated because Coombs believed that effective coordination between monetary and fiscal policy was best served by such a subordinate arrangement. Coombs was also confronted for much of the time by a domineering Treasury Secretary, Sir Roland Wilson. According to John Phillips, 'Wilson thought the Bank amounted almost to an irrelevant outpost and insisted that there was only one real line of advice to the Treasurer ... the Head of Treasury.'[63] In such a context, Coombs, by temperament, was inclined to avoid conflict, and he made sure the Bank kept a low profile in policy debates. The Bank's *Annual Reports* reflected this approach and were for the most part bland and uninformative about the Bank's thinking or strategy.[64] In 1967, the *Sydney Morning Herald* complained that: 'Dr. Coombs's reluctance to say plainly what he had to say about policy has sometimes driven observers to distraction. There have been periods when the Reserve Bank has seemed a tower of mediocrity, an institution too much subordinated to the government's other interests.'[65]

Coombs summed up his position on the question of central bank independence: 'Perhaps the ideal arrangement would be for a central bank which was substantially independent, by statute, of the government but which recognised the necessity to subordinate its general policy to that of the government ... in matters of major policy the bank would conform to the views of government.'[66]

Compared to images of independent central banks overseas, such as the German Bundesbank or the US Federal Reserve, central bank independence in post-war Australia amounted to a kind of statutory fiction. The Bank could get on with day-to-day operations, but would defer to, or at best collaborate with, the Treasurer and the Treasury. Generally speaking, however, the relationship with Treasury during this period was a tense one.

NEW CHALLENGES: THE 1970S AND ONWARDS

It was not until the 1970s that major new issues and challenges arose about the Australian financial system and the role of the RBA. First, there was a major surge in inflation, climaxing with inflation rates at around 18 per cent by the mid-1970s. The stability of the international financial system and the stability of the exchange rate system in Australia also became major issues following the United States-led movement towards financial deregulation and the scrapping of the Bretton Woods system in 1971. And on the domestic front, the post-war system of regulation of credit and liquidity that had focused primarily on the banks was being challenged by the rapid growth of the unregulated, non-bank financial sector; a sector whose growth had been overseen by Coombs from the 1950s.

The new context would see the power and influence of the RBA slowly increase. We will review this and the main monetary policy dynamics of this period in the next chapter, but here we can note one change, which occurred in 1977, was when the Fraser government brought monetary policy into the cabinet arena by establishing a Cabinet Monetary Policy Committee. By shifting monetary policy more formally into the cabinet arena, Treasury's grip on policy was weakened. Part of the reason for the shift was that tensions between the Fraser government and the Treasury saw the government keen to seek alternative economic advice. As Weller explains: 'The Monetary Policy Committee was responsible for issues that had traditionally been kept isolated in the Treasury. It brought crucial decisions into the cabinet arena, so that departments other than the Treasury became involved.' Weller also argues that this change saw the 'Reserve Bank become more influential'.[67] Ian Macfarlane questions this interpretation.[68] He suggests that the Bank had a degree of influence with the Treasurer that was weakened when monetary policy was thrown open to the Cabinet Committee and the broader cabinet.

In any case, encouraged by advisers (especially John Hewson), Fraser began to explicitly seek the opinion of the Reserve Bank Governor (1975–82), Sir Harold Knight, in the Monetary Policy Committee. This was a shift away from the prior convention that had seen only the Treasury Secretary address the committee, while the Governor sat mutely on the sideline.[69] The move annoyed Treasury. It was a move that expanded the Bank's channels of communication with the government, channels which had been widened earlier when Sir Richard Randall had taken over from Wilson as Treasury Secretary in 1966 and suggested that the RBA begin to formally brief the Treasurer after its monthly Board meetings.[70] This was the origin of the formal 'debriefs' that have continued to this day. As John Phillips explains: 'the practice developed of the Bank going down to see the Treasurer after the Board meetings, usually within a few days of the meetings ... And that was regarded as fulfilling that part of the Act that says that the Bank would keep the Treasurer informed ... So we would go down and talk to the Treasurer and his advisers.'[71]

It was in this context, in 1978, that the Fraser government formally commissioned the Campbell Committee to enquire into the operations of and prospects for the Australian financial system. The Campbell Committee was the first major financial system enquiry since the establishment of the Monetary and Banking Royal Commission in 1935. The economic and financial turbulence of the 1970s, plus the burgeoning growth of the unregulated non-bank financial sector had helped place a financial enquiry on the policy agenda. Neither the Treasury nor the Reserve Bank was keen on the idea of a full-scale enquiry into the financial system and worried about where it might lead. Prime Minister Fraser did want an enquiry but was not an advocate of large-scale financial deregulation; which is what the Campbell Committee ended up endorsing. The push to establish the enquiry had been promoted by Ed Visbord in the Department of Prime Minister and Cabinet and by free market ministerial advisers such as John Rose (adviser to the PM) and John Hewson (adviser to the then Treasurer John Howard).[72] As we will see in later chapters, Hewson was later to become Leader of the Liberal–National Opposition, a position from which he would launch a series of attacks and reform efforts directed at the RBA.

Not surprisingly, the Campbell Committee was also tasked with examining the role of the Reserve Bank. The central questions regarding the RBA were, how well had its institutional design served Australia and, most significantly in the context of the Campbell Committee's deliberations and recommendations, how well might it adapt to a deregulated and more market-oriented financial system?

CAMPBELL GIVES A TICK

The Campbell Committee's report, handed down in September 1981, charted a new deregulated course for the Australian financial system, as its first sentence makes clear: 'The Committee starts from the view that the most efficient way to

organise economic activity is through a competitive market system which is
subject to a minimum of government regulation.' In the context of the reckless-
ness of the banks, the financial calamities and major failures of prudential regulation that were to unfold later in the decade, this was to prove an optimistic
view, although the report did advocate a tightening of prudential regulation.

The report's major findings were that the post-war system of regulatory controls was too complex and inefficient, and that the system was failing to cope
with the rapidly expanding non-bank financial sector. Yet the committee did not
seriously consider rebuilding and expanding the regulatory system; instead,
reflecting the emerging ideological tenor of the times, it endorsed the market.

Surprisingly, the report considered that the RBA, although largely created
and moulded under post-war regulatory conditions, was ideally suited to a new
deregulatory era. This, if nothing else, is a striking commentary on institutional
flexibility.[73] Some of the submissions to the enquiry saw the Reserve Bank as a
closed, secretive organisation dominated by Treasury. But the Campbell
Committee gave a tick to the RBA's institutional framework – including Board
control, the Keynesian-inspired dual goal charter, limited independence, and the
disputes powers.

The report endorsed Board control, with the Treasury Secretary remaining
on the Board to promote policy coordination (especially between monetary and
fiscal policy). It endorsed the long-standing ban on those from the banking
industry sitting on the Board and recommended extending this ban to those from
businesses who were wholly or mainly financial intermediaries. It rejected other
suggestions regarding the Board – having more full-time members and extending the term of non-executive members – seeing 'no particular benefits flowing
from any changes to the legislative prescription of the Board's composition'.[74]

The report endorsed the dual goals of the RBA, although they might at times
be difficult to reconcile: 'the Committee does not consider it appropriate to seek
to confine the Bank to a narrower, more exclusive objective, such as price stability'.[75] The Bank's policy objectives were 'inextricably linked', and were not
wholly within the Bank's powers but required active policy coordination with
other arms of government. This need for consultation and coordination implied
an interdependent or bipartite policy relationship with government, not a starkly
independent one. The report recognised that governments might manipulate
monetary policy for political ends (expanding credit or reducing interest rates
prior to an election), but argued that in a deregulated environment, financial
markets were likely to impose sufficient discipline on governments and the
Bank.[76] The report took the Westminster view that 'ultimate determination of
and responsibility for overall economic policy – including monetary policy –

cannot be effectively divorced from government and the Parliament ... The Bank cannot rise above the source of its power ...'[77] Moreover, 'there is a reasonable presumption in favour of the Bank, Government and Parliament reaching consensus on important issues of monetary policy'.[78]

> Proposals to make the Bank fully independent of government would ... amount to the substitution of bureaucratic for political discretion which would be inconsistent with the processes of democratic government. Quite apart from constitutional limitations, it would be thoroughly undesirable for the Bank to hold a monetary policy which did not have the support of the Government and the Parliament.[79]

Three central themes guided the Campbell Committee's view on the policy relationship between the RBA and the government. First, it reasserted the 1945 Westminster view that government and parliament should retain ultimate authority for policy (as embodied in the disputes power). Such a view could conceivably accommodate a policy process whereby policy was conducted solely and routinely by the Bank but subject, *in extremis*, to government override, but the committee implicitly rejected this stronger form of independence for the Bank. Instead, its second theme was active collaboration and policy partnership between the Bank and the government. This *bipartite* pattern of policy-making was to be largely followed during the 1980s, though it faded in the 1990s. Third, as a safety check on this arrangement, the committee anticipated that under deregulation, financial markets would provide a strong measure of policy discipline.

In the wider financial system, the Campbell Committee pointed to extensive inadequacies in existing regulations, particularly the growth of the unregulated non-bank financial sector and the increased capacity of burgeoning financial markets to side-step the post-war regulatory regime. Given its pro-market stance, the committee recommended deregulation, particularly in exchange rate controls, interest rate ceilings, and the government's traditional controls over the volume and direction of bank lending.[80]

The Fraser government responded cautiously if not coolly to the Campbell Committee's radical agenda.[81] Prime Minister Malcolm Fraser's instincts were conservative; there were concerns within the coalition's National Party; and there was resistance from – of all institutions – the Treasury. Treasury did want a more market-oriented and efficient financial system and opposed rigid interest rate controls and regulation of the non-bank financial sector. Nevertheless, Treasury, and its intellectually fierce Secretary during this period, John Stone, did not advocate wholesale deregulation. It would threaten existing macroeconomic controls and allow markets too much say. In particular, Treasury did not agree with abolishing the exchange rate system and floating the dollar (see below).

The RBA was also cautious. Its leaders, including the Governor, Sir Harold Knight, wanted to enhance market efficiency. They de-emphasised the old, regulatory controls (such as interest rate controls) in favour of market-based instruments (such as the more active use of open market operations and the trading of government securities) in order to shape the demand and supply of funds and the level of liquidity in financial markets. On the other hand, the Bank's leadership was also deeply conservative. Harry Knight was a senior lay figure in the Anglican Church and his use of biblical allusions when addressing bankers and economists earned him the nickname Preacher Harry.[82] He did not wish to undermine the Bank's established regulatory instruments, which any far-reaching form of deregulation would do. On balance, the Bank preferred to retain a strong measure of policy control (such as the Statutory Reserve Deposits which controlled the banks) and saw market-based policy instruments only as a useful supplement for direct controls.[83]

These issues had been debated within the Bank through the 1970s. It was generally conceded that market-based instruments were potentially more broad and effective than regulatory controls. The argument for even bolder forms of deregulation was being pushed by a group in the Bank's Research Department, led by Austin Holmes, Bill Norton and Peter Jonson. They argued that many of the old direct controls were inefficient and that a floating exchange rate could enhance the efficacy of monetary policy. This would assist domestic monetary management by freeing monetary policy of responsibility for exchange rate management, allowing it to concentrate on domestic adjustments aimed at price stability. Slowly the Bank would move in this direction and the Campbell enquiry provided a useful opportunity for those within the Bank pushing for more wide-ranging deregulation. A further important impetus was the appointment of Bob Johnston as the RBA's Governor by Treasurer John Howard in August 1982.

This drift towards market advocacy reflected a deeper shift in mood within the Bank. Schedvin writes that central bankers tend to oscillate historically between trust and distrust of financial markets. Distrust is driven by the ever-present danger of financial market instability, if not systemic collapse, born of excessive optimism or pessimism among investors and the tendency for markets to overshoot. The experiences of the 1930s and 1940s had created suspicion of markets, but this view altered as the post-war economic climate proved generally stable and financial markets grew in scale and complexity. As Schedvin writes:

Running through the story of monetary management was a gradual swing in the pendulum of central banking philosophy towards liberalisation and to reliance on markets as a fulcrum of action. As the memory of depression and war faded, suspicion of the markets receded … the myth of market invincibility emerged that helped dismantle the remaining tangle of regulation and create a largely free environment for financial institutions.[84]

Although hesitant about deregulation, the Fraser government did take some notable steps. It abolished certain interest rate ceilings and, more importantly, shifted the system of financing government debt from the RBA more fully into the market in successive moves in 1979 and 1982. Thus the RBA was no longer required to fund that portion of government debt not taken up by the market at government-prescribed interest rates. Other deregulatory steps included the removal of interest rate ceilings on bank deposits and the removal of quantitative controls over bank lending.

FINANCIAL DEREGULATION

These initial deregulatory moves were completed in spectacular style by the Hawke government – or more particularly by Hawke and Keating and their advisers – in December 1983. They floated the dollar and abolished exchange controls. It was a volte-face for Labor, historically the party of regulation. It also catapulted the RBA into a new position of policy prominence.

Treasury, and especially John Stone, resisted the move, but by the end of 1983 both the RBA and the government were championing deregulation, along with some within Treasury (including senior officers such as Bernie Fraser, who would later become the RBA's Governor). Peter Jonson, the head of the RBA's Research Department in the 1980s, recalls:

You know, Treasury opposed the float, famously. And the Bank fought for it. And in my opinion this was bureaucratic politics at its best. Both sides understood that under the fixed exchange rate, fiscal policy, and the Treasury had more power. And with a flexible exchange rate, monetary policy and the Bank had more influence …[85]

The election of the Labor government in 1983 fostered a stronger policy alliance between the government and the Bank. Bob Johnston, who became Governor in late 1982, says, 'Keating and I had a very good relationship … it flourished really, over the exchange rate and all the paraphernalia about financial deregulation.'[86]

Johnston had been the Bank's Secretary and many, including Johnston, were surprised by his appointment as Governor.[87] The journalist David Marr wrote at the time:

> Absurdly high hopes were raised by the appointment of the urbane Robert Johnston as Governor of the Reserve Bank in August. Bankers praised him for quick wit, candour and grasp. These are not at once apparent, but this is banker's praise and this is the Reserve Bank, a world where gradations of grey can seem like vivid bursts of colour.[88]

Johnston was appointed over the head of the Bank's astute and more senior Deputy Governor, Don Sanders, seen as a conservative and too much a creature of the regulatory era. As one financial analyst said at the time: he is 'very capable but very cautious. He can think of 100 reasons for saying "not yet".'[89] Johnston, on the other hand, was willing to sign up to financial deregulation. Howard had been more impressed by Johnston, who had served as the Bank's representative on the Campbell enquiry and had later worked closely with Howard in deregulation discussions and planning. Johnston's experience in London and Washington in the late 1970s had convinced him that a more deregulated financial system was desirable. Having witnessed the machinations in Australia in the 1970s over monetary policy and attempts to regulate the exchange rate, he was not convinced that governments could effectively manage the monetary system.

John Stone had served at the International Monetary Fund in Washington, and his experiences of international financial markets led him to the opposite view. The financial turmoil of the 1970s had made Stone fear the increasingly untamed world of international finance and the burgeoning markets. He wanted to hang on to as much policy control as possible; and this certainly meant not jettisoning an exchange rate system and capital controls, especially for a small economy like Australia.[90] It is also probably true that Stone did not trust politicians to run a tough anti-inflation policy and saw control of the (overvalued) exchange rate in this context as a useful means of fighting inflation.

The problem with this Treasury line, however, was that it was becoming increasingly difficult to control exchange rates in the face of the burgeoning financial markets. The new Hawke Labor government considered floating the currency, and finally moved when powerful speculative assaults on the Australian dollar created a currency crisis in late 1983. The context was the growing integration of Australia into the international financial system and the explosive growth of global financial markets that followed the US decision of

the early 1970s to float its exchange rate and move towards a deregulated financial system. The growing strength of the markets and the rising volume of speculative trading were overwhelming Australian efforts to fix the exchange rate. In
the wake of the US deregulation, Australian authorities had attempted to fix the
Australian dollar first to sterling, then to the US dollar, and then to a basket of
currencies. These attempts at management were defeated by the growing
volume of funds moving in and out of the country. In March 1983, the new government devalued the dollar by 10 per cent in an attempt to deal with the market
gyrations, but by the end of that year market pressures had reversed the devalu-
ation. The authorities were losing control.

As the exchange rate became almost impossible to manage, financial flows
also added volatility to interest rates and made it more difficult to manage the
money supply. The moment of truth came in December 1983, after a week of
heavy pressure on the dollar. The RBA informed the government that speculators
were targeting the dollar. Australia had two options: deregulation or massive re-
regulation. Deregulation meant capitulation and handing more power to the markets. Treasury head John Stone, although a strident neo-liberal, clung to
economic nationalist sentiments on this issue, arguing that exchange rate policy
was too important a lever to sacrifice to the markets, that deregulation would
increase the volatility of the dollar, and that Australia was essentially surrender-
ing itself to the financial sector.[91] But the Reserve Bank doubted whether unilateral attempts to impose new controls would work, given the size, influence and
manoeuvrability of the burgeoning markets. In the end, with the support of
Johnston at the RBA, Treasurer Keating and Prime Minister Hawke took the
plunge. The senior Labor minister, John Kerin, recalls: 'Stone was dead-set
opposed to floating the dollar and it was only when Bob Hawke and Paul Keating
talked to Johnston – rather than Stone – that suddenly we decided to float the
dollar.'[92] In the bureaucratic firmament it was a win for the Reserve Bank, its first
policy triumph in the post-war period, especially in relation to Treasury. John
Stone later recanted his opposition, and in 1984 he called the float the single most
important decision made by a federal government since World War II. As Keating
recently commented: 'I was taking power off the cabinet table and giving it to the
markets.'[93] This was a historic turnaround for a Labor Treasurer. On the other
hand, deregulation, and later the entry of foreign banks, would shake up the conservative Australian financial establishment, something which Keating relished.
During the post-war period, the regulatory structure had moved, as Rowse puts it,
'from Chifley's disbelief that the banks could ever assume public responsibilities,
to the Hawke and subsequent governments' scepticism about any central bank
action that was not mediated by markets in finance and currency'.[94] The markets

were delighted. In 1984 Treasurer Keating got a special prize from *Euromoney* magazine – Finance Minister of the Year.

In the early hours of 9 December the decision to abandon one of the central elements of the regulatory framework was taken: to float the dollar and abolish exchange controls. In one stroke, the Australian financial system was thrown open to world market forces as part of the process of global financial liberalisation. Deregulation would make the economy increasingly subject to the test of financial market confidence: failure to meet the policy preferences of the markets could see an exodus of capital, or a sell-off of the dollar, or both. Keating later explained the decision to float the dollar:

> You can't defend an exchange rate against the market. There's too much money out there. Why, if we tried to defend an unsustainable exchange rate against the market, we'd have to sacrifice our foreign exchange reserves. What for? Trying to stop an exchange rate from going where the market sends it. That would be just crazy.[95]

The logic of deregulation was carried further during the 1980s with decisions to abolish interest rate controls on home loans and to allow foreign banks to set up in Australia.

Deregulation increased market discipline, and it fuelled a wild credit and asset boom later in the decade. The immediate implication for monetary management was that deregulation redefined the role and main instruments of policy. Deregulation, and especially the float, freed monetary policy from its former focus on the exchange rate and enabled it to focus on domestic demand management; especially, as it would eventuate, in fighting inflation. The main means of implementing monetary policy prior to deregulation was through quantitative controls on private bank lending and by setting the interest rate on government securities. Both processes required approval by the Treasurer. Similarly, cabinet determined exchange rate policy, and routine exchange rate adjustments were taken daily by a group of officials (only one of whom was the RBA Governor). Later, in the late 1970s and early 1980s, in the monetarist era, decisions about money supply and the targeted rate of monetary growth were usually determined by the Monetary Policy Committee of cabinet. In effect, the RBA had no real policy independence; as in the post-war era under Coombs, it was the Treasurer and Treasury, not the Bank, who were at the centre of monetary policy action.

Deregulation abolished all these monetary policy instruments, and thus saw a shift from controlling the *volume* of short-term credit to controlling its *price*. Henceforth, monetary policy was to operate through manipulation of the cash rate, an instrument controlled by the Bank that required intimate knowledge of the financial markets. The only institution capable of performing such a role was the RBA. Suddenly, control over monetary policy had shifted from Canberra to Martin Place in Sydney, the headquarters of the RBA and the financial hub of Australia. Treasury was the big loser. As the Bank came out from under the Treasury's wing, the policy relationship between Treasurer Keating and the Bank became much closer.[96]

The current Governor of the RBA, Ian Macfarlane, has argued:

> The Reserve Bank, by virtue of its Act in 1959, was always given a high degree of general independence as an institution. The fact that it had been unable to exercise this independence in monetary policy for much of the post-war period was due to a practical impediment – it did not possess the instruments of monetary policy. In the heavily regulated financial world which characterised most of the post-war period, virtually all the instruments – in the form of interest rate controls on government debt and on bank lending and borrowing rates – were vested with the Treasurer .... The big change for the Reserve Bank was financial deregulation. It swept away the interest rate controls, freed up the exchange rate and made it possible to finance the budget deficit fully at market determined interest rates. This left open-market operations, which effectively determined short-term money market rates, as the only instrument of monetary policy. This was entirely within the hands of the Reserve Bank, which put us operationally in the same position as the US Federal Reserve or the Bundesbank. For the first time, the intentions of the Act and the capacity of the Reserve Bank were in accord.[97]

CONCLUSION

Central banking and the institutional make-up of Australia's central bank were highly contested in the first half of the twentieth century amidst a series of highly politicised legislative changes. The major conflicts slowly abated during the post-war period, a time when financial markets were distrusted and the legitimacy of financial controls and regulation became widely accepted. In this period the idea of central banking first received proper statutory recognition in Australia.

The fluctuating power and influence of the Bank stand out. Its early independence and its policy assertiveness in the early 1930s were repudiated by the Chifley government, and during most of the post-war era the Bank played a junior role in policy. In 1983, after Bob Johnston's appointment as Governor, the *Australian Financial Review* editorialised about 'crude bullying from the

Treasury' and hoped the Bank would overcome its 'years of timidity and sub-servience'.[98] The Bank began to emerge as a substantial player in the late 1970s under the Fraser government, and made a leap towards becoming the central institution of monetary policy after financial deregulation in 1983. It showed greater willingness to rely on markets and market-based policy instruments, combined with a more circumspect view about the potential for effective or detailed regulation. As we will see in later chapters, the events of the 1980s pre-saged shifts towards a substantial measure of central bank independence in Australia.

CHAPTER 2

Into the Monetary Policy Wilderness

I guess we were in a monetary policy 'wilderness'; enlightenment from on high was a long time in coming.

Former RBA Governor, Bob Johnston[1]

The fight against inflation and the growing prominence of monetary policy (and the Reserve Bank) have been central features of economic policy in recent decades. This chapter begins in the early 1970s and examines the dynamics that followed the collapse of the post-war monetary order. The RBA's search for a stable monetary policy framework during the 1970s and 1980s was largely unsuccessful, although much was learnt along the way. Indeed, the 1980s was a baptism of fire as the government and the RBA searched for a path in a deregu-lated financial environment while attempting to control an increasingly wayward economy. The steep learning curve and economic gyrations of this period would have challenged any set of policy-makers.

As in many other economies, inflation began to rise in Australia in the early 1970s after the Bretton Woods monetary system broke down and the prices of oil and other commodities soared. Inflation was also driven by growing wage pres-sures, and by what at the time was a relatively loose or accommodating monetary policy. This combination was followed in the mid-1970s by a crisis of stagflation. Amidst what appeared to be a failure of the post-war economic order, politics shifted to the right and neo-liberal policies were embraced.[2] 'Fight inflation first' became the policy mantra, especially under the Fraser government.

Fiscal policy, monetary policy, wages policy and for a time exchange rate policy were all used to fight inflation. Over time, however, this range of policy options narrowed. For example, the government's direct control over the exchange rate was lost after financial deregulation in 1983. Fiscal policy is rela-tively inflexible on the taxation side because politicians have concluded that tax adjustments are politically risky, although there is more scope for cyclical man-agement on the expenditure side.[3] Wages policy too (more specifically, wage restraint policy) is difficult to orchestrate, although during the 1980s Labor's Accord with the trade unions was reasonably successful in dealing with inflation.

Over time, however, for a range of reasons, the burden of fighting inflation has increasingly fallen onto monetary policy. It can be adjusted quickly and flexibly, but it is a blunt instrument because it works by slowing or even recessing the entire economy. The rising prominence of monetary policy marks a shift from the post-war era, when fiscal policy dominated macroeconomic policy. Even in the early stages of our story, in the mid-1970s, monetary policy, according to the current RBA Governor, Ian Macfarlane, 'was not held to be very important' in the policy scheme of things.[4] Monetary institutions were also inadequate and the monetary policy machinery that could be deployed against inflation was increasingly a relic of the post-war regulatory order.[5]

STAGFLATION AND 'FIGHTING INFLATION FIRST'

Faced with high inflation, rising unemployment and wild gyrations in the economy in the 1970s and early 1980s, policy-makers struggled for control. Suddenly, they were dealing with a new type of economy.

One major change was wrought by international financial deregulation. The post-war international monetary policy order had been constructed as a response to the disastrous financial gyrations of the 1930s and the problems of free market finance. The Bretton Woods system of fixed exchange rates and regulated capital movements began to unravel in the early 1970s. Financiers and bankers had been chafing for greater market freedom, but the main change came when the United States began printing money to help pay its Vietnam War debts and was forced off the gold standard. The United States lost the will and jettisoned the capacity to regulate and oversee the international financial system. As we have seen, the United States deregulated in the early 1970s by abolishing exchange controls and floating the dollar,[6] and other countries were obliged to follow in a process of competitive deregulation. Once a major arena of financial freedom had been opened up, countries found it increasingly difficult to resist the impact of speculative flows in currency markets or to police capital movements across borders. By 1979, Britain had abolished controls over capital movements, and during the 1980s other countries, including Australia, floated their currencies, liberalised their financial systems and deregulated various interest rates. By the early 1990s this had created an almost fully liberalised financial system across the advanced capitalist economies, in which the activity of financial markets grew explosively. Financial interests became powerful players in the new deregulated political economy of free market finance.

Another major change was the outbreak of inflation. By 1975, a deep recession came with an extraordinary increase in prices. In Australia, the rate of inflation surged to almost 18 per cent. Policy-makers were attempting to deal with an unprecedented crisis of 'stagflation'. Recession, rising unemployment *and* high inflation were certainly not part of the post-war macroeconomic script.

A number of factors contributed to the new inflation. The collapse of the Bretton Woods system suddenly gave governments greater autonomy in relation to monetary policy, particularly the capacity to print money liberally and expand domestic credit supplies.[7] Governments initially did this because they were confronted by strong 'cost-push' inflationary pressures. There were freakish 'exogenous' events, such as the price increases in OPEC oil and other commodities of the 1970s, and distributional conflicts over the economic pie. The post-war era of high growth had muted these tensions, but when this slowed in the 1970s conflict broke out over wages and profit shares. A series of bitter strikes, large wage increases and the inevitable price increases led to a virulent wage–price spiral.[8] The combatants were stronger and more determined. The corporate sector had become more powerful, and on the labour side, several decades of full employment had improved confidence and bargaining power. These inflationary consequences of full employment had been predicted in the 1940s by the Polish economist Michel Kalecki, who in a now famous article argued that full employment posed a fundamental threat to capitalism because business would become 'boom tired' as full employment and tight labour markets strengthened the bargaining power of workers, threatened profits, weakened employer control and slowed productivity growth.[9]

Policy-makers and economists were initially baffled by stagflation. The standard Keynesian macroeconomic thinking of the post-war era pointed to an inverse relationship between inflation and unemployment. If one went up, the other would go down. But now both were rising together. The standard Keynesian response to a recession and rising unemployment was to stimulate the economy, but stimulation threatened even more inflation.[10] Labor's Treasurer, Bill Hayden, stated in the August 1975 Budget speech:

> We are no longer operating in that simple Keynesian world in which some reduction in unemployment could apparently always be purchased at the cost of some more inflation. Today it is inflation that is the central problem. More inflation simply leads to more unemployment.

The Whitlam government (1972–75) had been mired in conflicts about whether to tackle rising unemployment or rising inflation. It pursued various anti-inflation strategies, such as the 1973 tariff cuts and a sharp tightening of monetary policy in 1974, together with an upward revaluation of the dollar. In contrast, fiscal policy was expansionary, to promote Whitlam's social agenda and defeat rising unemployment. The combination was contradictory and did not work. In desperation, the Hayden Budget of late 1975 finally tightened both monetary and fiscal policy.

This marked a shift in orthodoxy towards a disinflationary policy – 'fight inflation first' – that continued (although often timidly) under the Fraser government until the early 1980s. A disinflationary policy essentially chloroforms the economy through tight fiscal or monetary policy or some combination of the two, although increasingly monetary policy has been the favoured weapon. Bernie Fraser, Governor of the Reserve Bank between 1989 and 1996, has argued: 'monetary policy everywhere operates on inflation by creating slack in the economy'.[11] A central aim was to limit wage-push inflationary pressures by driving up unemployment, thus 'disciplining' labour. 'Fight inflation first' was part of a wider neo-liberal policy mobilisation. It marked the demise of Keynesian orthodoxy and the quiet abandonment of the post-war commitment to full employment.[12]

The collapse of Bretton Woods and the shift to 'fighting inflation first' called for a new monetary policy regime. During the post-war period, the guiding principle for monetary policy was established through adherence to the Bretton Woods system of fixed exchange rates. Routine adjustments of domestic fiscal and monetary policy maintained a fixed exchange rate between the Australian and the US dollar. The system imposed an external discipline and, as Ian Macfarlane puts it, this 'effectively formed the centrepiece of Australian monetary policy'.[13] With the abandonment of Bretton Woods in the early 1970s, various ad hoc systems were used to try to stabilise the exchange rate, but lacking a solid external anchor, monetary policy was adrift. Macfarlane has argued: 'Some guiding principle, or rule, that limited the capacity for discretion in monetary policy was essential to keep it from falling under the influence of expediency or succumbing to populist pressures for an excessively expansionary stance.'[14]

This search for some kind of rule or formula to guide policy has long framed one of the central technical debates in monetary policy, 'rules versus discretion'. It is argued that a rule-based policy system that specifies the appropriate responses to given situations will usefully limit the discretion of policy-makers. The reasons for this, in part, relate to Macfarlane's comment above: policy-makers need the help of a rule-based system to fend off populist pressures. Rules also provide economic actors, including financial markets, with more transparency and predictability regarding policy and help condition inflationary expectations. In practice, most central bankers prefer to maintain a degree of discretion in policy-making, but they have also tended to try to pin down the policy system with a rules framework.[15] In the jargon, such a system is seen as more 'credible'.

MONETARISM

Enter monetarism. This doctrine dusted off some earlier monetary theories and was championed by the well-known Chicago economist Milton Friedman, who made a high-profile visit to Australia in 1975.[16] Monetarism caught on early in Australia. Its central thesis saw inflation driven by an excessive supply of money in the economy. Monetary contraction, aimed at aligning monetary growth with real growth in the economy, was thought to reduce inflation. Under such a regime, monetary policy would seek to control the growth of the money supply, typically guided by an annual monetary growth target (usually specified as the growth of a measure such as 'M3' or some related measure of 'broad money').[17] The practice became known as 'monetary targeting' or, more meekly in Australia, a 'monetary projection' or even a 'conditional projection'.

The Fraser government adopted this policy in 1976, with the support of the Treasurer, Phillip Lynch, and (somewhat less enthusiastic) the Treasury and the RBA.[18] The RBA was sceptical of monetary targeting because it doubted whether the government would adopt a sufficiently flexible approach to interest rates and the exchange rate to make targeting work. But the Bank did not resist the policy, insisting that its view of monetarism was 'pragmatic rather than doc-trinal'.[19] Monetarism caught on elsewhere too, with almost all central banks converts to 'pragmatic monetarism' by the end of the 1970s.[20] The practice of fighting inflation by regulating the money supply appealed to policy-makers (though they had reservations). In the wake of the collapse of Bretton Woods, it reintroduced a rule or formula into monetary policy determination. Officials in the Bank and Treasury also hoped that targeting would help discipline the 'nat-ural profligacy' of governments and reassure business and the markets that the government had a handle on monetary policy.[21] Simon Guttmann, whose PhD thesis is the definitive account of the rise and decline of monetary targeting in Australia, writes: 'The choice of the term "conditional projection" [to describe monetary targeting] is best seen as an attempt to reconcile a general scepticism concerning targets with the discipline and policy reinforcement a target would bring.'[22] The arrival of monetarism gave new prominence to the role of monetary policy, unmatched in the post-war history of macroeconomic policy.

Monetarism and other strands of free market economic analysis repudiated post-war Keynesian thinking, especially the view that stimulatory policy (tax cuts, government spending, lower interest rates) could promote employment.[23]

By the 1970s, mainstream economists rejected the Keynesian belief that lower unemployment could be traded for higher inflation and vice versa. In the short term, it was agreed, reducing inflation (say, through higher interest rates) would slow growth and increase unemployment. But in the medium to long term there was no trade-off. Higher inflation could not be traded for lower unemployment because eventually, so the argument goes, growth and employment gains would be cancelled out by higher inflation. Arguments about 'inflationary expectations' claimed that any short-term employment gains through policy stimulation would be neutralised through higher inflation. The 1970s and 1980s were the high point of this type of thinking. In recent years some central banks have aimed for a more balanced approach than that implied by the 'no trade-off' argument. Still, the more doctrinaire central bankers continued with this line even in the late 1990s. For example, according to the former Governor of the Reserve Bank of New Zealand, Don Brash:

> there is in fact no evidence that monetary policy can, by tolerating a little more inflation, engineer a sustainably higher rate of growth, or a sustainably higher level of employment ... To be sure, monetary policy can engineer faster growth and higher employment in the short term – by tolerating a bit more inflation right now, there is not much doubt that growth and employment would be a little higher ... than otherwise ... Most of that faster growth and higher employment would be bought at the cost of tricking workers into accepting a reduction in their real wages, as prices rose ahead of wages. However, it would not last. Before too long, people would recognise the deception and would demand compensation in the form of higher wages and salaries. Within a very short time, inflation would be rising, growth would be back to its previous, lower level and we would be left contemplating the cost of reducing inflation again ... Not only is there no evidence that tolerating more inflation can engineer a sustainable faster rate of growth, there is now overwhelming evidence that high inflation positively damages the way in which the economy works ...[24]

A related set of ideas about the causes of unemployment also rejected post-war Keynesianism, especially the view that expansionary policy could create employment. Neo-liberal economic thinking argued that unemployment was largely 'structural' – caused primarily by inflexible labour markets burdened with skill shortages, inflexible workers or 'excessive' wage claims. In this view, attempts to reduce unemployment below a certain level are likely to ignite wage and other inflationary pressures. This resembles the concept of the Non-Accelerating Inflation Rate of Unemployment or NAIRU, a level of unemployment seen as consistent with low and stable inflation. In the RBA's jargon, this 'structural unemployment rate sets a limit on how low the unemployment rate can fall in response to cyclical expansion before upward pressure on labour costs and inflation appear'.[25] As the Bank's Stephen Grenville put it in 1996, 'there is no point in attempting to operate with unemployment less than the NAIRU'.[26] If the priority is given to fighting inflation, the 'structural unemployment rate' essentially becomes the 'full employment rate'. 'Once this stage is reached,' the RBA argues, 'macroeconomic policies cannot successfully stimulate activity and reduce unemployment any further, unless structural impediments to lower unemployment can be removed.'

According to such thinking, the solution to unemployment does not lie with macroeconomic policy at all, especially with Keynesian-style stimulation. Unemployment is not a 'cyclical' problem whose remedy involves faster economic growth; rather, it is redefined as a microeconomic or 'supply-side' problem, rooted in the structure and operation of labour markets (or, more precisely, workers). According to this view, unemployment is best tackled through programs to improve labour market 'flexibility' (especially wages cuts and labour market deregulation).

Although many Keynesians reject these ideas and argue that unemployment is mainly a 'demand-side' issue, best tackled through faster economic growth,[27] the neo-liberal, supply-side view of unemployment has shaped policy. Accordingly, inflation is to be purged from the economy through a 'restrictionist' policy – the tough medicine of deflation or even recession. Employment growth, it is argued, could resume after a period of fighting inflation first, reducing inflationary expectations and, above all, disciplining the labour market. This approach makes employment conditional on successfully fighting inflation, and it has come to dominate the world of central banking. The often unstated corollary is that successfully fighting inflation has relied – and continues to rely – on a degree of 'slack' and insecurity in the labour market which effectively cows labour.

The Fraser government said it was fighting inflation first, but its miserable macroeconomic policy record offered little endorsement of monetarism. Although monetary policy had come to prominence under the post-1976 monetary targeting regime, its uncertain application and limited policy disciplines failed to achieve most of the monetary 'projections' and raised doubts about the efficacy of the approach. 'Over time', Guttmann writes, 'the Reserve returned to its initial opposition to the projections. An important reason for that was the difficulty in persuading the government to take measures – such as reducing the budget deficit, increasing interest rates and re-valuing the exchange rate – that would allow the projection to be achieved.'[28] Nor was the government impressed with monetary targeting. Treasurer John Howard even announced in the 1982 Budget speech that 'the government in fact gave serious thought this year to formally abandoning the announcement of a monetary projection'.[29] Given the problems with targeting, it is remarkable that it persisted for so long. It lasted because it suited a range of interests. For the government, monetary targeting had become the centrepiece of its economic strategy and, as Guttmann points out, 'an alternative approach for structuring monetary policy, let alone one that was credible, was absent'.[30] The government had an instrument that did not work, but it was afraid to jettison it. Besides, targeting could be paraded as a useful discipline in relation to other arms of policy; for example, reducing government expenditure. Targeting was still in vogue internationally, the financial markets liked it, and the government was unwilling to antagonise the markets.[31] To the markets, targeting implied policy discipline by the government and the target was thought to be a useful way of reading the RBA's policy stance. Neither of these views was necessarily correct.

Besides these policy dilemmas, the economy was going badly. There was an incipient 'resources boom' late in the decade, but tentative bouts of monetary policy restrictionism and an uncertain fiscal policy saw economic growth generally remain sluggish as unemployment rose to post-war highs; it hovered between 5 and 7 per cent, and rose to 10 per cent in 1983 after the severe recession of the early 1980s. The restrictionism, though not full-blown, was nevertheless unpopular. The Victorian Chamber of Manufactures, for example, complained in 1977 that 'it would indeed be a tragedy if the battle against inflation were won only to find industry had died fighting the battle'.[32] But little was achieved on the inflation front. By the beginning of 1982, after six years of 'fighting inflation first', the inflation rate was over 11 per cent. The battle to discipline labour had largely failed, as the wages explosion of 1982 (in the midst of recession) illustrated. The recession was partly driven by international factors, including oil price shocks and the US Federal Reserve's high interest rate attack on inflation in the early 1980s (known as 'the Volcker deflation', after the Fed's chairman, Paul Volcker). But Australia's recession was also driven by domestic factors, including a severe drought and high domestic interest rates (official rates averaged 15 per cent in 1982) and other forms of monetary tightening in the face of high inflation and mounting balance of payments problems. Significantly, however, and this emerged as the pattern of the 1970s and 1980s, the Bank and the government were simply unwilling to get too tough on inflation.[33] In its 1979 *Annual Report*, for example, the RBA stated that it was aiming for 'a rate of monetary growth which keeps downward pressure on increases in money incomes and expectations about inflation', but it added that the 'rate of growth should not, of course, be so low that it unduly restricts activity'.[34] And in the wake of the early 1980s recession, in its *Annual Report* for 1983, the Bank stated:

> given the state of the economy, it was judged inappropriate to tighten the screws ... and, as it were, chase the economy down ... a significantly tougher monetary policy might have hastened [bringing] ... inflation down more quickly but it could also have ... resulted in further cuts in employment and increases in bankruptcies ... and jeopardised the longer run acceptability of sensible policies.[35]

Clearly, the Bank (and the government) were concerned about the legitimacy of policy. There would be no Volcker deflation in Australia. This relatively dovish approach was not to be repeated in the next major recession in the early 1990s.

LABOR'S NEW BROOM

The Hawke Labor government took office in March 1983, with Treasurer Paul Keating later referring to the 'failed dogma of high monetarism'.[36] The government's platform promised an end to 'fighting inflation first'. The electorate, weary of the Fraser government's perceived austerity and its confrontation with the unions, embraced Labor's promise to give priority to employment growth. In fact, Labor recast the policy mould. It boldly promised to stimulate the economy through a broadly expansionary fiscal and monetary policy and, simultaneously, to deal with inflation through a policy of wages restraint through consultation and bargaining with the unions. This deal was embodied in the 1983 Accord and subsequent revisions. Corporatist wages policy had arrived in Australia.[37]

The Accord amounted to an official rejection of monetarism, signalling a new stance in which wage restraint would be worked out through consultation rather than restrictionism. Treasurer Keating boasted that, armed with the Accord, the Labor government was in a unique position to pursue growth *and* low inflation. Labor could run the economy harder without a collapse into recession. Exchange rate flexibility, after the float, through import and export price adjustments, was also expected to help with, if not eliminate, any current account problems that might arise under an expansionary program. Throughout the 1980s, compared with OECD countries, Australia's high GDP growth, its relatively high employment growth, and its growing current account deficit (CAD), were indicative of an expanding economy. But by mid-decade the restrictionist screws were being tightened as the markets lost faith in Labor's expansionism and dumped the dollar. The government responded with tighter fiscal and monetary settings.

Significantly, under Labor's new approach to wage restraint, monetary policy (and the RBA) operated in the shadow of the Accord, playing only a supportive role.[38] Indeed, the Bank was out of the loop regarding the Accord negotiations, its role being mainly to advise on and implement monetary policy after the Accord-based macroeconomic targets had been set.[39] The significance of this should not be overlooked: throughout the 1980s, wages policy and the Accord, not monetary policy, were the key anti-inflation weapon. Hence, the Bank did not feel it had the prime responsibility for fighting inflation[40] and its policy role was subservient to the wider Accord framework.[41] In its 1983 *Annual Report,* in a remarkably rapid endorsement of the new approach, the Bank signalled its distaste for disinflation and argued that, 'Because it should entail a lower cost in terms of unemployment, income restraint achieved through processes of consultation is much to be preferred to restraint enforced through tough monetary policies.'[42]

The Accord prevented the wage breakouts that had derailed both the Whitlam and Fraser governments. Its weakness, at least according to dry neo-liberal critics, was that it relied on the uncertain instrument of union cooperation and was likely to be ineffectual or too slow in bringing down inflation.[43] Nevertheless, many within the RBA, the Treasury and other agencies supported the Accord.[44] As events unfolded, however, monetary policy moved to a much larger role in fighting inflation than envisaged by the architects of the Accord.

During Labor's initial years in office, both the government and the Bank grudgingly endorsed monetary targeting. As Guttmann argues: 'The absence of a projection would have signalled an unwillingness on the part of the government to submit to what was widely seen as an important policy discipline. The press and the financial markets would have quickly concluded that the Hawke government was likely to be a rerun of the Whitlam government.'[45]

Nevertheless, achieving annual monetary targets was hit and miss. In part, this was because of insufficient policy discipline in other areas, but also the monetary control instruments were not up to the task. Before financial deregulation, the Bank's main policy instruments were the post-war machinery of quantitative regulations and credit controls on the banking system, such as controls over the volume and direction of bank lending, various interest rate ceilings, and the banks' Statutory Reserve Deposits.[46] These were failing to operate effectively or efficiently. As the Campbell Committee of 1981 had pointed out, the system was open to evasion in the face of an increasingly sophisticated and complex financial system. The Bank even doubted whether the regulatory controls were up to the task of a significant tightening of monetary policy. In the words of Ian Macfarlane, 'significant structural deficiencies in the system ... meant that no one could be confident that a tightening could be achieved with any reliability'.[47]

The main problems with the old control system were, first, that it did not cover the large and rapidly expanding non-bank financial sector. Second, under the fixed or semi-fixed exchange rates of the 1970s, currency trading and other trade and investment flows could lead to significant offshore injections of money into the Australian monetary system. Third, instead of financing government budget deficits through public borrowing, under the old system the RBA directly funded a substantial part of the deficit by printing money. In short, controlling 'money' was becoming more and more difficult.

Governments solved some of these problems. The problem of financing the deficit was largely dealt with through policy changes in the late 1970s and early 1980s that increasingly funded government debt directly via the market at the going interest rate. However, other decisions, especially deregulatory moves to remove interest rate controls on the banks, undermined monetary targeting and weakened the links thought to exist, in the monetarist conception, between monetary aggregates, economic growth and inflation.[48] As the Bank admitted: 'by early 1985, it was clear that M3 was giving very misleading signals on the stance of monetary policy, and, as a result monetary targeting was suspended'.[49] Ian Macfarlane reports that 'Treasurer Keating made no secret of his lack of enthusiasm for this approach to monetary policy.'[50] The Treasurer announced the termination of targeting in January 1985.

The RBA's attempts to establish (an admittedly loose) rule-based system had broken down. Its endorsement of an increasingly deregulated financial environment made its quest to control money impossible: the goals were incompatible. The Bank now concedes monetarism's 'comprehensive failure as a practical guide to policy',[51] although at the time there were concerns within the organisation about what would happen if the targeting regime were dropped. The markets, predictably, reacted negatively. As Simon Guttmann puts it: 'With no projection, the financial markets concluded that monetary policy must be loose. This created further impetus for the depreciation of the Australian dollar',[52] which became the major issue of 1985 and 1986. Inside the Bank, the question was what would replace targeting as a formula for policy? Given the travails of targeting over the preceding years, it is surprising that more thought had not been given to this question. The Campbell Committee had recognised but not probed the issue of how targeting would cope in a deregulated environment. As for the Bank, Guttmann argues that it was reluctant to canvass the monetary policy implications of financial deregulation or, for that matter, to think about what would replace a targeting regime; the reasons being both uncertainty within the Bank and a reluctance to come clean and potentially unsettle the markets.[53] 'The Reserve's increasing opposition to projections should have led it to investigate how policy could be structured in the absence of projections. Yet the Reserve gave such matters extremely limited attention.'[54]

FURTHER INTO THE POLICY WILDERNESS

Labor's expansionary settings (partly inherited from the electorally inspired expansionism of the Fraser government) saw the economy rebound in 1983–84 and the recession ended. Inflation was also coming down and the Accord seemed to be moderating wages. But Labor soon encountered problems. The chief one was that the Accord was a solution to the macroeconomic problems of the 1970s, not the 1980s and beyond. Stagflation and wage blow-outs had been replaced by chronic balance of payments problems – rising national debt and growing current account deficits – together with mounting pressure from financial markets. Although schools of thought vary, a current account problem loosely reflects an imbalance between savings and investment, and/or structural problems with the country's productive and export capabilities. Starting in the late 1970s, Australia's current account problems began to mount; by the mid-1980s it faced a major current account crisis. The current account deficit approached 6 per cent of GDP, foreign debt ballooned, and the markets dumped the dollar: between early 1985 and mid-1986, the dollar slid about 40 per cent on a trade-weighted basis. The markets were conveying a negative judgement about Australia, the first major message of this kind since financial deregulation and the float of the dollar.

The government and the policy authorities became preoccupied with the current account problem. The Bank's researchers pushed the issue with Keating and offered the bad news that Labor's expansionism was likely to be derailed by mounting current account and debt problems, not to mention the negative market reaction. But Keating was committed to an expansionary program. In a meeting in early May 1986 between Keating and officials from the Treasury and the RBA, Peter Jonson, the Bank's Head of Research, recalls: 'We told him [Keating] he was off track and he's not a man that likes to be told he's off track ... Paul found himself having to do a back flip because of the Bank.'[55] Keating initially resisted the Bank's advice, but in the wake of more bad news on the current account he began to accept its views. Treasury was also urging fiscal discipline.

In April 1986, Keating shocked the nation by announcing that Australia could become a 'banana republic' if the current account was not addressed. Keating rapidly became a convert to CAD mania. The required short-term response was to restrict the economy and stem the flow of imports – an emergency measure, akin to bandaging a burst blood vessel. Fiscal, monetary and wages policy were substantially tightened in this period. It was a major setback for Labor's expansionism.

Macroeconomic policy was plunging into uncharted waters.[56] Financial market deregulation had ended attempts to impose direct regulation or quantitative controls on the monetary and credit system, all but terminating the capacity to control the exchange rate and the money supply. This narrowed the choice of policy instruments to one monetary policy weapon, the Reserve Bank's ability to influence short-term interest rates through its 'open market operations' in the short-term money market. The Bank set a target for the overnight interest rate or 'cash rate', and then operated daily in the market, buying and selling securities in order to hold short-term interest rates as close as possible to the target or 'official' rate. Through various 'transmission mechanisms' this official short-term rate in turn influences, for instance, the mortgage rate and the 90-day bank bill rate. Although long-term interest rates are determined primarily by the bond market and assessments of inflation and other forms of risk, at the short end of the market the official interest rate effectively establishes the *price* of money. This is potentially a potent weapon, albeit with various timelags, in shaping the behaviour of consumers, borrowers and businesses in the real economy.

During 1985 and 1986 the RBA was under extreme pressure. It was feeling its way in the new deregulated financial system since monetary targeting had broken down. In confronting the mid-1980s current account crisis, the Bank used its influence over short-term interest rates to try to reel in the economy. From the government's and the Bank's perspective, the rising CADs were placing strong downward pressure on the exchange rate and thus upwards pressure on inflation.[57] The CAD crisis was likely to cause capital flight and a run on the dollar. The aim of policy was to attempt to reduce the CAD by slowing the economy, thus supporting the exchange rate and reducing pressure on inflation. But the Bank was also concerned about the volatility of the exchange rate and, through policy, sought 'greater stability in the foreign exchange market than market forces alone were likely to produce'.[58] Attempts to stabilise and support the exchange rate in the face of the current account crisis became the focus of monetary policy.[59] As the then Governor, Bob Johnston, explains:

> We in the Bank were getting a bit concerned about the current account. The terms of trade were terrible ... we couldn't go on the way we were. Interest rates would have to rise very substantially ... So I think in those years ... we sort of had quite an orthodox belief about the importance of inflation but we were distracted by the terms of trade.[60]

Figure 2.1   Cash rates, Australia (quarterly averages), 1980 to 1990

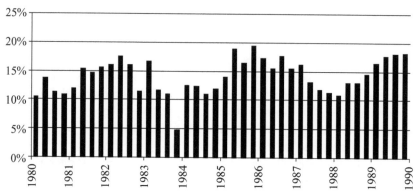

Source: Reserve Bank of Australia Bulletin.

The Bank began to push up interest rates sharply, knowing it was using a largely untested instrument in a new context. As Figure 2.1 shows, cash rates were raised during 1984 and 1985, peaking at a decade high of 18.4 per cent in December 1985.

In contrast to the previous era of quantitative controls on the behaviour of the banks, the new regime operated via the responses of burgeoning financial markets to changes in the official cash rate. The Bank operated through the markets, via the little-understood processes of the transmission mechanism. As the Bank commented in its 1986 *Annual Report*: 'with further experience of a deregulated system, more reliable readings of the likely size and speed of financial market responses [to changes in the official interest rate] may emerge. But, at present, there is still much uncertainty.' Matters were 'complicated by the tendency of markets to overshoot' or react in other skittish ways.[61]

The operation of the interest rate weapon was uncertain; so too were the principles that would guide its use. With monetary targeting suspended, the Bank scrambled for a policy rationale, and in May 1985 it concocted the 'checklist' policy. The initiative came from the Bank, not the government.[62] It was a sign that in the monetary policy wilderness the Bank would increasingly make the running on policy. According to the Bank, the checklist would focus, in some way, on all of the following: 'money and credit aggregates, interest rates, the exchange rate, external accounts, economic activity and inflation'.[63] Peter Jonson, an architect of the checklist, argues that the 'use of a checklist is a way of formally recognizing the many complex and interrelated elements of economic development'.[64] Pointedly, the Bank added that it did not have a 'target' for any of the checklist items. The earlier rough adherence to a monetary policy rule (via monetary targeting) had been dropped, but now it was not clear, at least from the checklist, what the Bank's priorities were. As the Bank now puts it, this was a period of high policy discretion.[65] Bob Johnston explains that, in the wake of the failures with monetary targeting, 'there followed a period of ad hocery'.

> It was well understood that addressing price stability was what monetary policy does best. But there were problems. Partly because economic reform began with financial reform, interest rates were already generally high. Interest rates are a powerful but blunt instrument. Monetary policy was operating with other policies out of kilter. So reforms elsewhere were needed quickly to take some pressure off monetary policy. [Also] the economy was less than robust. The current account was following a roller coaster path … At the time it was considered the balance of payments could not be ignored.[66]

Interest rates were raised sharply in late 1984 and 1985 and then lowered in 1986 and 1987, all in direct response to shifts in the exchange rate. As the Bank's *Annual Report* for 1987 put it, 'The exchange rate became the pressure point.'[67] The Bank not only manipulated interest rates in response to currency shifts during this period, but also actively intervened in the market to buy and sell the currency.[68] It was a partial retreat from the orthodoxy of 1983 that had assumed the float would be 'clean'. The Bank declared it was 'testing the pressures at work and their strength', but it was obviously concerned about where the currency was heading at various points.[69] Its 1987 *Annual Report* stated, 'A major fall in the value of the Australian dollar at the time would have been unhelpful both practically and psychologically.'[70]

But the checklist amounted to policy on the run, a kind of holding operation until something better was formulated. According to Peter Jonson, there was no rush to adopt another formulaic or rule-based approach to policy and there was a kind of 'elegant scepticism' among the Bank's leaders about such matters: 'this tradition in my view explains why most senior people in the Bank accepted the "checklist" – what could be wrong with looking at everything? Having been "burnt" with monetary projections, anyone suggesting a "new rule" would be ruled out of court.'[71] Bob Johnston confirms this: 'partly because of the unhappy experience with monetary targeting, there was some wariness about quickly embracing a new "anchor"'.[72] He explains:

> We were in a transitional phase of having unhooked from monetary targeting, and we had some bruises from that, and we were not wanting to make another mistake. It was a bit like a battalion that had suddenly run into the enemy and was bruised

and retired a bit to think, 'now just how *are* we going to take this lot on?' And you had to, you know, get by on a day-to-day sense.[73]

Yet the checklist was roundly criticised because it could not convey a clear sense of what the Bank was doing or why, and provided no public indicator of the stance of monetary policy. As Ian Macfarlane now admits:

> The problem was [the checklist] did not have a sufficiently well thought-out economic rationale or any criteria for determining which indicators were more important. In particular, it failed to distinguish between the instrument of monetary policy, intermediate targets and ultimate targets … they were all in there … The checklist was introduced in haste … It had not undergone close analysis within the Bank, and had not been exposed to public scrutiny … In defence, it has to be said that the circumstances were very turbulent … There was a feeling that something had to be done.[74]

Macfarlane concedes it was a difficult situation that was handled badly. Getting rid of monetary targeting was the right decision, 'but we weren't prepared for it. We then floundered around with the checklist which just brought ridicule on us.'[75] The journalist Paul Kelly puts it bluntly: 'Monetary policy management in the mid-1980s became an exercise in chaos management.'[76]

> Financial deregulation had destroyed the 1970s orthodoxies in monetary policy and left central banks around the world bereft of any new approach to guide their conduct. The economic and political history of the 1980s is indissolubly linked to the inability of central banks, typified by the Reserve Bank, to identify a new star to guide their monetary management during the initial years of deregulation. It was not just a failure of practice or courage, it was a comprehensive failure of economic theory worldwide.[77]

For a time, it seemed that the restrictionism of 1985 and early 1986 was working. The current account improved on the back of improving terms of trade and exchange rate shifts. Wages were held in check and inflation was trending down. Fatefully, the policy lesson seemed to be that restrictionism and high interest rates did not lead to a recession. Interest rates at the dizzy level of 18 per cent had not crunched the economy: 1987 proved to be a 'soft landing'. As the Bank's former Deputy Governor, Stephen Grenville, explains: 'The exchange rate crisis of 1985 and 1986 had shown policy-makers that interest rates could be shifted sharply without dramatic consequences for [economic] activity.'[78]

MANAGING THE BOOM?

Instead of a slump, 1987 and especially 1988 saw the economy take off in a spectacular boom, driven by the major rebound in commodity prices and improving terms of trade which added as much as 2 percentage points to national income in 1988. Stimulus was also provided by profit growth and improving investment resulting from Accord-based wage moderation. The most important stimulus, however, was an unprecedented credit explosion born of investor exuberance and an increasingly liberalised credit supply in the deregulated context. Credit customers threw off the shackles of earlier credit rationing and surged forth to borrow. Easier credit, combined with the effects of inflation on borrowing and investment decisions, a strong dose of greed-driven asset appreciation, and a tax system that favoured debt, created a feeding frenzy in credit markets. And the banks were only too happy to lend; it seemed like a new bonanza. The banks had been spooked by the entry of foreign banks into the domestic market as part of the deregulation package. But they were professionally unprepared for the hothouse competition of the new deregulated context. John Phillips recalls: 'the banks had been cosseted away for so long. And when they were set free to operate in what became a very free and open market, they were like a bunch of kids set loose for the first time in a lolly shop.'[79] Credit growth had averaged around 20 per cent per annum since deregulation and by late in the decade had reached an extraordinary annual growth rate of almost 30 per cent.

Amidst the frenzy, the Reserve Bank was also unprepared for the new environment. It had failed to gauge the dangers of the credit explosion and subsequent asset price boom. The Bank knew that deregulation would possibly lead to an expansion of credit and it did make an effort to monitor credit growth aggregates. Yet as Bob Johnston admits, the numbers were hard to interpret and the Bank had difficulty in assessing the full measure of the credit expansion.[80] Beyond this, the banks were extending increasingly risky and dubious loans and in some cases were not adequately monitoring the true state of their loan portfolios. By 1986 the Bank had obtained the right to inspect the external auditors' reports of the major banks, but it was not up with the game. A key problem was that the Bank itself was caught up in optimism about deregulation. The operating assumption was that the markets knew best: it was assumed that the banks and lenders would be prudent. At the Bank, Johnston's banking background had helped shape this prevailing assumption. Moreover, any notion regarding strict prudential supervision from the RBA seemed philosophically incompatible with deregulation and the new market freedoms the banks were supposed to be exploiting. But the banks, frightened by the new competition and the entry of foreign banks into 'their' domestic market, began chasing market share and started to lend aggressively, to almost anyone. Several of the major banks (such as Westpac) adopted very large risk exposures to the business high-rollers of the late 1980s. The traditional concept of bank prudence, it seemed, had been abandoned in the chase for market share. The old, close contact between the RBA and the banks was also diluted. After off-the-record interviews with senior insiders in the early 1990s, the journalist Max Suich offered the following observations:

> The Reserve Bank of Australia must be judged to have been asleep at the tiller ... The RBA, which during regulation had firm control of the banks, changed from nanny to couch potato, issuing instructions but taking little intelligent interest in how they were being observed – not least where the quality of bank lending was concerned ... The old intimacy between the RBA and the banks might have revealed at least anecdotal evidence of the extraordinary surge in high risk lending. But the monthly meetings had been replaced with quarterly discussions with individual chief executives and their advisers. The Governor of the RBA since 1982, Bob Johnston, did not always attend these meetings. While the sessions were rigorous and often resented by the banks, the objectives of the meetings were not well defined. If the RBA was no longer a supervising nanny, what was its job and what was it entitled to ask? It spelled out in detail the tasks of the banks in maintaining prudent lending but it had not established any effective way of knowing what the banks were doing ... With almost 30 banks to supervise now, the RBA found it difficult to maintain liaison with them all.[81]

In 1989 the RBA obtained stronger prudential and regulatory capacities via amendments to the *Banking Act*. The main changes were the right to make on-site inspections of the banks and a strengthening of the capacity to secure information from the banks and their auditors. The Bank noted that it sought to continue with a 'flexible and consultative' approach to prudential regulation, with the 'changes to the Act ... providing reserve powers to underpin current practice'.[82] The problem remained, however, that current practice had clearly failed; the horse had already bolted when the legislative revisions closed the stable door.

To compound the problem, the banks preferred to chase market share and profits than to listen to the RBA. In a deregulated environment, even if the RBA had been more proactive on the prudential front, it had no tools except moral suasion. Raising interest rates seemed too tough (at least initially), and the Bank knew that if it got heavy with the banks, credit demand would simply spill over into the non-bank sector or even move offshore. As we will see in chapter 9, the role of central banks and prudential authorities in dealing with credit and asset booms is still one of the central dilemmas of deregulated financial environments.

In Australia in the late 1980s the new faith in unregulated markets helped fuel a wild, debt-driven, speculative boom in which asset inflation took off. It was Australia's first experience of a bubble economy in the wake of deregulation. First the equity market boomed; when it crashed in late 1987 it spilled over into the property markets. By early 1989, credit growth was at record levels; asset prices were soaring; GDP growth was running at an annualised rate of almost 10 per cent; and the current account, as in 1985–86, was rapidly worsening on the back of surging imports and mounting foreign debt. The situation was considered unsustainable, although in contrast to previous booms, both wages and aggregate or CPI inflation were held in check; indeed, underlying CPI inflation *fell* throughout this period. There was no wage blow-out – a testament to the Accord. The budget surpluses of the late 1980s also implied that fiscal policy was reasonably tight: this was certainly Treasurer Keating's view, although it was not shared by some others, including finance minister, Peter Walsh.[83] In any event, the burden of restricting what was mainly an asset boom thus fell onto monetary policy, a policy arm that had overseen a flood of credit in the economy and was now trying to restrict credit by jacking up its price with high interest rates. Compounding these problems were several major errors of monetary policy.

First, the government and the authorities did not move quickly enough to slow the boom. They misread its scale and underestimated what it would take to stop it. There was little understanding, in the new deregulated context, of how hard the interest rate brake would need to be applied. The nature of the brake itself had also changed. In the old regulated system, the authorities could control the volume or availability of credit, and its price. But in the new system they could only control its price.

A complicating factor was that the share market crash of late 1987 had spooked Keating and the authorities. They were reluctant to tighten policy in case liquidity dried up and plunged the economy into a recession, 1930s style. They thought that the share market crash would help slow the economy of its own accord, thus negating the need to tighten policy. As the Bank's *Annual Report* for 1988 stated:

> The crash had two effects on immediate policy. The first was a decision to underpin adequate system liquidity to avoid disorder and instability. The second was a preliminary assessment that the size of the market fall would check growth in demand and credit and remove the need for any re-tightening on monetary conditions. That assessment proved to be wrong.[84]

Another problem was the policy easing that had occurred *prior* to the crash, in the first nine months of 1987. The Bank now accepts that it also erred in this, but argues that the easing occurred because fiscal policy was seen as tight and there was also a concern not to further raise the exchange rate via higher interest rates (and thus potentially unsettle the current account and wreck the government's hoped-for J-curve effect).[85] Also, the Bank did not want to inhibit the rising business investment that had been a long time coming.[86] The thinking (or at least hope) at the time was that a gentle slowing might stabilise the economy without crashing it and without wrecking much-needed investment.

Early 1988 saw intense debate among Keating and his advisers, the Bank and Treasury over appropriate action. As John Edwards explains, Keating was in front of the consensus in the Bank and Treasury.[87] Keating states that he wanted to raise rates early but both Treasury and the RBA advised caution. Both Bernie Fraser, then head of Treasury, and Governor Bob Johnston at the Bank, were reluctant to tighten. According to Keating:

> They were slow putting the rates up. The popular wisdom is that the Bank wants to put the rates up and the Treasurer wants to keep them down ... in my lifetime it was the opposite. I wanted the rates up and the Bank was slow to get them up. In the period after the 1987 stock market crash, when the property market took off, I wanted them up then and it took a long time to get them up.[88]

Bob Johnston recalled:

> On the Bank's initiative interest rates rose, fell and were held steady at various times while I was Governor but always, as far as I can recall, with the acquiescence of the Treasurer. It may have been that the Treasurer at times deferred to my judgment while privately having reservations. I cannot answer that. I guess that, looking back, he is conscious of relying on advice that at times was faulty, as indeed we all were. I do not think there is enough evidence to say anyone was consistently ahead of or behind the game. In any case the Bank recognised that it had been slow to raise rates after the share market crash and it has properly taken full and sole responsibility for that.
>
> 30 March 1988 was a turning point. This was the first meeting between the Treasurer and Bank at which a proposal to tighten monetary policy was tabled. The Treasurer instantly supported the proposal. Then occurred a misunderstanding. Management of moves in the marketplace customarily was in the hands of the Bank. My recollection is that action was delayed at my request to allow markets to settle down after the normal disturbances associated with the oncoming Easter period and a 'Greenspan' like concern for public (non bank) liquidity. But the delay continued, unfortunately, until my return on 21 April from meetings in Basle and Washington.

The Treasurer, not unreasonably had expected instant action to follow the 30 March meeting. He was extremely disappointed by the delay. While valuable time had been lost, it has to be seen in the context of a long preceding period when monetary policy was not tough enough. The episode however put the Bank temporarily on the wrong foot. It might well loom large in the Treasurer's impressions, as it does in mine.[89]

Ian Macfarlane recollected:

> What happened was we had decided we should lift interest rates, we sent it to the Board, we went along to the debrief with Keating and said we should do it, and Keating agreed immediately, so there was no conflict ... [But] Bob Johnston had misinterpreted the meeting, and he didn't realise he had the Treasurer's agreement. He then went overseas for a few weeks and nothing happened. He then came back, and had another conversation [with Keating] then we acted. And Paul Keating and his team are aware of that delay – that mechanical delay – which was a misunderstanding, and they have built it into something much bigger than it should have been.[90]

When Paul Keating returned from the 30 March meeting with the Bank, he reportedly told his staff, 'I've finally got the Bank to put interest rates up',[91] although the first rate rise did not occur until late April 1988. Tightening continued thereafter, eventually pushing the cash rate to 17.9 per cent by late 1989. The rates stayed high for almost a year and a half, the first cut not occurring until January 1990. The only thing that selectively softened the impact of the high rates was a deal worked out between Keating and the major banks, whereby the full rate increase was not passed on to home mortgages. In the late 1980s the mortgage rate was in the unusual position of being lower than the cash rate.[92]

With the benefit of hindsight, it is clear that rates should have been tightened earlier. The Bank has since argued that it was one of the first countries (following the United States) to significantly raise rates during this period, but the Bank's leaders, such as John Phillips, acknowledge the failure. 'I think the Bank was too slow in putting rates up; there is no doubt about that, no doubt about that at all ... in retrospect, we misread the situation badly. One might say we made a hash of it.'[93]

The second policy mistake was that the Bank did not publicise rises in interest rates. It lost the so-called 'announcement effect', the signal to high-rollers and speculators that the Bank was going to get tough and stop the asset and spending boom. This practice of secretly 'snugging' interest rates in a cat and mouse game with the markets was overturned in January 1990 when, under its newly appointed Governor, Bernie Fraser, the Bank began to formally announce its target cash rate and explain policy changes. Fraser recalls:

> I remember on a couple of occasions the Reserve Bank had operated to raise the cash rate by snugging in the market. Some commentators had divined that and made news of it. The market quickly picked it up only to have Paul Keating, when asked, say, No, the Bank is not tightening monetary policy, thus adding to the confusion. It was that tremendous confusion that led me to change the practice.[94]

Many see the announcement of rate changes as a pivotal shift that has given monetary policy more clout and made interest rate setting more predictable and transparent. Prior to this, however, the Bank was secretive. In the mid-1980s, for example, it seemed unwilling even to admit that it controlled short-term interest rates.[95]

Both Treasurer Keating and Prime Minister Hawke compounded the problem by explicitly denying that rate rises were occurring. In 1988, in a bout of wishful thinking, Hawke was saying that rates would be 'down before Christmas'. Rate hikes are supposed to change economic behaviour, but the behaviour of Keating and Hawke reduced this effect. One of Keating's defences is that he wished to comply with the wishes of the Bank not to announce the policy changes. Others, such as Keating's former adviser John Edwards, claim that Keating could have pushed the issue but chose not to.[96] But the Bank itself was also in a difficult position: how could it announce the rate rises (even if it had wished to) when the Treasurer and the Prime Minister were denying them in parliament? The financial journalist Laura Tingle presents a withering critique of Keating's actions:

> Keating's argument that he had to push the authorities to raise rates sits uncomfortably with the fact that he did not acknowledge – for months – that policy had changed, nor did he try to curb the community's perceptions of boom times ahead ... This is probably the point of Paul Keating's greatest culpability in the events that led up to the recession because throughout 1988 he repeatedly lied about the fact that the government was lifting interest rates ... His own justification of this was that he did not want to cut off the investment boom.[97]

Yet it is also true that the Bank was not keen to telegraph its policy because it was groping; it was looking, as usual, for cues from the markets and how lenders and borrowers would respond to rate changes. As Barry Hughes, a one-time Keating adviser, argues:

The Bank carried some very heavy baggage from the earlier days of quasi-monetarism and commitments to free markets. The rhetoric about setting quantities and letting markets look after prices remained for some time after 1985, let alone 1983. This is one reason why the Bank made such heavy weather of admitting its cash rate decisions in the later 1980s. Setting a price stood out like an ugly outcrop in a sea of free markets.[98]

Bob Johnston concurs:

> I have to take a lot of the responsibility. I wasn't advocating a public explanation of the tightening of interest rates. I was beguiled by the view of allowing markets to have more say in what happened and I was really urging the markets to tell us what they thought should happen with interest rates[99] … What did the players in the market really think? … It's all very well pontificating about rates … but why shouldn't the market players have some influence on the rates? Say the Bank decided, we'll put rates up and see what happens. Is that going to turn borrowers off? What's it going to do to lenders? And how do we find equilibrium in this market? And that, you know, was called snugging up, because we just took the view of what the market was doing, and in a sense went along with it … [100] But the markets had gone to water and they were looking for leadership. In hindsight I should have been open and bolder and said we were putting rates up[101] … I suppose it was pretty foolish of us but we were, we were in that, you know, transitional period without much to go on.[102]

The third problem was policy coordination, especially in the critical period of 1989. As Keating and the Bank were trying to slow the economy with higher interest rates, Keating was simultaneously offering stimulatory tax cuts in return for wage moderation under the Accord, to reduce the likelihood of a wage blow-out. As Kelly writes, 'Keating was a car driver who used interest rates as a brake and tax cuts as an accelerator.'[103]

A final problem, and another reason for the authorities' failure to stem the boom, was simply that the RBA lacked market 'credibility'. Despite the high rates, the Bank was not perceived to be 'tough', and there was a widespread view that the Bank and monetary policy would prove to be weak instruments. Believing this, borrowers and speculators were inclined to carry on regardless.

FIGHTING INFLATION SECOND

Looking back on the 1980s it is clear that the monetary authorities were attempting to tackle a series of interlinked problems. Figure 2.2 plots official interest

Figure 2.2   Cash rate versus current account deficit (% of GDP), Australia, 1974/75 to 2000/01

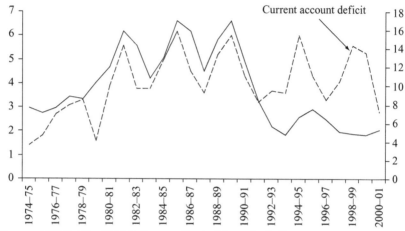

Current account deficit (% of GDP)   Cash rate (%)

Source: ABS Cat No. 5302.0; *Reserve Bank of Australia Bulletin.*

rate shifts against the current account deficit from the mid-1970s onwards. It must be viewed with caution because the two variables interact. Nevertheless, it suggests that monetary policy was highly attentive to the current account situation during the 1980s, including the late 1980s, but that this policy focus lapsed, as we see in the next chapter, after the recession of the early 1990s.

The credit boom and asset inflation (especially in the property market) were probably the major issues for monetary policy during this period. The corollary, of course, was that fighting CPI inflation was not always the primary aim of policy. The rhetoric of 'fighting inflation first' under the Fraser government became the reality of fighting inflation second under Labor in the 1980s. Even during the monetary tightening of the late 1980s, it is clear that CPI inflation was a second-order issue, largely because it was falling during this period. Across the 1980s more broadly, Bob Johnston recalls,

> On the whole it did not seem practical to single out price stability as *the* focus of monetary policy. Interest rates certainly needed to resist inflation but it was hoped that as other policy reforms 'kicked in' [fiscal restraint, microeconomic reform, etc.] inflation could be worked down in a co-ordinated way – steadily but not spectacularly.[104]

As in the early 1980s recession, the Bank was reluctant to go in too hard on inflation. In fact this amounted to the monetary policy orthodoxy in Australia in the 1980s. A king-hit against inflation or Volcker-style disinflation was seen as too damaging and counter to Labor's expansionism. Instead, inflation would be worked down slowly; over time, microeconomic reforms partly aimed at improved productivity would kick in and assist the process. In a paper reviewing the monetary policy of the period, Stephen Grenville argues that in the 1980s, low inflation was essentially something to be achieved on a 'best endeavours basis'.[105] He explains that anti-inflation policy confronted a series of 'policy distractions' (financial deregulation, exchange rate shifts, current account crises and asset booms). Significantly: 'While there was a desire to get inflation down, there was never a sense of pressing urgency. Low inflation was not an overwhelming priority ... Inflation was never seen as "out of hand".' Even more significantly, 'there was never a clear readiness to incur the significant output cost that was required to shift inflation down in a definitive way'.[106]

Yet neither the Bank nor the government was especially dovish in the 1980s. Aggregate or CPI inflation had been reduced during the 1980s, even during the boom late in the decade. The Accord played an important role here. According to Paul Keating:

> The Accords could have been about growth and all sorts of things. They didn't have
> to be about price stability but this one was! Because Kelty [the key union
> negotiator] and I both understood that for working Australians the thing, the monkey
> on their back that matters most in terms of weight is inflation. That is what drives up
> interest rates and cuts their savings.[107]

Monetary policy nevertheless played a role in restraining inflation. Real interest rates in Australia averaged almost 6 per cent in the 1980s, the highest rate in the OECD countries. Figure 2.3 shows the significant falls in underlying inflation from the mid-1980s.[108] The pattern of disinflation is clear. Indeed, as Barry Hughes asks, 'One wonders what monetary policy-makers thought they were doing throughout this period if they were not serious about disinflation.'[109]

So, monetary policy in the 1980s was neither hawkish nor dovish. Inflation was falling under the combined impact of the Accord and the restraint imposed by monetary policy. Peter Jonson thinks that if there was a 'policy wilderness, it produced pretty good outcomes'.[110] Clearly, the intent of both the RBA and the government was to push forward with a number of policy instruments, and they were unwilling to confront inflation if this meant substantial costs for growth or jobs.

Figure 2.3   Annual change to underlying Consumer Price Index, Australia, 1985 to 1997

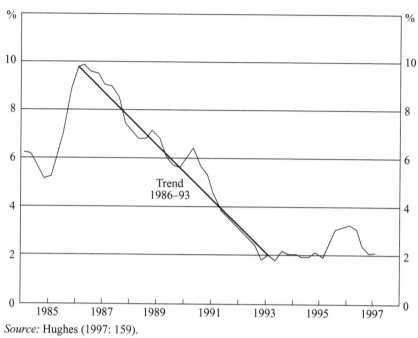

Source: Hughes (1997: 159).

Figure 2.4   Inflation in Australia and the OECD group, 1970/71 to 2002/03

Inflation rate (%)

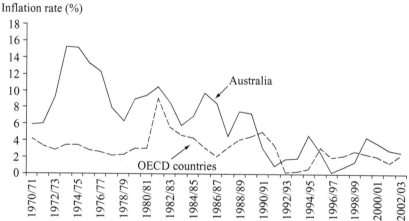

Source: International Monetary Fund, *World Economic Database.*

The key remaining issue, however, was that Australia's inflation rate in the 1980s was consistently higher than the OECD average, though, as Figure 2.4 shows, the difference was narrowing by the late 1980s.

CONCLUSION

In the 1980s the RBA rose to new prominence in the wake of financial deregulation, but its debut was mired in uncertainty. The period is aptly described as a policy wilderness because of high levels of uncertainty surrounding the operation of monetary policy and because of a lack of a settled or consistent policy regime. As Bob Johnston recently commented: 'I guess we were in a monetary policy "wilderness"; enlightenment from on high was a long time in coming.'[111]

Using nautical metaphors, Governor Ian Macfarlane has argued the RBA needed to be made more 'sea-worthy' with a new 'navigation system'. But after a series of experiments and setbacks, including the failure of monetary targeting and the short-lived checklist, Macfarlane admits that 'the Bank entered 1988 with no articulated framework for monetary policy'.[112]

If the RBA was facing uncertainties and difficulties, so was Labor's bold attempt at economic expansion. Structural weaknesses in the economy – major current account problems, large swings in the exchange rate, the forces unleashed by financial deregulation – eventually derailed Labor's expansionist ambitions. Labor's claim that it could drive the economy hard without it collapsing into recession proved to be wrong. Ironically, despite the travails with monetary policy, Labor did manage to reduce inflation in the 1980s. The Accord was central here, but the restraint imposed by monetary policy also helped.

The major calamities for Labor in the 1980s were severe current account problems and eventually a runaway economy. Late in the decade the poorly handled process of financial deregulation came home to roost in the form of a boom in credit and asset prices. As we shall see in the next chapter, the resultant monetary tightening of the late 1980s, and the crash of the early 1990s, formed a watershed. Policy-makers were keen to pull something from the wreckage of the recession, and lower inflation seemed the obvious candidate. The turn of the decade would mark a period when monetary policy stopped playing second fiddle to wages policy on the inflation front and when monetary policy and the RBA were catapulted into the policy cockpit.

CHAPTER 3

Snapping the Stick of Inflation

I will not abrogate responsibility for the stance of monetary policy from the elected government to unelected and unrepresentative public officials in the name of fighting inflation first.

Treasurer, Paul Keating, 1990[1]

After a wild ride during the 1980s, the Australian economy crashed in 1990. On most measures, the subsequent recession was the worst since the 1930s. It proved a defining moment for the Reserve Bank, which finally attacked inflation head on. The Bank emerged from the recession having seemingly conquered inflation, and with new power, focus and resolve. The *Australian Financial Review* eventually concluded that 'The Reserve Bank is now a more powerful force for low inflation than at any time in its history.'[2] This chapter explains how and why the Bank (and Keating) broke the stick of inflation.

CREDIBILITY CRISIS AND RECESSION

Two major factors prompted the Reserve Bank's new resolve about inflation. First, the Bank's uncertain performance in the 1980s, its difficulties in articulating a clear policy framework, and allegations surrounding its relationship with the government, plunged the Bank into a credibility crisis in the late 1980s. For a central bank, lack of credibility is an institutional disaster. A credible central bank has a firm policy stance, an undoubted commitment to low inflation and a track record in dealing with inflation. Financial markets, central bankers and governments all take credibility seriously.[3] Early economic models of credibility tended to focus on the response of labour markets to changes in monetary policy, but increasingly, actors in financial markets have also featured in such models.[4] Credibility is seen as increasing the clout of monetary policy, in part, so the argument goes, by reducing the costs of disinflation by reducing inflationary expectations (but see chapter 5). Former Governor of the RBA Bernie Fraser argues: 'In theory, the more credible a central bank's anti-inflationary credentials, the less it will have to raise interest rates to pursue its [anti-inflation] objective.'[5] If the central bank is seen as serious enough, wage bargainers, it is said, will act moder-

ately (through fear of being crunched by higher interest rates), and financial markets will most likely reduce market risk premiums and long-term interest rates.
This is one reason central bankers watch wage bargainers and bond markets so
closely; they are important guides to inflationary expectations and hence how
monetary policy is travelling and how risks are perceived.

The problem for the Reserve, however, was that it did not have much credibility by the late 1980s for several reasons. As Figure 2.4 showed, Australia's
inflation rate in the 1970s and 1980s had been substantially higher than most
other OECD countries. In the 1980s it had averaged 8 per cent against the average for the leading seven OECD economies of just over 5 per cent.[6] There was
no clear monetary policy framework, and the monetary targeting and checklist
approaches had been found wanting. The Bank's policy framework was seen as
too 'discretionary', especially regarding the vagaries of the checklist. The Bank
had also openly endorsed the Accord as an important weapon against inflation,
but orthodox financial circles, especially overseas, frowned upon incomes
policy (which relied on continuing trade union cooperation). The Bank had also
failed to control the boom. And hawkish critics were concerned that the dual
goals in the Bank's charter, and particularly its statutory obligations regarding
'full employment', were confusing the agenda and diluting the Bank's efforts at
reducing inflation.

Markets perceived Australian monetary authorities as too dovish compared
to the high-profile, hawkish approach adopted in 1989 by New Zealand. The
New Zealand model, as it became known, included legislative changes granting
formal operational independence to the central bank; a formal, and very low,
inflation target (0–2 per cent); a single statutory goal of containing inflation; and
a performance contract for the Bank's Governor.[7] This model rapidly became the
benchmark in central banking and international financial circles, and Australia
compared poorly. As Bernie Fraser recalls:

> The problem was that, in those early years, New Zealand was very much the flavour
> of the month and Don Brash [the Bank's high-profile Governor] and others were
> running around all the financial capitals of the world saying look what a tremendous
> model we have here, and we're streets ahead of the Australians ... well all that was
> unhelpful.[8]

The RBA was also seen by a coterie of critics to be in the government's pocket
(see chapter 5). Initial studies in the field rated its independence poorly, which
damaged its credibility.[9] Perceptions of softness and politicisation were fur-
thered by the appointment of Bernie Fraser as RBA Governor in September

1989. Paul Keating had appointed Fraser as Treasury Secretary in 1984 (when John Stone resigned), and gave him the nod as Governor on Bob Johnston's retirement. Fraser was seen as an inflation dove and as wary of the power of interest rates; in 1988 and 1989 he had argued against tough interest rate measures, urging instead more action on the fiscal and wages front. Fraser was also keen on the Accord and close to Treasurer Keating.[10] Keating had said before Fraser's appointment that he wanted someone in the Bank who was not afraid to push rates down.[11] The decision to appoint an 'outsider' also raised eyebrows within the Bank: John Phillips, strong-minded and much-respected, though somewhat hawkish, had been passed over. Keating admired Fraser's capacities; they were close friends and trusted each other. But those who knew him understood that Fraser was his own man – and he was soon to prove this.

Meanwhile, the Opposition Leader, John Hewson, his shadow Treasurer, Peter Reith, and other critics denounced Fraser and championed a long list of reform proposals regarding monetary policy and the RBA. The Opposition charged that the interest rate reductions that occurred during this period were politically motivated. It also argued that the Bank was too soft on inflation (never mind what the Bank was about to do to inflation) and not independent enough. Indeed, the Opposition declared war on the RBA and proposed, on winning office, to tear up the *Reserve Bank Act* and start again. The blueprint for change was the New Zealand model, which Hewson admired. Within the Bank there was understandable alarm; its institutional foundations were under attack and the fate of senior staff was uncertain.

In the face of this onslaught, Fraser dug in. He even fuelled the fires of contention by openly supporting the government's Accord strategy and, in behaviour which many saw as 'political', took periodic pot-shots at various Opposition policies. In the campaign for the 1993 federal election, he attacked the Opposition's centrepiece Goods and Services Tax (GST), and claimed that comments by John Hewson might have destabilised the dollar.[12] On the GST, Fraser thought the tax would stimulate wage-push inflation, but he also recalls: 'My criticism of the Opposition at different points arose out of my frustration over criticism of the lack of independence of the Bank.' On the Opposition's attack, he says:

> They were political criticisms, but they were the things that were picked up … They got on the front pages of the *Financial Review* and that's all that people in the financial markets in London and New York see. You know, what flashes across the headlines. They didn't understand what the reality was. They didn't see inflation coming down in the way that it was or the way the Bank was operating. So I thought

Hewson, Reith and his like-minded critics who got onto the bandwagon, were doing a great disservice to our international credibility.[13]

Matters were worsened by infamous off-hand comments by Keating in 1989 and again in 1990, which suggested that the Bank lacked independence.[14] In short, as Governor Macfarlane has commented, 'there was clearly great distrust of monetary policy, the government and the Reserve Bank – or, in modern parlance, a lack of credibility'.[15]

The second factor that prompted the Bank to seize the initiative on the inflation front was the early 1990s recession. The recession stands as a policy blunder because of the damage wrought and because it was not planned or expected. But the recession also provided a major opportunity – and the Bank seized it.

Hewson had warned the federal parliament as early as March 1989 that 'there is a very substantial risk of another bust'.[16] Don Russell, Keating's key adviser, thought he heard the economy 'snap' in late 1989.[17] The first major signs of a downturn began to emerge in 1990, with figures revealing a contraction in the December quarter of 1989. Peter Jonson became concerned about a severe downturn (after canvassing the experiences of company insolvency experts), and in May 1990 he outlined his concerns in a letter to Treasury Secretary, Chris Higgins, and to Ian Macfarlane, then Head of Research at the RBA.[18] In July, BHP chief John Prescott gave a speech warning the government about the impact of the high interest rates and the likely severity of the downturn. Criticism of the high rates from different perspectives began to mount, as did criticism of Keating's handling of the economy.[19] A series of worrying statistics on jobs and investment began to accumulate. Keating, though not panicking, became more concerned. The then Industry Minister, John Button, recounts that 'late in the year misery and despair descended on the country … businessmen beat a path to my door. Investment was declining rapidly.'[20] The prevailing view, however, pushed strongly by the Treasury, was that there would be a 'soft landing'. A recession could be avoided.

The high interest rates started to fall, in a long series of reductions, from January 1990. Bernie Fraser, who had taken over as Governor in September 1989, was keen to get rates down. By December 1989 the Bank and Keating had decided to cut rates, but the actual cut was delayed, because of Keating's absence overseas (he wanted to be in Australia for the rate cut) and because of the Christmas season. The cuts were justified on economic grounds. But the rate reductions that occurred prior to the March federal election, plus the announcement (by Prime Minister Hawke) of expected rate cuts after the election, were all grist to the mill for an Opposition claiming the cuts were 'political'. Rates were reduced by about 2 percentage points between January and April 1990; then there was a pause until August after a momentary brightening in the economic data. The Bank and especially the Treasury were concerned not to pull down rates too quickly. Treasury, in particular, was concerned that the economy could surge back. Most advisers still thought there would be a soft landing. Keating and Don Russell were still also concerned about the current account. Russell had insisted in November 1989 that to get the current account down, 'we must not let the monetary screws off too early'.[21]

But doubts were brewing about the current account as a policy focus, and whether monetary policy could effectively deal with it. The former view was expressed during 1989 by the prominent ANU economist, John Pitchford.[22] It turned out to be an influential message for many policy-makers, a 'consenting adults' view of the current account deficit. If the offshore debt that was driving much of the CAD was the result of considered market judgements, why should that concern policy-makers? This argument, plus the build-up of evidence during the 1990s that the debt servicing seemed sustainable, was the start of the decline of official concern about the CAD. Then, in June 1990, the RBA's Deputy Governor, John Phillips, hit the front pages with the latter view: that it was 'blindingly obvious' that monetary policy was a specialised instrument that should be used primarily to fight inflation – that was monetary policy's forte. Ross Gittins of the *Sydney Morning Herald* saw this as 'the Reserve's reaction against the folly of its checklist period', where monetary policy had tried to address all sorts of objectives.[23] More pointedly, Phillips argued that monetary policy should *not* be used to tackle the current account. Phillips's views reflected a growing consensus in the Bank that higher interest rates would most likely inhibit investment and lead to exchange rate appreciation, making it more difficult to export and cheaper to import, thus *worsening* the CAD.[24] Phillips also argued that monetary policy should not be used as a short-term economic tool, but instead should be pitched at medium-term changes, notably on the inflation front. Opposition Leader John Hewson weighed in, agreeing with Phillips.[25] This signal of change to a medium-term policy focus was a critical step for the Bank; it was increasingly willing to accept short-term demand fluctuations – perhaps even a prolonged recession – if this meant making gains on medium-term goals, especially inflation.

Keating was furious. Phillips's views challenged his long-standing policy commitment to the current account. Several journalists suggested[26] that Keating was using tight policy to attack inflation but masking this with CAD rhetoric, because this was allegedly more saleable to the public, but this view stretches credibility: the CAD was rapidly rising while CPI inflation was falling during this period. Keating even had a private briefing with journalists, one of whom later told Phillips that Keating had said he would cut Phillips 'off at the knees'.[27] The internal policy consensus that Keating had worked to achieve was fracturing. Keating publicly attacked Phillips, arguing he would not 'abrogate responsibility for the stance of monetary policy from the elected government to unelected and unrepresentative public officials in the name of fighting inflation first'.[28] Keating was parting company with the Reserve over policy. In a speech to the Metal Trades Industry Association in Sydney, which amounted to a public rebuke of Phillips, Keating said that 'the government would continue to use monetary policy as a central element in its strategy to reduce the current account deficit which remained a key policy target'. He also signalled his wish to get interest rates down quickly and his unwillingness to adopt a heavy-handed monetary policy and to 'fight inflation first'. The government's approach of combating inflation and other policy targets with a range of policy instruments (including the Accord) was 'more real and more comprehensive'. Crucially, hinting at pressure from the hawks within the Bank and Treasury, Keating also said:

> As to the view that interest rates should stay higher for longer, this is being urged on us by those who wish to return to the days of fighting inflation first. This amounts to no more than a strategy of keeping the economy comatose over a long period of time to grind inflation out of the system.[29]

Despite growing doubts, the current account remained a major focus of policy for most of 1990. Indeed, in August Governor Bernie Fraser devoted an entire speech to reaffirming the commitment to tackle the CAD. He argued that worsening current accounts and growing external debt made Australia vulnerable to adverse market reaction. 'Confidence, as we all know, is a fragile thing', he warned. 'Even countries without large foreign debts can be subject to adverse re-assessments by international markets.'[30] Significantly, Fraser also argued that tight monetary policy had substantially reduced imports over the course of 1989/90, and that, in a short-term cyclical sense, 'monetary policy has clearly improved the current account deficit'.[31] This looks like an attempt to appease Keating, although Fraser says it was mainly aimed at calming the financial markets.[32]

However, it was also clear that the Bank was shifting to a view that any *structural* improvement in the current account could only occur over the medium term; that it would not be achieved by monetary policy; and that real improvement would require structural shifts in other parts of the economy (such as more exports and more saving). But some time passed before this view became the consensus within the wider policy elite, especially within the Treasury.

Yet a gradual rethink was occurring on the current account. During the 1980s, Don Russell had said: 'we should set ourselves tests we can pass. The current account is the obvious test – inflation is not.'[33] But with the growing realisation that monetary policy was only at best a short-term emergency palliative for the current account, and at worst counter-productive, the Bank, and eventually Keating, concluded that monetary policy should not be used to directly pursue the current account problem

In a detailed review of this period, former Deputy Governor Stephen Grenville has criticised the lack of consensus among the policy elite during this period, even partly blaming it for the slowness in reducing interest rates in the run-up to the recession:

> Clarity of analysis was not helped by some of those involved in the policy discussion who did see monetary policy as the appropriate instrument to address the current account deficit – this may have encouraged policy to stay firmer for longer into the second half of 1989, in the face of the recognition on the part of the Bank that the economy was slowing.[34]

In a footnote, Grenville quotes the journalist Laura Tingle: 'There was a growing rift between the Treasury and the Reserve Bank on the appropriate use of policy. Treasury was more aligned with Keating's position of explaining changes in interest rates in terms of balance of payments, a position some of the Reserve Bank thought was ridiculous.'

For his part, Keating became increasingly concerned about the economy by mid-1990 and soon started pushing the Bank to cut rates further. Following the March 1990 federal election, which returned Labor, Keating was furious with the Bank for a press release that appeared to hem him in and postpone further cuts indefinitely.[35] The Bank, he thought, was attempting to set the agenda and had not briefed him. He says he gave the Bank's leaders a 'ferocious pasting' over the matter, 'the only one in my whole period'. Tensions between the Bank and Keating were boiling over. Normally the Bank would consult with the Treasurer on such matters, and Keating regarded the Bank's unilateral move as a 'very large breach of the protocol ... it was a decidedly silly thing to do, and this they did without consultation'.[36] Yet even in July Keating was saying publicly that there was no need to panic and no urgency about pulling rates down. Following the release of numbers showing an improvement in the current account, he said: 'While, of course, the government is conscious of the pressures of a firm monetary policy, we cannot risk rekindling demand in a way which would threaten the downward trend in the current account and inflation.'[37]

Finally, amidst clear signs of a downturn, rates were finally reduced in August. Both Keating and the Bank thought a cut of 1 per cent was appropriate, with Keating explaining that 'we are not trying to recess the economy'.[38]

Yet Treasury, hawkish to the end, strongly resisted the cuts. It was convinced there would be a soft landing, 1987 style; that policy-makers should not panic; and that further gains should be made on the current account and inflation. Treasury's analysis of the situation in the August Budget Papers even spoke of monetary policy being directed towards *restraining* domestic growth, expecting that employment would only be minimally disrupted. The message was repeated in September. The Treasury Secretary, Chris Higgins, took the extraordinary step of arguing against his minister's preference for a rate cut at the Bank Board meeting that endorsed the August interest rate cut.[39] Tensions were mounting within the official family, an issue we take up again in chapter 5.

What stands out during this period are the misjudgements and doubt among all concerned. They were uncertain about the state of the economy, about the setting of interest rates, about whether to cut rates, and subsequently, about the size and pace of rate cuts. Part of the problem was faulty economic forecasting. Too little growth was forecast prior to the recession and too much once it started. There was also the lag – often a year or more – between changes in interest rates and effects on the real economy. By the late 1980s policy-makers also thought that microeconomic reform might make the economy more flexible and resistant to a recession. This assumption proved incorrect. The boom and especially the subsequent recession were also misread because there was no wage blow-out, as had occurred in the major downturns of the 1970s and early 1980s. Also, the share market crash of 1987 appeared to indicate that an asset price bubble could burst without doing much damage to the real economy. There was also the false impression generated by the experience of 1986–87: that very high interest rates could be followed by a soft landing. Nor was there sufficient recognition that the late 1980s boom was driven by a new and virulent form of asset inflation, first in equities and then subsequently, and more powerfully, in the property market. Finally, there was the basic problem: nobody knew exactly what the effects of high interest rates would be in a deregulated, credit-saturated financial system. Policy-makers were flying blind. As the Bank now puts it, there was an ongoing 'calibration' problem with the interest rate weapon. Some insiders have also claimed that the policy-making procedure at the time was myopic and tended to look backwards at existing data for guidance on the effects of policy that would not impact on the economy till as much as a year later.[40] Keating was more forthright. In 1989, reflecting on the monetary policy process and the Bank's role, he said to a colleague, 'They go on with all this bullshit, because they won't admit

it's an art, not a science.'[41] Several years later Bernie Fraser gave a speech entitled 'The Art of Monetary Policy'.[42]

As 1990 wore on, talk of a recession became common. In September and
October economic news continued to worsen. Keating denied there would be a
recession and resisted calls for faster reductions in interest rates. Interest rates
were cut again in October; again Treasury opposed them. Most official forecasts
predicted the economy would begin to lift in 1991. Uncertainty was rampant.
The September quarter figures revealed a production slump of 1.6 per cent, the
biggest slide in seventeen years. Profits were well down, and the farm sector was
hit hard. Several prominent economists formally warned the government of a
pending crash.[43] Industry Minister John Button recalls that Prime Minister
Hawke 'seemed incapable of believing that a recession was about to happen'.[44]
Finally, in early November, the figures showed Australia had entered a recession.
After insisting there would be a soft landing during most of 1990, Keating was
forced to use the R word. Labor, the anti-recession party, had brought on the
worst recession since the 1930s. In desperation, Keating at a press conference
on 29 November infamously proclaimed 'it was a recession Australia had to
have'. Keating loved pithy one-liners and sometimes regretted them. This one
was a major gaffe.

Displaying the benefits of hindsight, in early 1992 the Bank's newly
appointed Deputy Governor, Ian Macfarlane, gave the most candid official post-
recession assessment of the situation: 'The dynamics of a modern capitalist
economy are such that it is hard to believe that this excess [the boom] could have
been followed by a gentle slowing.' So much for the soft landing! 'It was far
more likely', Macfarlane continued, 'that it would be followed by an absolute
contraction. Some people think that if only the instrument of monetary policy
could have been adjusted in a more skilful and timely manner we could have
avoided the recession. But I very much doubt it.'[45] This is close to saying it was
the recession we had to have.

FIGHTING INFLATION FIRST

As we have seen, the Bank and the government had shied away from a frontal
assault on inflation in the 1980s. The Bank had taken a back seat to the Accord
and its wage–tax deals in managing inflation. When Bernie Fraser became
Governor in 1989 he talked about 'policy coordination', implying that the same
formula would continue, with monetary, wages and fiscal policy working in
tandem, but without a major new commitment to fighting inflation. The Bank's
caution, or at least Fraser's caution, as well as Labor's quest for jobs and expan-

sionism, were important factors here. But there were also concerns about the political feasibility of a frontal assault on inflation, and the large mortgage belt was sensitive to increases in interest rates. The costs of fighting inflation were likely to be high, and the anti-inflation constituency in Australia was not strong. Fraser had argued in 1984 that it was difficult to see how monetary and fiscal policy 'on their own' could significantly reduce inflation 'without incurring socially and politically unacceptable levels of unemployment'; the implication was that a gradualist approach supported by an incomes policy was the best route.[46] Moreover, by the late 1980s, Keating was publicly attacking the Opposition over its 'scorched earth' approach to fighting inflation. Even the banking sector, supposedly the anti-inflation hawks, were bleating about the punishing impact of high interest rates after their lending spree and bad loans of the late 1980s.[47] John Phillips observed late in the decade, 'there appears to be no organised group in the community spearheading a campaign against inflation'.[48] As Bernie Fraser put it: 'People generally feel that inflation is bad, but ... not so bad that they want the authorities to get too serious about eliminating it.'[49] Michael Stutchbury, a financial journalist, provided the best summary:

> The problem with Australia is that everyone has come to believe that the central
> bank will never be serious about extinguishing inflation. This means the Reserve
> Bank would have to deliberately engineer a deep recession to tame inflation ... And
> there is no constituency in Australia – be it voters, the farmers, the miners, the
> retailers, the builders, the manufacturers or the unions – which wants to get rid of
> inflation that badly. This is Bernie Fraser's mission impossible.[50]

It was the recession that finally drove policy-makers beyond this political impasse. There is no evidence that the recession was foreseen, despite Macfarlane's clarity of hindsight above. It was a policy blunder wrought by those who, post-1986, thought high interest rates could end with a soft landing. So the recession was a turning point.

Nevertheless, even independently of the dynamics that spun out of the recession, the Bank was beginning to worry about inflation. It had thought that inflation would continue to trend down as it had through most of the 1980s, but as Stephen Grenville puts it, the 'mindset' within the Bank began to change.[51] Bernie Fraser agrees: 'I think there was more urgency and more desire too to try harder to do something about inflation.'[52] Clearly, the 1980s Accord-based strategy was starting to look too gradualist. In the context of the speculative boom of the late 1980s, the Bank had begun to realise that inflation was seriously distorting investment and savings decisions, promoting a speculative culture, and undermining the kind of investment that was required to effectively restructure the real economy. Other factors were the Bank's poor credibility and mounting external criticism and pressure on the Bank regarding inflation, especially from the Opposition. Ian Macfarlane recalls:

> At first, there was little pressure from the markets, the press or the economic community to deliver a new [monetary policy] framework because by 1988 the currency woes of 1985 and 1986 seemed to be behind us. But that soon changed as critics began to focus on the fact that Australian inflation had not returned to relatively low rates as it had in most OECD countries. This [was a] period of intense criticism – roughly from 1989 … The main charge of the critics was that Australia was still an inflation-prone economy, and that its central bank was never going to improve the situation … Other high inflation countries such as the United Kingdom and New Zealand and Canada were doing something about 'stiffening up' their monetary policy frameworks, but Australia appeared to be doing nothing.[53]

Some of the Bank's senior insiders were becoming frustrated. Peter Jonson, the Bank's Head of Research, resigned in 1988 and began writing articles about why the Bank should be more independent and strengthen its resolve to attack inflation.[54] He argued that 'greater weight should be given to the longer-term view and that our central bank should be more independent and more outspoken in providing that view'.[55] He had argued in 1988 that 'monetary policy seems to have performed well',[56] but as the wider anti-inflation campaign intensified Jonson began to write about the need not just to reduce inflation, but to 'eliminate' it. He even suggested a change to the Bank's charter to enshrine the low-inflation goal and endorsed the view that the short-term costs of cracking inflation would be outweighed by the long-term gains.[57] According to Jonson, 'having a credible former insider making these points in public had a positive impact on the debate – it certainly kept the insiders honest and got under Paul Keating's skin'.[58] John Phillips and Ian Macfarlane were also pushing within the Bank. In the late 1980s senior Treasury officials – such as Des Moore and David Morgan – called for a lift in interest rates even higher than the 18 per cent rates of the period as a king-hit against inflation.[59] Fraser was also becoming irritated by the attacks on the Bank. As Peter Jonson puts it, 'he had me out there giving him a bit of stick … and a lot of people saying in effect to him "you know, well show us what you're made of mate".'[60]

The first clear signs of the Bank's strengthening resolve on inflation appeared in April 1990, in a speech by Fraser simply entitled 'Inflation'.[61] As Ross Gittins later wrote, 'It was Bernie Fraser who, earlier this year, delivered the most detailed and persuasive speech we've heard in years about exactly how and why inflation harms Australians.'[62] At the time, however, the Bank's credibility was so low that the speech was greeted with ridicule. The *Australian* commented that 'it is just a pity that the Governor, Mr. Fraser, has taken so long to express the ... elimination of inflation as his main concern'. For too long, the *Australian* railed, 'the Bank has acted as a tame appendage of government policy – a role for a central bank which is not conducive to the defeat of inflation'.[63] But the Bank's *Annual Report* for 1990 was shot through with anti-inflation rhetoric, much more than had been the case. The pressure was clearly on the Bank to up the ante on inflation. Some have argued that the Bank attacked inflation in an opportunistic sense, only once there were clear signs that it was falling.[64] Grenville rejects this. 'Some have argued that the Bank's inflation focus came as a result of the (implicitly accidental) success in reducing inflation. The clearest refutation of this view is in the mid-1990 *Annual Report*, with its singular attention to inflation, at a time when inflation had not yet fallen substantially.'[65]

Nevertheless, the Bank's forecasts were predicting falls in inflation and, as the scale of the recession became clearer during 1990, the Bank made a further crucial calculation: the unexpected recession could be a one-off opportunity to defeat inflation once and for all. As the recession rapidly worsened, it was a new resolve. Initially, the view within the Bank was that the high interest rates of the late 1980s should be milked to help lower inflation, but as the economic news worsened, a more determined view emerged. It was a two-stage process: policy blunder, followed by a calculated, strident attack on inflation. Yet the policy calculations (and miscalculations) were always mediated by uncertainty about the true state of the economy; in addition to forecasting errors, the Bank failed to anticipate the depth and impact of the recession. The Bank was slow in pulling rates down. There was a fear that inflation could return. But as the scale of the recession became clear, the view emerged, as John Phillips recalls, that 'we needed to get the benefits from the recession'.[66] Former Treasury Secretary, Tony Cole, concurs: 'there was a view that, right, we've got to get something out of this. We'd been through a hell of a lot of pain.'[67] Indeed, the dramatic use of high rates had resurrected a belief in the potency of monetary policy, and the Bank could now seemingly make major gains on, if not crack, inflation, at a time when its credibility and reputation were at a low ebb. Ultimately, Australians would get low inflation whether they wanted it or not. It was classic elite-led policy-making, and the elites were in the Bank and the wider official family. Grenville argues:

> The key to establishing price stability was that the 1990/91 recession provided the *opportunity* ... and the monetary policy framework was ready (in a way that it had not been in earlier recessions, such as 1982/83) to use the opportunity ... The Bank did not set policy with a view to producing the sort of inflation-busting downturn

that had occurred in the United States in 1979–80 (the Volcker deflation) ... But, when the recession came ... the policy response was quite different from the recession of 1982–83 and the slowdown of 1986, when the Bank had been a passive player in the unfolding events – in 1990 the Bank was prepared to use the opportunity to achieve a *structural* downward shift in inflation ... This required that policy should focus, much more sharply than before on inflation.[68]

Bernie Fraser also recalls 'we wanted to seize the opportunity to really make some progress on inflation'.[69] 'It was not a matter of crudely "fighting inflation first" but of seizing the opportunity to hold onto the gains flowing from the recession while also trying to revive the economy.'[70] In late 1990, when he was predicting that 'the downturn could be a bit deeper and more protracted than some forecasters envisage', Fraser also said the Bank was not only concerned about the short-term demand situation in the economy (dealing with the recession) but was also looking to make gains on 'medium-term' objectives, especially on inflation. 'If we were concerned about demand alone, maybe we'd have interest rates lower than they are now.' But, Fraser continued, 'our judgement at the moment is that we need to ... keep demand running along at a *subdued pace* for some time to make progress on inflation'.[71] In September 1991, Fraser followed up in a speech:

> When the economy is running hot, everyone can agree on tighter policies; it is when the economy slows, and the stance of policy *remains* relatively firm, that policymakers demonstrate their resolve to wind back inflation. This resolve has been demonstrated in Australia of late ... We remain deadly serious about ... hanging on to recent gains on inflation but also to improving on them.[72]

Suddenly, it seemed, even the so-called doves were 'deadly serious' about inflation. The *Australian*, now running to catch up and rapidly revising its approach to Fraser, commented: 'While Mr. Fraser continues to endure attacks from monetary policy purists for being a monetary policy dove [an attack made by the *Australian* not long before], the Reserve, under his governorship, has one of the tightest monetary policies in the world.'[73]

It seemed that Keating's nightmare, 'keeping the economy comatose over a long period of time to grind inflation out of the system', was coming true. Referring to policy 'tensions' in this context, John Phillips recalls:

> I think it was only resolved actually because we, you know, we got the interest rates and held the interest rates long enough that in fact it started to have an impact ...
> When the forecasts suggested it [inflation] was going to come down, everybody got

on the bandwagon. I mean it wasn't that much earlier that I'd been talking about how impossible it was to find a lobby for lower inflation.[74]

Probably the frankest statement of the new resolve, explicitly acknowledging that policy had prolonged the recession, came from Macfarlane in 1992:

It may have been possible to have a somewhat smaller recession if all the policy guns had been quickly turned towards maximum expansionary impact. But if we had followed this course how could people credibly have believed we were serious about reducing inflation? ... The central point is that on this occasion we had to run monetary policy somewhat tighter than in earlier recessions and take the risk that the fall in output would be greater than forecast. To do less than this would be to throw away a once-in-a-decade opportunity for Australia to gain an internationally respectable inflation rate.[75]

As Macfarlane also acknowledged, the Bank was willing to take 'risks' with unemployment in an attempt to make major inroads on inflation. The older, 1980s orthodoxy of slowly reducing inflation on a number of fronts had been dumped amidst the trials and opportunities presented by the recession. In contrast to the previous recession, the Bank was clearly willing to pursue inflation and chase the economy down amidst the worst recession since the 1930s. For his part, Bernie Fraser recalls that achieving gains on inflation was a major aim during this period, but he was also pushing against hawkish colleagues in the Bank and the Treasury for a policy stance that took economic activity into account.[76] The Bank's 1992 *Annual Report* sums up this view, claiming that policy had been 'pursued with an eye to the implications for activity and employment', with the aim of 'pursuing a *balance* between inflation and activity'.[77] We will return to this issue in chapter 5.

Macfarlane explains that during this period the authorities were also concerned about adverse market reaction if the Bank eased off the brakes too quickly and forced the pace of interest rate reductions. Bernie Fraser says that opinions about the degree of market constraint on policy varied within the Bank, although Fraser too 'thought the markets important'.[78] In a telling commentary about the constraints (or perceived constraints) on policy imposed by the markets, Macfarlane explains that: 'the financial markets set a corridor in which monetary policy can act'.[79] It was the exchange rate market and the long-term interest rate or bond market that mattered most in this respect. Grenville recalls:

the speed of interest rate reduction was influenced by judgements about how the market's inflation expectations were moving – as measured by the exchange rate and the long bond rate … For the most part the Bank was pushing at the edge of what the market would accept in terms of rate reductions.[80]

As the Bank argued in 1993, 'if financial markets had sensed that policy had "lost the plot" or was giving too little weight to inflation control, long-term interest rates could have responded adversely with unfavourable consequences for activity'.[81] From late 1990 and increasingly in 1991, short-term cash rates and long bond rates finally began moving down together, evidence that the markets were lowering their inflationary expectations.

Meanwhile, as Laura Tingle says: 'the push for a change of policy focus came from the Reserve Bank, backed by some in Treasury, to get Keating to stop focussing so exclusively on the current account, and to turn his rhetoric more to link monetary policy to fighting inflation rather than imports'.[82] John Edwards adds that 'the possibility that there would not be good news on the current account but good news on inflation, combined with the realisation that the recession was quite deep, induced Keating to accept a significant change in his public line'.[83] Officials within the Bank and the Treasury had also been urging Keating to adopt a 'medium-term' policy focus, to downplay the short-term pain of the recession and to focus on the medium-term goal of cracking inflation. Keating resisted the argument during 1990, although the Bank was upping its anti-inflation rhetoric. But in early 1991 Keating changed focus and backed his bureaucrats in the face of gains on both inflation and the current account, encouraged by the Bank's arguments that low inflation might also prove useful in tackling the structural problems of the current account in the medium term. As the Bank argued: 'Monetary policy can best contribute to a sustainable external positioning the same way that it can best contribute to overall growth, namely by providing an environment of low inflation.'[84] Keating had been using fiscal surpluses and increased public savings to try to fight the CAD during the late 1980s, but this 'fiscal rock' was smashed by the recession. In the depths of the recession, the good news on the inflation front looked like a minor salvation. It was something the government *could* achieve. After meeting with the Bank's leaders, Keating announced the new priority in a speech in February 1991:[85]

> I want to put at the head of our agenda another great task in reforming the
> Australian economy. I don't just want to bend inflation a little and see it spring back.
> I want to snap the inflation stick and bring Australia back into the community of its
> OECD partners.[86]

Ross Gittins analyses Keating's new inflation zeal:

Keating started giving these speeches about snapping the stick of inflation. He'd never been very big on inflation. But he could see it coming, and his advisers could see it coming ... and it occurred to me this is a fabulous political trick. You can see it ... all you do is stand up and say 'I command the waves to fall back', and that means you've caused it and you get the credit ... 'I'll predict it and I'll demand it and I'll command it and I'll lump it, and then I'll get the credit'.[87]

Keating had always sought to reduce inflation, but it had not been the priority during the 1980s. Keating's preferred method was the negotiations of the Accord and the slow process of reform and structural change in the economy, not a bitter process of disinflation. Inflation only became the priority for Keating once the recession took hold and he felt trapped by circumstances. In a glib concession, Keating said that the recession would 'de-spiv' Australia. But he was never whole-hearted in the push to keep the economy running at a 'subdued pace' and pushed the Bank for faster rate reductions.[88] When interviewed, he blamed the Bank for the severity of the crunch. They 'were exceptionally slow about bring-ing them [interest rates] down. In other words, they prolonged the recession by being very slow to pull them down ... The problem about the Bank is it was always too slow on the way up, and far too slow on the way down.'[89] But at other points (in the same interview), Keating appears happy to be cast as the inflation fighter and as the Bank's major ally.

The Bank had to have a standing in the world and at home. And I was about building that standing by successfully fighting inflation ... And in the end, if I had not been prepared in 1990 to push or hold the rates up, we would never have hammered inflation into the ground ... That was the priority. The priority was I was not going to see the wage restraint [of the Accords] wasted.[90]

Via circumstances, it seemed, Keating had shifted from fighting inflation second to fighting inflation first.

Although inflation was falling, all the rate reductions during 1990 and 1991 were assailed by a storm of criticism from the Opposition and sections of the media for being too dovish, 'political', or premature. The flak annoyed the Bank, especially Bernie Fraser. There was even speculation that Fraser would be forced to resign should the Opposition win the 1993 federal election.[91] At one point in late 1991, in response to a tedious stream of criticism from shadow Treasurer Peter Reith, Fraser famously snapped back, saying: 'I won't go to appease some dickhead minister who wants to put Attila the Hun in charge of monetary policy.'[92] Fraser explains:

Reith would have been inclined to try to sack me if they had won the 1993 election and that prospect largely prompted my response. I was not going to resign, so they would have had to sack me, and to have a good reason for it ... This would have required the disputes procedure to be invoked, but that would have been a very high-risk strategy for the government.

I was actually in Tokyo when the Attila the Hun response hit the news and Reith's office was feverishly trying to track me down to get me to retract, which I could not. The Bank was pushing interest rates down, and these characters were saying we were going to re-ignite inflation and boom-bust conditions; by implication, the Bank shouldn't have been pushing interest rates down. So, Reith's Governor would have been holding interest rates steady, at best, as the economy's nosediving; a prescription for torching the economy.[93]

The Opposition's attack seemed to imply that interest rates should not have been reduced in the early 1990s or, at least, should have come down even more slowly than they did. As we have seen, Fraser had first suggested cutting rates in December 1989 but there was a delay because of Christmas and Keating's absence overseas. Fraser was also cautious about reducing rates, and in a letter to the Board in January had suggested that lowering inflation should remain an important focus of policy.[94] Interest rates began to fall in January 1990 before the full brunt of the recession hit. But it was the lags between rate reductions and effects on the economy and the gradual pace of the policy easing that were to prove fateful. Looking back on the fifteen rate reductions between January 1990 and May 1993, Fraser concedes: 'In retrospect, of course, we should have eased earlier and faster.'[95] The prominent economist John Quiggin points out that almost three years passed from the first signs of a slowdown in 1989 until 'a shift in fiscal and monetary policy to a stance that could reasonably be described as stimulatory'.[96] Indeed, beyond the high interest rates of the period, a renegotiated Accord in 1991 had brought wages policy to bear on inflation, and fiscal policy too remained relatively tight, especially for a recessionary context.[97]

In its 1992 *Annual Report*, the Bank announced that underlying inflation had fallen below 3 per cent, the lowest rate for two decades. 'A critical threshold has been breached', the Bank said. It marked a structural shift towards lower inflation. Australia recorded one of the largest comparative falls in inflation among the advanced economies in this period (see Table 4.1), and emerged from the recession with one of the lowest rates of inflation in the world. Governor Fraser announced that 'price expectations, which are now seen as occupying a central role in the inflationary process, have been cracked'.[98] The stick of inflation had seemingly been snapped. Bernie Fraser's 'mission impossible' had been achieved.

Figure 3.1   Unemployment and inflation, Australia, 1970/71 to 2002/03

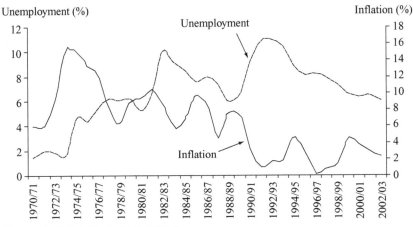

Source: ABS Cat. No. 6203.0, 6401.0.

Moreover, the inflation gains were locked in during the 1990s. Having delivered a king-hit against inflation, the Bank was still concerned about community support for low inflation. In 1993, for example, Bernie Fraser commented that: 'The high inflation rates of earlier years were lamented widely, but our re-entry to the low inflation club has not brought out large numbers of cheering fans ... Our role as guardians of low inflation is important in part because there is no strong natural lobby for it in Australia.'[99] By default, it seemed, the policy elite at the RBA had become the new policy guardians.

WHAT ABOUT EMPLOYMENT?

The damage wrought by the recession was immense: high unemployment, thousands of failed businesses, and a major loss of output. The associated banking crash racked up about $25 billion in bad loans, intensifying the malady: in fact, the losses were worse (relative to GDP) than the 1980s savings and loans crisis in the United States. Bernie Fraser made several speeches about the 'recovery' during this period, but there was no denying that low inflation had been bought at a high price. Unemployment peaked at around 11 per cent in December 1992. Almost one million people were officially unemployed.

Figure 3.1 shows the policy priorities of the 1990s. The battle against CPI inflation had been largely won, but the battle against unemployment (to the extent there was a battle) had been less successful. During the 1990s the unemployment rate averaged 8.9 per cent. Clearly, most of the risks in the system, especially in the first part of the decade, were being taken on the employment front.

Bernie Fraser argued that, with lower inflation in a post-recessionary context, the employment could recover: 'such losses can in fact be made good'.[100] But progress was slow. The 1990s recovery, though lasting longer than the 1980s recovery, proved a hard road in terms of job creation – especially full-time, well-paid jobs.[101] Moreover, assessing the impact of major recessions on employment depends on one's view of the labour market. The theory of labour market 'hysteresis' suggests that the labour market, once significantly perturbed, may fail to readjust; the damage is likely to be long-term. Indeed, some recent studies have shown that recessions tend to create high levels of structural and long-term unemployment and that it is very difficult for the economy to return to its pre-recession state.[102]

The experience of the RBA in the early 1990s typifies the default position of central banks around the world: prioritising low inflation. But where does this leave the second of the RBA's dual goals, its obligation to pursue full employment? The message from the Bank was that the two could not be pursued simultaneously and that it would always fight inflation first.

Does the Bank pay mere lip-service to the full employment part of its charter? Following the recession, the Bank detailed its views on unemployment in a 1993 paper, *Towards Full Employment*.[103] The Bank rehearsed the theme that most of the unemployment problem was not a macroeconomic issue at all, but was a 'supply-side' or 'structural' issue related to the workings of the labour market. It was best tackled through programs of labour market 'flexibility'. The Bank also argued that low and stable inflation is the best recipe for *sustaining* an expansionary economic cycle, and therefore the best macroeconomic therapy for unemployment. In other words, the Bank seeks what it sees as the highest *sustainable* rate of GDP and employment growth consistent with maintaining low inflation. Central bankers in the RBA and elsewhere have attempted to establish this as the new 'common sense' about the nature of unemployment and about the links between unemployment and inflation. The Bank has sought to equate its response to employment with its preferred inflation-first policy.

In this context, the Bank, and particularly Bernie Fraser, defended the Bank's dual goals. At the time, Chris Eichbaum considered this 'manifestly exceptional' for a central bank, although these days more central banks are slowly acknowledging the need for some kind of policy balance.[104] In Australia, the issue became politicised in the late 1980s and early 1990s amidst strident calls by the Opposition and other critics for the Bank to drop its charter and follow

New Zealand's lead of 1989 by establishing a tough single goal of low inflation. The aim was to focus the Bank's attention more firmly on inflation and to make assessments of the Bank's performance easier and more transparent. John Phillips, the Bank's Deputy Governor during this period, said 'fighting inflation deserves top billing',[105] and now recalls that he always thought the dual goals were 'a bit of nonsense, to be honest'.[106] Fraser, however, rejected such calls and clearly believed in the dual goals. But why? Twin goals were increasingly out of step with international trends in central banking at the time. And certainly, the Bank had shown considerable resolve in crunching inflation. So was dualism 'a bit of nonsense'?

Fraser, just before his retirement from the Bank in 1996, argued dovishly that central banks, 'should not be fixated solely with inflation, and we should not be loading the dice even more in that direction'.[107] Debate about the efficacy of dual goals versus the single goal of inflation relates to orthodox debates in monetary economics about whether policy should be conducted mainly within a medium-term framework, having little regard for fallout in the short term. The prevailing view among central bankers and economists is that policy should pursue a medium- to long-term approach aimed at the *unitary* goal of low inflation, largely because orthodoxy holds that in the medium to long term there is no trade-off between inflation and unemployment.[108]

Fraser remained unconvinced. 'The problem with this [orthodox] argument … is that the long term can be quite long indeed – five years or more. In the short term – that is, in the year or two ahead, which is clearly a highly relevant period for most people – trade-offs do arise.'[109] Significantly, Fraser insisted the RBA's policy stance would have been even more hawkish without the dual goal charter. Ian Macfarlane agrees: 'We were worried that if central banks were to be judged *only* by inflation results, there would be a tendency to over-achieve' on the inflation front.[110] Discussing the early 1990s, Fraser points not only to what he saw as his strategic use of the dual goal charter, but also to some tension within the Bank over policy:

We should have moved faster to cut rates yet there was a lot of resistance to moving even as fast as we did. This is where the dual goals become important because if we didn't have them and were stuck with inflation as the sole objective, as in the New Zealand or European model, it would have been easier for those in the Bank who were uncomfortable about moving as rapidly or as often as we did to lower interest rates to point to such a single objective [i.e. a low-inflation one]. I was able all the time to counter with the argument that we were also legally charged with a concern about growth and employment. Without the dual goals I don't have any doubt at all (particularly given the media and political criticism of many of the rate cuts) that it would have been very much harder to make those rate reductions. Equally, there would have been more pressure than there was to start increasing rates in mid-1994, and to go further than we did. There were a lot of people wanting the Bank to raise rates further in 1994 and 1995, including in the Treasury. I think it made an enormous difference to have those dual goals.[111]

As to the tensions within the Bank during this testing period, Fraser recalls:

Central bankers traditionally think in terms of fighting inflation above all else, and the RBA was no different. The various public comments during this period by Ian Macfarlane, John Phillips and others bear this out. I did not grow up in this culture, and did not share it. This made for some on-going tensions within the Bank, but, with some effort, these were manageable.[112]

Fraser and others within the Bank have also defended the dual goals on what can only be described as 'political' grounds. Notwithstanding the events of the early 1990s, the Bank considered it important not to appear too hawkish. Hawkishness might appeal to financial markets, but there is also the issue of wider community legitimacy; here the Bank looks better, so the argument goes, if it can articulate some connection between what it does and improvements in growth and employment. Non-financial business interests in the real economy generally favour the retention of the dual goals.[113] Glenn Stevens, the Bank's current Deputy Governor, recalls that in the early 1990s: 'The RBA was, from the start, honest enough to say that it cared about inflation but not *only* inflation. We were always conscious of avoiding being ... called "inflation nutters".'[114]

The institutional life of a central bank has been depicted in terms of this potential tension between market credibility, on the one hand, and wider community legitimacy on the other.[115] In the RBA's case, a positive approach to employment seemed appropriate. As Bernie Fraser said in 1996:

A lot has been written about the Reserve Bank's 'credibility' in the narrow context of the Bank's credibility with the financial markets for delivering low inflation. This is important, but to actually deliver low inflation the central bank needs credibility [legitimacy] in labour and other markets more than it does in financial markets. To build this broad community support for its anti-inflation objective, the Bank also needs to build credibility in relation to its other objectives. Community support for low inflation is likely to dissipate unless the Bank can help to deliver some gains in employment and living standards.[116]

This implied, at least since the recession, that the Bank would try to avoid crunching the economy and that it would have regard for employment and economic activity. Stephen Grenville has argued: 'there is a presumption that central banks, which are responsive and accountable to the public, should take activity into consideration in setting policy ... in practice (although not always in rhetoric) no central bank ignores activity'.[117] The level of this concern clearly varies among central banks, however, and critics are quick to point out that central banks (and governments more generally) don't pay sufficient attention to unemployment.[118] The main criticisms are that the use of monetary policy and disinflationary strategies to control inflation are too blunt and damaging, and that other methods of controlling inflation – such as the use of fiscal policy in tandem with an effective wages or incomes policy – are preferable.[119] This was certainly what Bernie Fraser argued in the 1980s, but this approach was headed off by the opportunities presented by the grim recession of the early 1990s. As Fraser used to say, fighting inflation through monetary policy relies heavily on creating 'slack' in the labour market. There seems to be a connection in Australia's case between, on the one hand, bringing inflation down in the 1990s and, on the other, official unemployment that averaged almost 9 per cent across the decade and the normalising of long-term unemployment and job insecurity. It may be true, as we will see, that the Bank in recent years has shown a propensity to test the growth envelope, but important components of the new political economy of inflation still stem from various imposed forms of labour market 'discipline'.

CONCLUSION

Amidst the initial plunge into recession in the 1990s, the RBA independently concluded that the new context provided an opportunity to speed up the pace of reducing inflation. As the full depths of the recession were plumbed, this resolve strengthened. This strategy marked a departure from Labor's gradualist approach of the 1980s. The RBA (and the Treasury) were the prime movers. Treasurer Keating eventually endorsed snapping the stick of inflation but was always more concerned than his officials (except perhaps Bernie Fraser) about the fallout from the recession, and was somewhat slower to join the front ranks in the fight against inflation than was the RBA. Surprisingly, Labor managed to win a federal election in 1993 in the wake of the inflation-crunching 'recession we had to have'. The recessionary king-hit against inflation and the new resolve to fight inflation set the Bank on a new path.

CHAPTER 4

'A Measure of Peace'?
Monetary Policy in the
1990s

We have reached some kind of stable resting point.
Stephen Grenville, former RBA Deputy Governor[1]

During the 1980s and the early 1990s, the RBA sought to establish a measure of control over the economy and define its role in a difficult monetary context. It had been assailed by neo-liberal critics and immersed in political controversy over its performance and perceived lack of 'credibility'. The charges, to reiterate, were that the Bank was too close to the government, that is, not independent enough; that it was soft on inflation; and that it lacked a coherent policy framework.

We will deal with the independence issue in later chapters, but on the second charge, crunching inflation certainly helped take much of the steam out of the criticism that the Bank was soft on inflation. In a short period, the Bank had clarified its goals and tackled inflation head on. As Ian Macfarlane observes: 'while all the debate was going on, inflation was actually falling to its lowest level in a generation. From the Bank's perspective, it was this outcome that ultimately ended the debate in our favour.'[2]

The Bank had also been quietly working at a new set of 'post-checklist' operating procedures to guide its behaviour and make its actions more accountable and transparent. These changes helped to 'normalise' monetary policy in the 1990s, a major shift from the uncertainties and policy groping of the previous two decades. The framework changes, the crunching of inflation, and the shift towards independence, all helped the Bank to beat off its neo-liberal critics and avoid the sort of radical institutional surgery that had been applied to its counterpart in New Zealand. It is these policy framework changes, how monetary policy has travelled through the 1990s and since, and the general improvement in the Bank's fortunes that are the focus of this chapter.

TELLING THE PUNTERS

The first step in sharpening the monetary policy framework occurred in January 1990 when the RBA began to publicly announce and explain interest rate changes. This was a major shift from the earlier more secretive approach to policy. The move was a step towards greater transparency and accountability. By telling the punters about interest rate changes it took advantage of the 'announcement effect', the assumption that economic actors would act more compliantly if they had a greater understanding of the Bank's motives and intentions.

Another reason for the shift was politics. Bernie Fraser had taken over as Governor in September 1989 and it was felt that a more open policy stance might ease the political controversy surrounding the Bank. As Ian Macfarlane now says, 'a big change of policy occurred when we started to put out an announcement, because there was so much suspicion around it just had to be done. So it was policy-making on the run. It turned out to be a very good piece of policy-making.'[3] The timing of this reform is also of interest. The first explicit announcement of policy change coincided with the first of a long series of interest rate reductions. Also, though not too much should be made of it, the shift towards announcing policy (reductions) occurred just two months prior to the March 1990 federal election.

TARGETING INFLATION

The Bank became confident enough about inflation to adopt an explicit inflation target in 1993. Being upfront was thought to help guide policy, anchor inflationary expectations, improve policy credibility, and cement in the government's mind the Bank's policy priorities.

The establishment of an inflation target was a partial shift back towards a rule or formula basis for policy. Central bankers generally agree that policy works best when it has some nominal anchor. Although previous regimes of exchange rate and monetary targeting have come and gone, central banks have increasingly linked monetary policy decisions to a formal or informal inflation target, and many countries, especially in the 1990s, set inflation targets to anchor policy.[4] Some hoped that such targets would also influence inflationary expectations, but policy authorities generally recognise that it is results, not targets, that count. A survey of ninety central banks in 1998 found that fifty of them had adopted an explicit inflation target during the 1990s, typically of 1–3 per cent.[5] The European Central Bank has one of the most stringent, aiming to keep inflation below 2 per cent. Advanced economies that have adopted inflation targets include New Zealand (1989), Canada (1991), Britain (1992), Finland, Sweden and Australia (1993), France and Spain (1994), and Italy (1995). The strategy has been to manipulate monetary policy to keep the economy broadly within the target range of inflation. Because monetary policy can affect inflation only after a considerable timelag (perhaps as much as one year), manipulation has come to rely on the accuracy of inflation forecasting.

Although it gradually endorsed the idea of an inflation target, the RBA also wanted to retain some discretion. Hence, the RBA set its target at a comparatively generous (for a central bank at least) 2–3 per cent. Significantly, the Bank also stated that its target was medium-term, to be achieved *on average* over a run of years – typically, over an economic cycle. Thus the target was an average, not a strict band restricting inflation in the face of short-term contingencies, such as a shock in the terms of trade or oil prices. As the Bank notes, its approach to targeting 'allows for the inevitable uncertainties that are involved in forecasting, and the lags in the effects of monetary policy on the economy'.[6]

The adoption of a target was part of the Bank's wider efforts to establish a clearly defined, credible, transparent policy framework, aimed at domestic economic actors but particularly at offshore financial markets. The RBA's discretion was limited by the need to win market credibility.

The Bank initially treated the adoption of rigid inflation targets with caution if not scepticism, especially after the earlier failure of monetary targeting. But, after problems with the checklist approach, the Bank began quietly working out the details of an inflation target regime. For a time its public statements dismissed the idea of an explicit inflation target. In 1990, for example, Bernie Fraser described targets as 'a pre-determined commitment that limits the room of the authorities to manoeuvre, especially in the face of shocks to the economy', adding 'none of this has much appeal me'.[7] Fraser later said that setting a target amounted to a form of 'incantation'.[8] What mattered was not targets, but results: 'we have to be tough as well as talk tough'.[9]

The Bank nevertheless went on to adopt an inflation target as part of the gradual process of aligning itself with fighting inflation as a main goal. According to Ian Macfarlane, 'Bernie put his toe in the water'[10] and endorsed (obliquely and with caveats) the concept of a target in a speech in March 1993: 'if inflation could be held to an average of 2–3 per cent over a period of years, that would be a good outcome'.[11] It was a low-key announcement: Fraser avoided the term 'target' and reiterated that he was still 'rather wary of inflation targets'. But, over time, the Bank's commitment to the target became clearer and firmer. In September 1994, after several pre-emptive interest rate rises, Fraser said: 'In our opinion, underlying inflation of 2 to 3 per cent is a reasonable goal for monetary policy.'[12] By October 1995, the Bank was using the term 'target' to describe its approach to policy.[13]

In most other countries, official inflation targets are prescribed by government or formulated jointly between the government and the central bank. Paul

Keating, who by 1993 was the Prime Minister, argues that the Bank worked out the target in consultation with the government.[14] The Bank, however, claims that it formulated and announced the target unilaterally.[15] According to Macfarlane, 'The government didn't introduce it, we introduced it.'[16] Fraser concurs: 'It evolved within the Bank without any active government involvement.'[17] It was not until late 1994 that a government minister, Treasurer Ralph Willis, publicly acknowledged and endorsed the Bank's inflation target.

The initial reaction from the markets and other critics to the target was sceptical. The announcement seemed tentative. The target was loosely defined; it was an average to be achieved over time, not a tight band. Not long after, Stanley Fischer of the IMF visited Australia. In a meeting with the RBA staff and selected journalists, he congratulated the Bank's leaders on adopting a target, but then proceeded to lecture them on its excessive 'vagueness'.[18] Macfarlane comments: 'people said that this was a sign of weakness. So ours was definitely regarded – of the half dozen models available – as being the softest of the spectrum.'[19] Nor was Australia's move associated with the formal institutional or legislative changes like those in New Zealand.[20] Macfarlane says, 'some of the books on inflation targets don't include Australia because we didn't change the Act'.[21] Critics also pointed out that the RBA's target was on the high side and praised the more hawkish 0–2 per cent inflation targets of New Zealand and Canada.[22] According to Macfarlane: 'We regarded this as probably too low, and certainly too narrow a range. No country had achieved this sort of inflation performance over any significant time interval in the past fifty years.'[23] Bernie Fraser comments, 'The target was seen as weak by those that favoured the New Zealand benchmark; we chose very deliberately *not* to adopt such a benchmark.'[24] Significantly, however, the RBA's target of 2–3 per cent was tougher than the 3–4 per cent tentatively suggested in the government's *One Nation* policy manifesto of 1992.

Several factors prompted the shift to a target. As suggested above, the search for credibility was one. International pressure played a role, with similar moves around this time in Britain, Canada and Sweden. 'I mean you couldn't go anywhere in the world without people giving you a speech on why didn't Australia have an identical set of monetary institutions as New Zealand', Macfarlane observes.[25] The Bank had been through years of wearing criticism, and Macfarlane says, 'the lack of a monetary policy framework that could command widespread support had had its costs'.[26]

But the Bank had been hesitant to move too quickly towards a target, and one reason was politics. Critics and the Opposition had been claiming long and loud that the Bank's policy framework needed tightening. Many, including the

Opposition Leader, John Hewson, were calling for new central bank legislation, and this was a plank in the Liberal Party platform in the 1993 federal election. The government had of course defended the Bank's monetary policy approach, and the issue had become highly politicised. Because of this, Stephen Grenville recalls that the Bank was 'unable to make a useful contribution without getting itself deeply politicised in the process'.[27] Macfarlane adds that the Bank retired to the sidelines because 'political circumstances contrived to make our participation in the debate marginal at best'.[28] 'It was a very difficult period for us because, you know, we had to stay out of the debate really.'[29] The Bank lay low until the political contest had been settled. It went public with its inflation target soon after the March 1993 federal election, which returned Labor.

A further reason for the delay in the setting of a target was inflation itself. Although countries such as New Zealand and Canada had announced inflation targets prior to achieving low inflation, the RBA had been unwilling to adopt a target until it was clear that inflation in Australia had fallen and was likely to stay low. Grenville notes that the Bank might have achieved a 'credibility bonus' from announcing an inflation target earlier, although, given the prevailing scepticism regarding the RBA, this is doubtful. Grenville also says that the Bank was 'too uncertain' in the early 1990s about where inflation would end up to commit itself.[30] Economist Barry Hughes draws attention to the timing. Musing on the possibility of introducing an inflation target in Australia in the 1980s, he argues:

> It seems fairly obvious that it is a lot easier to be transparent about maintaining low inflation than about the ultimate intent of disinflation when the inflation rate is near double digits ... It is an open question what the public at large would have thought of Bob Johnston had he said that ultimately what he wanted was inflation to be at two point something in 1986. Certainly he would have made a rod for his back and aroused major suspicions about the Bank's agenda ... More to the point it is not at all obvious that such candour would have advanced the cause of monetary policy at the time.[31]

Another reason for the Bank's delay in setting an inflation target is the interaction between monetary policy and wage bargaining. Until recently this link was little explored in the technical literature on central banking.[32] In Australia's case, the general strengthening of monetary policy and the shift to inflation targeting reflected a changing relationship between monetary policy and wages policy. By 1993 it was becoming obvious that the shift in wages policy towards decentralised enterprise bargaining was likely to weaken the capacity of the Accord to promote coordination and wage restraint.[33] Increasingly, instead of monetary policy acting in the shadow of the Accord, the opposite would occur. This shift first occurred, dramatically, during the recession of the early 1990s. As Stephen Grenville has argued:

> The relationship with wages policy had almost been reversed: in the 1980s, monetary policy had supported wages policy in putting downward pressure on inflation; in the 1990s, monetary policy was directed primarily to price stability and, in doing this, had an important influence on the economic climate in which wages were determined.[34]

This was a big change on the inflation-fighting front. Indeed, in 1995 Accord Mark VIII explicitly agreed that wage bargaining would be conducted within the RBA's 2–3 per cent inflation target.

Despite the flexibility and discretion implied by its approach to targeting, the Bank has adopted a conservative approach. It was initially concerned that inflationary expectations might gravitate to the top of its target band; this led it to be 'a little ambiguous on how much variance in inflation policy could expect to tolerate'.[35] The Bank added that 'less variance is better'. Since the adoption of the target, inflation has rarely been allowed to stray too far above the target range, as Figure 4.1 illustrates. Only once, during 1995/96, has inflation substantially exceeded the target range. The initial specification of the target, an *average* of between 2 and 3 per cent inflation over the course of an economic cycle, seems to have gone out the window. Indeed, the Bank's ongoing commentary about

Figure 4.1 Quarterly year-ended inflation in Australia and the 2–3% target rate, 1993 to 2003

Inflation rate (%)*

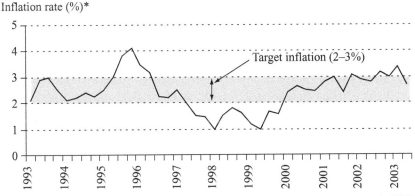

* RBA estimate, adjusts for tax changes associated with the Howard government's GST.
Source: Reserve Bank of Australia Bulletin.

inflation is not even expressed in terms of an inflation average. Ian Macfarlane comments: 'We accept that at times it [inflation] will be outside this range. But if we think that is going to happen more than briefly, it calls for adjustments to monetary policy which will return inflation to the target and keep it there.'[36] This sounds less like managing an inflation average over the course of an economic cycle and more like restraining inflation within a *target band* most of the time.

FORWARD LOOKING, MEDIUM TERM

Another significant change in the policy framework in the 1990s was the explicit adoption of a medium-term policy stance. There are several implications.

First, the Bank will not focus on the short-term consequences of its anti-inflation policy; it will not 'fine tune' or react to every shift in the economy. As Bernie Fraser put it in 1994, 'our main aim is to maintain price stability, while doing what we can to smooth the cycle'.[37] The Bank may still take into account short-term issues or costs, but the overall balance of policy is geared to achieving results in the medium term. This shift was first displayed when the Bank stayed its hand during the early 1990s recession to extract low inflation; it was a medium-term strategy.[38]

Second, a medium-term focus deals not with current inflation but with *forecast* inflation, and policy is pre-emptive. The idea is to act before inflation takes hold. This marks a shift from the policy approach of the 1980s, which the Bank admits was 'backward-looking', based on the analysis of 'past data'.[39] The new approach was displayed not only in the recession of the early 1990s, but also in 1994, when interest rates were tightened pre-emptively by 2.75 percentage points in three rate rises, two of 1 per cent. Clearly, Bernie Fraser was not mucking about. The Bank's credibility was still on the line. He would jump on inflation and was not about to retreat from the tough stance of the early 1990s. He comments:

> There was an understanding by that time that significant pre-emptive action could perhaps avoid the need to do as much as you might otherwise need to do if you were more leisurely in approaching these problems. I think the government also realised that a more leisurely approach, a more staged approach, might have been more uncomfortable for them in relation to the electoral cycle or whatever. So, there is something in the argument that if you are pre-emptive and if you create a bit of surprise, then you are likely to get a bit of an extra bang.[40]

The Bank's commitment to an inflation target also strengthened in this period. During the tightening critics claimed that there were no apparent signs of inflation, although the bond market had become concerned and sent ten-year government bond yields from 6.4 to 9.6 per cent. This was twice the increase in the United States and more than the rise in New Zealand during this period. The bond market was still not convinced Australia was running a 'credible' monetary policy. The Bank's moves were based on forecast inflation, the main indicators being an upswing in domestic demand and a tightening in the labour market. Fraser's intentions were clear: 'We will need to sustain low rates of inflation through the upswing of the current cycle to build real credibility.'[41] As Figure 4.2 shows, interest rates were held high during 1995 and the first easing did not begin until July 1996. The Bank's actions slowed growth, and inflation was pulled back into the target range.

A pre-emptive strategy depends on forecasts; hence the higher level of uncertainty now built into monetary policy. The Bank admits that policy involves the '*probabilistic* nature of the process of making forecasts and devising appropriate policy responses'.[42] The heightened uncertainty also extends to issues of policy accountability. The efficacy of a pre-emptive strike on (forecast) inflation is difficult to assess because the anticipated inflation may never materialise! As the Deputy Governor of the RBA, Glenn Stevens, comments: 'policymakers seeking to be pre-emptive do run some risk of responding to perceived problems which do not, in the end, eventuate'.[43]

BEATING OFF THE NEW ZEALAND MODEL

Although the RBA had been subjected to a welter of criticism during the late 1980s and early 1990s, the institutional surgery promised by the conservative

Figure 4.2   Cash rates, Australia (quarterly averages), 1990 to 2003

Cash rate (%)

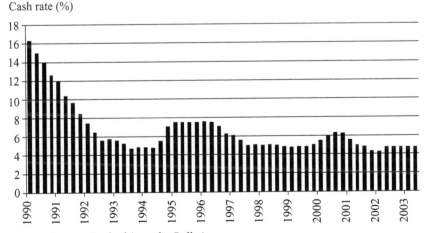

Source: Reserve Bank of Australia Bulletin.

Opposition never eventuated. The first reason for this was fortuitous. The Hewson-led Opposition, which had promised to rewrite the *Reserve Bank Act* and subject it to the radical surgery that had been applied in New Zealand, lost the 1993 federal election. It never got the chance to introduce its version of central bank reform. Second, the RBA's improving performance and policy credibility had blunted the attack. A symbol of the Bank's rising stocks was the decision by the Opposition in 1994, under its new Leader Alexander Downer, to drop the issue. Downer announced that a future Coalition government would resile from earlier Opposition efforts to install an inflation-only charter, adding that he did not want the Bank to become 'an inhuman organisation'.[44]

The RBA favoured the route of incremental institutional remodelling; it was not keen on the New Zealand model. Furthermore, as Macfarlane explains:

> we believed that we could achieve what our critics wanted – a return to a lower inflation environment – without radical overhaul or a complete rewriting of the *Reserve Bank Act*. In a sense, we believed that reform from within was possible and that this would gradually return Australia to being a low inflation country.[45]

The reshaping of the RBA and its role – the low-inflation priority, the 2–3 per cent medium-term inflation target, the shift to independence – flowed not from black-letter changes but from gradual, informal changes to institutional practices. New mindsets and conventions were accommodated within the original statutory framework. This demonstrates the scope for informal institutional flexibility and adaptation, and underlines the claim in institutional theory that informal arrangements often matter a great deal.[46] It validated the view of the Campbell Committee that the old legislative framework was highly adaptable. As Eichbaum points out, Australia's 1945 and 1959 central bank legislation had proved 'to be capable of accommodating an environment that few, if any, would have anticipated'.[47]

THE 1996 *STATEMENT*

Labor finally lost office in 1996, allowing the incoming Howard Coalition government to have its way with the Bank. But very little happened. By September 1996, Bernie Fraser's term as Governor had expired and he did not seek reappointment; nor, in all probability, would it have been granted, given his previous clashes with the Coalition. Instead, Ian Macfarlane, the Bank's Deputy Governor, was promoted. As we have seen, Macfarlane – sometimes referred to in the press as 'Big Mac' – was a long-serving senior officer of the Bank. He had been promoted to the deputy-governorship in 1992 and had a reputation as one of the more hawkish of the Bank's leaders. As it eventuated, however, partly through good fortune and partly by design, Macfarlane has charted a broadly expansionary monetary policy.

The Howard government's other initiative was when the incoming Treasurer, Peter Costello, co-signed a document with Ian Macfarlane, entitled *Statement on the Conduct of Monetary Policy*. It was designed partly to reassure the markets, particularly overseas, about the 'soundness' of the new government's policy intentions. It was also a means for the Bank to formally register with the new government the policy framework it had been evolving through the 1990s. As Macfarlane explained soon after, 'the previous Treasurer had endorsed the inflation target and the Reserve Bank's independence, but not in a public statement and not by formally relating it to the *Reserve Bank Act*'. So the *Statement* 'was a means of clearing up any ambiguity about the relationship between the government and the Reserve Bank'.[48]

The *Statement* endorsed the Bank's inflation target. It also formally endorsed the policy independence of the Bank, overturning the implicit policy convention of the post-war era. As we will see in chapter 5, the RBA had gradually achieved a substantial measure of policy independence before 1996, but the *Statement* now formally and publicly recognised this. The *Statement*, while reiterating the broad objectives of the Bank's charter – including the dual goals – added: 'Price stability is a crucial *precondition* for sustained growth in economic activity and employment.'[49] This gave the inflation goal 'top billing', making the other goals conditional on it. Interestingly, reference to the Bank's statutory goals – including full employment – was removed from the front matter of the Bank's *Annual Reports* from that point on.

The markets and economic commentators widely praised the *Statement*. Macfarlane informally approached Bernie Fraser about the content of the *Statement* during its preparation, and later Fraser publicly endorsed it: 'because it essentially formalises current practices, it has a sweet ring to it for me. It suggests that we are all marching to the same tune now, something that seemed impossible only a few years ago when the government was in Opposition.'[50] But Fraser had reservations about the *Statement*, although he did not mention them publicly at the time.

I wasn't a fan of the *Statement*. It wasn't something I would have pursued, for two main reasons. One, it gave more prominence to inflation than I thought the Charter justified and was appropriate – that issue of balance had been an ongoing theme in my term at the Bank. And the second thing was that the *Statement* was essentially an accord between the new Governor and the Treasurer; the Board wasn't involved at all. I thought the Board was a significant part of the Bank's policy process. So it was on those two scores that, as I say, I wouldn't have been hankering after such a relationship with the new government.[51]

In any event, the *Statement*'s positive reception was a sign that the Bank's neo-liberal critics had largely been silenced and that the Bank now had bipartisan support. Macfarlane publicly noted that this was a huge improvement over the situation in the early 1990s.[52] The earlier campaign to alter the Bank's charter had been defeated. The Coalition had made its peace with the Bank and the *Statement* was the formal declaration. In Chris Eichbaum's words, 'the onus on the incoming government was to be party to an action that would help restore credibility that the Coalition, in Opposition, had, in part, been responsible for eroding'.[53]

One reason for the Coalition's revised stand was the Bank's strong results on inflation. Another was that any overt tampering with the Bank's dual goal charter might have damaged the government's and Bank's legitimacy in an era of high unemployment. As Eichbaum puts it, 'it was most unlikely that any government would want to visit upon itself the political opprobrium attached to removing the reference to full employment in the Bank's Charter'.[54] The minor parties which held the balance of power in the Senate would probably have opposed any such move. Plus, from the government's point of view, a legislative route to change involved uncertainties that would have become politicised, and the results were uncertain.

DOING OKAY?

By 1996, Stephen Grenville notes, 'the process of reformulating a "rule-based" framework (which had begun in 1989) was completed'.[55] On his retirement from the Bank in 1996, Bernie Fraser argued the Bank had achieved a stable 'four pillars' policy framework: the dual goals, the flexible inflation target, central bank independence, and a 'good Board' to oversee the Bank's operations.[56] By 1998, Ian Macfarlane was arguing that the Bank had 'entered a phase where a measure of peace has returned'. Monetary policy and the institutional framework had achieved a degree of credibility 'that seemed out of the question a decade ago'.[57] In 2001, Grenville argued that 'we have reached some kind of stable resting point'. The Bank's systems and procedures had reached 'an advanced stage of evolution', and 'there is no obvious or compelling logic which would move us to a subsequent stage of history'.[58]

Certainly, the markets seemed happy with the new framework, and with the Bank's anti-inflation stance and performance. Long-term lenders factor in an interest rate premium as insurance against inflation: the higher the rate of

Figure 4.3   Yields on 10-year Treasury Bonds, Australia and the United States, 1985 to 1999 (year ended April)

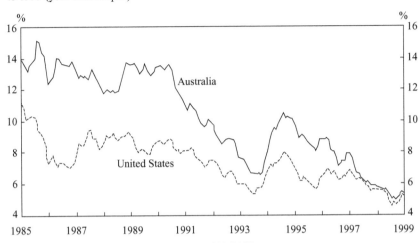

Source: Treasury, *Budget Paper 1*, Part 3, 1999/2000.

expected inflation, the higher the long-term interest rate. As the credibility of monetary policy improves, however, and expected rates of inflation decline, long-term interest rates fall, both absolutely and relative to other (low-inflation) countries. For almost a decade Australia lagged other economies, such as the United States, in bringing down inflation and thus suffered higher bond premiums for longer, as Figure 4.3 shows.

Australia's high inflation in the 1980s, together with inflationary expectations, generated relatively high bond yields. But as inflation improved and expectations were lowered, Australian and US bond yields converged. The change was a sign of growing market confidence in domestic monetary policy. After some further concerns as the economy tightened and the Bank breached its inflation target in the mid-1990s, a similar substantial narrowing in bond yields began to occur in 1996. When the Bank announced progressive easings of monetary policy, the bond markets reacted by lowering long-term interest rates. The Bank had achieved sufficient credibility to ease monetary policy without exacerbating inflationary expectations.

In 1997 and 1998 the Bank further improved its stocks by holding its nerve in the face of the Asian financial crisis. Indeed, the Bank, and especially its Deputy Governor, Stephen Grenville, went out on a limb and criticised the IMF's handling of the crisis.[59] The American authorities were not happy. Reportedly, the Deputy Secretary of the US Treasury, Larry Summers, telephoned Treasurer Costello to complain about the RBA's stance.[60] Macfarlane thinks the domestic handling of the crisis was a boost for the Bank. He commented in interview: 'I used to have a file at one stage called "Favourable Comments About the RBA", and I had it for about six or seven years, and it only ever had about two items in it. And then of course the Asian crisis came, and it filled up.'[61] During the crisis, market concerns about fallout in Australia, particularly on the export front, were reflected in a depreciating currency. The Bank could have attempted to defend the currency, ward off imported inflation and appease markets by raising interest rates, but it chose not to. It sat tight, although, as Macfarlane told the House of Representatives Economics Committee in late 1998, it did intervene in January, June and August to try to smooth the foreign exchange market, and the option of using interest rates was certainly 'on the table' during these periods.[62] Ultimately, the Bank's leaders did not think the falling dollar would pull in much inflation or that Australia's exports would be hit too hard. The net effect was to cushion the impact on the domestic economy and absorb the shock in the exchange rate. Crucially, interest rates were not raised – in fact, they were lowered several times – and domestic growth and employment were protected. John Edwards, now chief economist with HSBC, praises Macfarlane. 'A more easily rattled Governor, someone with less monetary experience, someone with more reliance on models and theories and less on accumulated wisdom, would quite easily have cost Australia billions of dollars in lost output and a hundred thousand jobs.'[63] Interestingly, Paul Keating claims some of the credit:

> I used to say to the Bank, look … we can never make a rate [i.e. an exchange rate]. Let's never try and make a rate. Smoothing and testing, yes. Never try to make a rate. And there was always this inclination in the system to try and make a rate. Now the Bank never went out at any point to make a rate, but they were always, in conversation, worried about the rate. They were always in the virility business. And I take a large measure of the personal responsibility for knocking that out of the Bank. If Ian Macfarlane – or whoever might have been Governor instead – at the time of the Asian crisis had been left to the orthodoxy, Australia would have been pushed into recession … we'd actually made the Bank cross the Rubicon of its own where it knew that the exchange rate could take the slack, and take the hit, and domestic demand could continue … [64]

The contrast with the hawkish stance adopted in New Zealand and Canada is instructive. Their central banks chose the orthodox approach, raising interest rates in order to support the currency and ward off imported inflation.[65] The move landed both countries in a policy-induced recession. It was a major blunder.

Table 4.1 Comparative gross domestic product, inflation, and interest rates for selected OECD countries, 1980s and 1990–2003

Country	Average GDP growth (%)			Average inflation (%)			Average interest rates (%)		
	1980s	1990–2003	Change	1980s	1990–2003	Change	1980s	1990–2003	Change
Australia	3.3	3.6	0.3	7.9	2.2	-5.7	15.2	6.4	-8.8
New Zealand	2.5	2.8	0.3	10.8	2.0	-8.8	17.3	7.4	-9.9
Japan	4.6	1.7	-2.9	2.1	0.8	-1.3	6.1	2.1	-4.0
Canada	2.8	2.7	-0.1	6.0	2.0	-4.0	11.2	5.7	-5.5
USA	3.0	3.0	0.0	4.7	2.8	-1.9	9.9	5.2	-4.7
Germany	1.8	2.2	0.4	2.6	2.4	-0.3	6.8	5.3	-1.5
France	2.4	1.7	-0.7	6.4	1.8	-4.6	11.3	5.9	-5.4
Italy	2.4	1.5	-0.9	9.9	3.8	-6.1	15.1	8.3	-6.8
UK	2.4	2.0	-0.4	6.2	3.2	-3.0	11.7	7.1	-4.6
OECD Major 7	2.7	2.2	-0.5	5.2	2.1	-3.1	10.3	5.7	-4.6

Sources: International Monetary Fund, *World Economic Database*; OECD.

The RBA's response in 1998, as well as its role in presiding over sound rates of economic growth in the post-recession 1990s, indicate that it is not one of the world's more hawkish central banks. That dubious honour would probably go to New Zealand in the 1990s or the European Central Bank. Table 4.1 shows inflation and growth across a range of leading economies.

Comparatively, Australia's numbers look good. In fact, the Australian economy in the post-recession 1990s headed the OECD's league table for economic growth, and outperformed the United States in both growth and inflation. Moreover, Australia, once a classic stop-go economy, now seems to have become more stable: the current expansion is over a decade long. Ian Macfarlane, once seen as a hawk (by Bernie Fraser, among others), now admits, 'I'm regarded among the central Bank community as being a bit of a wet.'[66] For a long time, the orthodox journal *Central Banking* gave the RBA a bad press over this. The RBA is certainly keen to rebuke critics who see it as too hawkish. Macfarlane argued in a speech in September 2000, 'the fact that Australia has been virtually at the top of the international growth league, while achieving a respectable middle order ranking on inflation, shows that we have not over-emphasised inflation control at the expense of economic growth'.[67]

The RBA's approach and performance raise the question of just what current central bank orthodoxy is these days. The hawkish New Zealand model, the single inflation target and the idea of bold pre-emptive strikes against any stirrings of inflation still hold sway among many central bankers and much of the financial community. However, the two major growth economies in the 1990s, the United States and Australia, appear to reflect a different tack. Both central banks have displayed a willingness to poke around at what they see as the edges of the growth envelope. Orthodoxy has also been challenged by the lacklustre macroeconomic performance of New Zealand and some large European countries.

Bernie Fraser (despite crunching inflation) always regarded himself as unorthodox, especially regarding his defence of the Bank's dual goals. As he commented upon his retirement in 1996,

> The multiple objectives of the *Reserve Bank Act* help make the trade-offs [regarding inflation and employment] explicit in Australia, which is one reason why I have always championed our approach over the more fashionable, inflation only objective of many other central banks ... I see the Bank's multiple objectives as a counter to the (understandable) preoccupation of central banks with low inflation.[68]

Reflecting on his experience in the Reserve Bank and among international central bankers, Fraser admitted during interview:

I felt a bit lonely on many occasions, and I argued with them about what they themselves most focused on – on low inflation. Unless the Bank can carry the broader community, not just the financial markets but the broader community, and that means having regard for employment and unemployment and growth ... unless you are credible in terms of what you are doing in these areas, you're going to lose support for low inflation with people ... And I don't think it's too far away before you see some more intensive questioning of inflation only in the European Central Bank.[69]

Commenting in late 2001, Ian Macfarlane thought there had been a shift away from earlier strict orthodoxy. He argued 'there's been a shift in our direction. There is no doubt about that.'

The single [inflation] objective is being questioned ... there was this sort of feeling that if you were a central banker and you were caught worrying about something other than inflation, well you know, you should be gotten rid of ... that has certainly changed. I think the other thing too that has changed is there used to be a lot of veneration for the Bundesbank ... its representing orthodoxy. And I think of the success of the Fed, the US Fed, during the 1990s ... the Fed has really got pragmatic ... it's got dual objectives. And so I think the success of the Fed and the demise of the Bundesbank have probably been the biggest single influences ... [Also] the New Zealanders have made some mistakes as you know. I mean they had the recession they didn't have to have in 98 ... You know the sort of economists who hang around the big financial institutions and a lot of the academics have still got in their mind that the New Zealand model is the right one, and the IMF's the same ... I mean the IMF did not trust us ...[70]

Interestingly, in 2002 Ian Macfarlane was voted Central Banker of the Year by *Euromoney* magazine.

For those central banks willing to push the envelope, the opportunity to ease up on the inflation front has almost certainly arrived. The economics Nobel laureate, Joseph Stiglitz, in a 1998 paper entitled 'Central Banking in a Democratic Society', questioned the prevailing hawkishness of central bankers and the empirical rationale for bold pre-emptiveness in monetary policy, arguing instead for a policy of 'cautious expansionism'.[71] He argued that the costs of inflation have been overstated and the costs of disinflationary policies understated. Indeed, he argued, as have others, that there is little evidence that moderate rates of inflation actually damage the economy.[72] He also opposed the 'premise of many inflation hawks that inflation is like a genie, once you let it out of the bottle it will just keep on expanding'. Stiglitz pointed out that for good reasons economic models rarely contain such an assumption, and that empirical testing does not confirm it. The costs of higher inflation incurred in driving unemployment somewhat below the so-called 'structural rate of unemployment' or NAIRU are likely to be small, he argued, compared to the gains based on a more expansionary stance. He also questioned the hawkish view that any increase in inflation is intolerable because reeling in inflation (assuming it has been allowed to expand) is always a high-cost policy. Stiglitz pointed to many episodes where monetary policy had 'trimmed the sails' without inducing a major slowdown in growth (for example, 1994–96 in Australia). For these reasons he cautioned against 'the arguments underlying the policies of aggressive, pre-emptive strikes against inflation, a stance that is the basis of the rhetoric if not the practice of so many central banks. These policies are based on articles of faith, not on scientific evidence.'[73]

Another reason for 'cautious expansionism' is that we have almost certainly entered an era in which inflationary pressures have receded.[74] Some are asking, and others are asserting, that inflation, or at least aggregate or CPI inflation, is now 'dead';[75] others fear not inflation but deflation. The RBA now has 'considerable confidence' that low inflation can be maintained.[76] The volatility of inflation has declined, and a new political economy of inflation has emerged as a result of structural, institutional and attitudinal changes:

- Central banks, including the RBA, have gone through a torturous process of achieving low inflation and are determined to hang onto it.
- This imposes a new discipline which alters behaviour. We know, in a mixture of fear and threat, that any significant rise in inflation will be crunched (painfully if need be) by the Bank.
- The labour market has changed; more wage bargaining is tied to productivity gains, and the labour market is more 'flexible'. Many workers have been effectively 'disciplined' by weakened bargaining power in the context of high unemployment and less secure work.
- Australia, with its high foreign debt and heavily traded currency, is particularly exposed to financial market sentiment providing an external discipline and pressure for low inflation.
- Globalisation, tariff reductions and other rising competitive pressures in product markets are making employers less willing to grant wage increases and workers less able to win them.
- Relatedly, rising productivity has helped promote low-inflationary growth.
- The exchange rate is now handled more flexibly and can take some of the adjustment in maintaining low inflation.

- The 'pass through' from exchange rates to domestic prices declined in the last five years, in part reflecting some of the changes noted above.
- Rapidly rising business and household debt have made economic actors more sensitive to interest rate rises and hence more averse to inflation. Relatedly, interest rate increases these days are generally small, with adjustments typically of 0.25 per cent.
- Culturally, and partly for the reasons above, the post-war consensus on low unemployment has shifted towards the current consensus on low inflation.
- Inflationary expectations have declined, and one-off increases in costs are less likely to feed into prices.

This new political economy of inflation emerged in Australia in the 1990s. In these new dynamics monetary policy, though used in the early 1990s to king-hit inflation, is now less central as a mechanism for ensuring that low inflation continues. Although it has not become impotent, its role has diminished as wider institutional and structural forces have made Australia less inflation-prone. Again, this provides a rationale for 'cautious expansionism'. Paul Keating, for one, thinks there have been big structural changes in this regard. Pointing to deregulation and increased competition, Keating suggested during interview:

> This is the thing, it's the productivity coming naturally from the skin of the economy which now keeps the inflation rate down. It's not a bit of shifty management up the top of Martin Place. That helps. But it's the building on those eighties policy changes. It's the structural changes which have broken the back of inflation, along with a good knock on the head in the 1990 period.[77]

Chapter 9 will examine whether monetary policy has a role to play in dealing with the latest twist in the political economy of inflation – the challenges of asset inflation.

IS EVERYBODY HAPPY?

In recent years the Bank has been making some effort to push the growth envelope in a context in which the threat of CPI inflation appears to have substantially receded. Nevertheless, complaints still surround the Bank's approach to monetary policy, especially from dissident MPs, the unions and some sectors of industry.[78]

Tensions also erupted between the RBA and the Howard government following a series of five interest rate increases during late 1999 and 2000 that moved the cash rate up from 4.75 to 6.25 per cent. These were the first rate rises since the government was elected in 1996, and they displeased the government which had boasted about presiding over low interest rates. The Bank initially argued that an upswing in the world economy and rising inflationary pressures had forced it to adopt a less 'expansionary' setting for monetary policy. In February 2000 the Bank added incipient wage pressures, strong credit growth and 'speculative activity in asset markets' to its list of concerns.[79] The Bank announced a rate hike of 50 basis points, its first (tentative) foray into combating credit growth and asset inflation since the late 1980s. Then, in April 2000, the Bank raised widespread concerns by justifying a further rate rise – this time 25 basis points – on the grounds of a weakening currency (and the implied imported inflation) stemming from a widening of the interest rate differential between Australia and the United States. As the Bank argued: 'The level of the exchange rate is not an end in itself, but is important insofar as it can affect future inflation.'[80] Critics pointed out that the tactic of using interest rates to support the dollar was likely to be futile, that similar efforts to defend the currency in New Zealand and Canada had failed, and that over the long term the slide in the Australian dollar during the 1990s had not ignited inflationary pressures.

Treasury Secretary Ted Evans entered the fray, publicly criticising the move to factor the currency decline into interest rate decisions. He argued that the currency movements were mainly driven by what was likely to be a short-term strengthening of the US dollar and that compensating domestic interest rate changes should be avoided. He saw developments as a story about the US dollar, not the Australian dollar. Treasury's view in the 2000 Budget Papers was that the economy was less inflation-prone than in the past – in part because of productivity increases and increased competitive pressures – and that concerns about imported inflation were exaggerated.[81] Evans reportedly argued unsuccessfully against the rate rises at various RBA Board meetings, a pattern of argument and Board defeat that has apparently continued under the current Treasury Secretary, Ken Henry (see chapter 8).

In contrast to the early 1990s, Treasury now seems more dovish than the RBA. Why the turnaround? Some have speculated that Evans was responding to pressure from Treasurer Costello or the government. Others put an institutional argument: it's the RBA role to worry about inflation; Treasury now deals primarily with fiscal policy. The first argument is hard to test and is not implausible. The second does not square with what happened in the early 1990s, when Treasury was more hawkish than the RBA. It's safer to conclude that Treasury's recent concerns reflect the independent policy calls that seem to characterise its dealings with the RBA (see chapter 8).

The differences between the government and the Bank spilled over into the public arena in late January 2000, when Prime Minister Howard publicly doubted the need for substantial interest rate raises.[82] For journalist Louise Dodson, this was a case of 'the battlers versus the Reserve Bank boffins in John Howard's re-election rule book'.[83] Treasurer Costello suggested that Howard's frankness underlined the Bank's independence. But in the markets, following Howard's statement, the dollar slid 3 cents and continued to lose ground. The slide appeared to be driven by market perceptions that the Prime Minister was challenging the RBA's independence, or worse, that the RBA had only limited independence to start with. Both views show that the markets have limited understanding of the relationship between the RBA and the government, or, perhaps, the skittish way in which markets react to political news.

Undeterred by Howard, the Bank announced a rise after its Board meeting in early February. As the *Australian*'s Alan Wood commented, 'by pushing rates up by 0.5 per cent, Macfarlane has made a virtual declaration of independence'.[84] The employment minister, Peter Reith, attacked the rate rise, aligning himself with small business critics of the Bank. The Bank was clearly unimpressed by all this, especially with Howard's January comments. Its May 2000 *Semi-Annual Statement on Monetary Policy* stated that 'some political comments on interest rates' had been partly to blame for the dollar's slide.[85] The real problem for the government, however, was that the Bank's rate rises were eroding the effects of the income tax cuts the government was offering as part of its July 2000 GST tax reform package, in the lead-up to the 2001 election.

The Howard government's GST created turbulence for monetary policy during this period. Ian Macfarlane was careful not to enter the policy debate surrounding the new tax, and was reticent about its impacts on the economy or on monetary policy, despite pointed questioning by members of the House Economics Committee, notably Labor's Mark Latham, during 2000.[86] But the link did seem clear to a range of commentators. For Tim Colebatch in the *Age*, 'the real reason the Reserve wants to raise rates soon is to exert maximum downward pressure on wage claims once the GST pushes up inflation to 5 per cent or more and the government's tax cuts inject an extra $6 billion a year into an economy already at full speed'.[87]

In response to the Bank's exchange rate rationale for raising rates, Prime Minister Howard again entered the debate in May 2000, suggesting that international developments (the strengthening US dollar and exchange rate falls in Australia) should not lead Australia to adopt 'knee-jerk' responses. Opposition Leader Kim Beazley chided the government for even talking about interest rates, although its right to comment on monetary policy had been set out in the 1996 *Statement on the Conduct of Monetary Policy*. Howard declared, 'I say to those people who suggested the Prime Minister of this country can't talk at all about monetary policy, that hey, this is a democracy.'[88] Howard's tactic was clearly to distance himself from the Bank and identify himself in the public's mind as one opposed to rate rises.

After the rate rises in 2000 and the negative impact of the GST on the housing sector, the economy slid into negative growth in the December quarter of 2000, the first contraction in nine years. The RBA was surprised by the scale of the housing downturn and hurriedly began to lower rates in early 2001. In March Howard criticised the Bank in the bluntest terms, claiming it had made 'an error of judgement' in the rate rises of 2000.[89]

These events highlight two things. First, never before has a federal government confronted an RBA of such power and independence. The Howard government was the first post-war government to openly endorse central bank independence, and now it was finding out what this means. Second, the tensions surrounding monetary policy in 2000, although public, were just that – tensions. They were not confined to the corridors of power in Canberra or in Martin Place; the government (and the Treasury) will *publicly* challenge the Bank. The Bank's policy independence gives the government an incentive to point the finger at the Bank for unpopular rate rises. For its part, the Bank has been careful not to criticise the government openly, but there is no evidence that it has been deterred from steering its own policy course. During the post-recession 1990s, the Bank built its stocks by presiding over an economy featuring low inflation and comparatively strong growth. It rejects claims that it has been fixated on inflation at the expense of growth. An exchange in June 2003 in the House Economics Committee is illustrative. Referring to reported differences on the Board between the Bank's leaders and the Treasury Secretary, Ken Henry, Labor MP David Cox commented:

> This is the second Treasury Secretary whom you have been at odds with to some degree on the stance of monetary policy. It seems from my observation that Treasury, perhaps under Ted Evans, had wanted to run the economy a little bit harder, and with productivity improvements that was possible.

Macfarlane responded:

> Just look at the record of the Australian economy over the last twelve years. We do not have to defer to any country in the world in terms of our economic growth ... So if you have got a better basic formula somewhere, tell me about it ... the one we have used has produced the goods.[90]

Indeed, the economy has had a good run, and so has the Bank. It has pushed the growth envelope, although some – including Treasury, at least in recent years –

would have liked it to do more. It has avoided policy blunders, although some commentators, such as Ross Gittins of the *Sydney Morning Herald*, have argued that the interest rate U-turn of 2000 and 2001 amounted to a miscalculation:

> over the past two years or so, the Reserve's been driving the economy like a dodgem car, spinning the wheel first one way then the other. First it tightened, then it loosened, now it's tightening again. Frankly, to be reversing the direction of policy so soon, twice in a row, is a tacit admission of error. Interest rate changes are notoriously slow-acting. It can take up to two years for their full effect to work its way through the economy. So if you're cancelling out policy changes before they've had much chance to work, it's an admission that you got it wrong the first time.[91]

The Bank argues that this period was hard to read (especially the unexpected size of the post-GST housing slump, which dragged the economy down). In testimony before the House Economics Committee, Macfarlane admitted: 'So yes, we plead guilty in having got those figures wrong ... we were dealing with a once in a lifetime or once in a generation change and we were not able to predict exactly what the outcomes would be.'[92] The Bank also says that its interest rate adjustments were less frequent and smaller than most of the other lead economies during this period.

Overall, however, the Howard government has been happy with the Bank. It reappointed Macfarlane in July 2003, with Treasurer Costello stating that Macfarlane 'has served Australia very well as Governor of the Reserve Bank. It has been a period of great success in the conduct of monetary policy.'[93] At Macfarlane's request, the reappointment was for three years; he wished to retire at age sixty. The current Deputy Governor, Glenn Stevens, is expected to succeed Macfarlane. The government also agreed with the Bank's request to reissue an updated (though essentially unchanged) *Statement on the Conduct of Monetary Policy*, which re-endorsed the Bank's independence. In relation to monetary policy, it confirmed the Bank's 'focus' on price stability, 'while taking account of the implications of monetary policy on activity'. In a press conference announcing Macfarlane's reappointment, Costello noted that the Bank had held inflation at an average of 2.4 per cent, almost the mid-point in the target band, since Macfarlane's appointment in 1996.[94]

In steering the Bank since 1996, Macfarlane has done a good job in building on the policy and institutional foundations laid by Bob Johnston and especially by Bernie Fraser. The Australian economy has experienced strong growth and low inflation – almost calm seas compared to what Macfarlane's predecessors confronted. But whether the RBA will achieve the 'measure of peace' that some of its leaders were talking about in the late 1990s is debatable. The world economy is unstable. The battle against inflation may have been won, but new challenges – soaring asset prices in equity and property markets, plus sluggishness in some major economies – pose threats.

CONCLUSION

The RBA's adaptations to the new economic world, working with an unaltered 1959 charter, illustrate the scope for informal institutional flexibility and adaptation.[95] This is a lesson the RBA now seems keen to talk about, especially in contrast to the less successful macroeconomic outcomes that followed radical institutional surgery in New Zealand.[96] In eschewing radical versions of institutional reform, in maintaining dual goals, and in not jumping too hard on the expansionary cycle since the mid-1990s, the RBA may be carving out a revised version of central banking orthodoxy; one which emphasises flexibility, discretion and some willingness to test the limits of the growth envelope.[97]

Paul Keating reflects on the Bank's institutional development:

> In the end what was left behind was not a Reserve Bank which was only an agent of the Treasury, but one that had standing internationally. That had processes which led the market ... that all the variables were properly considered; that had an attitude of cooperation with the government. It learned some things about not trying to make an [exchange] rate ... that we need to control inflation while optimising growth, and not the reverse because anyone can do that. And those things have happened, those lessons have been learnt ... Now, over time with these things, the standing of the Governor and the institution sort of rises. This is the best result, because governments are unlikely to be as participatory as the Labor government was. And in the event we get to a position where the government of the day is not managing policy, the manager, if it is the Bank, ends up managing it more – both ambitiously and thoughtfully ... So therefore the transition from a regulated system through the Johnston years to one where we're slaking inflation from the economy in the years I had Bernie there, and then on to where we're down to the even keel, two and a half per cent productivity and two and a half per cent inflation, and all we then have to watch for is exogenous shocks. Well that's what I wanted to see left behind. And I think that is what is left behind ... I was determined when I left that there stood an institution that was able to fend for itself.[98]

The RBA is now much stronger than at any time in its history. The changes in the monetary policy framework, not to mention the structural underpinnings of the shift to low inflation, have transformed the political economy of monetary policy in Australia. There is a case to be made for the RBA to exploit this transformation and be even bolder in pursuing growth.

On the other hand, new storm clouds are brewing, and the 'measure of peace' the Bank thought it had attained in the late 1990s may be evaporating. The RBA has already reversed policy sharply in recent years in the face of increasingly turbulent economic and financial conditions. And all central bankers, including those in the RBA, are worried about countering rising debt exposure, asset inflation and financial system instability. All four interest rate rises in 2000 cited consumer credit growth as a background consideration, and more recent rate decisions have been partly shaped by the overheated property market. Future monetary policy decisions are likely to be framed with the financial system in mind. The new political economy of inflation is already being eclipsed by an even newer political economy of credit growth and asset inflation born of financial deregulation, an issue we return to in chapter 9.

CHAPTER 5

Towards RBA Independence

An independent central bank ... would be an Australian Treasurer's
nightmare.

Max Walsh[1]

A world-wide shift over the last decade has seen governments grant greater
policy independence to their central banks. For the most part, central banks have
gained control over the instruments of monetary policy – 'instrument' or 'operational' independence – while governments have reserved the right to set central
bank goals (see also chapter 7). As MacLaury argues, central banks these days
are 'independent *within* the government, not independent *of* the government'.[2]
Thus central bank 'independence' can be defined as the institutional capacity –
typically derived from an institutional mandate, backed by government support
– to conduct monetary policy free from significant government input or 'meddling'. Governments may establish the goals of policy, or the 'rules of the
game', but an independent central bank is free to conduct routine policy within
this framework as it sees fit.

The global debate on central bank independence (CBI) began in the late
1980s. By 1993, one well-placed observer declared that it was 'now an idea
whose time has most certainly come'.[3] Several countries, such as New Zealand,
France and Britain, made high-profile legislative choices to grant policy-making
independence to their central banks. The European Central Bank is now one of
the most independent in the world: it is not formally accountable to any government. Spurred by financial crises, Russia, the transition economies of Eastern
Europe and countries in East Asia and Latin America have taken similar steps.
Maxfield cites over thirty cases in the 1990s where national governments legis-
lated to increase the statutory independence of their central banks.[4]

In Australia, there was little debate on central bank independence until the
late 1980s, when the conservative Opposition raised the matter, with the support
of the financial community and financial commentators. The RBA began to seek
independence and by the mid-1990s had achieved substantial operational independence and control over the instruments of monetary policy.

Of course, there is no such thing as 'full independence'. Nor, arguably, should there be. As McDonough argues, 'central banks neither can nor should be fully independent of government, since it is governments – and not central banks – that hold final responsibility for the economic and financial policy of a country'.[5] Governments will always retain legislative control of the central bank and typically appoint central bank leaders; central banks will always watch and perhaps respond to government initiatives in other areas of economic policy. So 'independence' is best understood as a substantial degree of policy *delegation* to the central bank. This may be done through legislation or informal arrangements. In Australia, the Reserve Bank has always possessed a high degree of formal, statutory independence and so the transition towards operational independence has been mainly by informal means.

The determining factor is not the formal arrangements but the evolving policy relationship worked out on the ground between the government and the central bank. This has varied markedly over time. As we have seen, the Bank had little policy independence in the post-war era; the government, not the Bank, made monetary policy. That situation began to change in the 1980s. Under Governor Bob Johnston, the Bank gained more policy clout in the wake of financial market deregulation, and gradually it was given, and began to assert, more policy independence. Although the government, and especially Paul Keating, continued to be involved in the making of monetary policy during the 1980s and 1990s in a policy partnership role, this chapter shows that the policy relationship gradually evolved to a point where the Bank was routinely *making* monetary policy and became relatively 'independent'. The final step, formal recognition of this independent status, was taken by the incoming Howard government in 1996. Interestingly, most of the key changes occurred under the regime of Treasurer (and later Prime Minister) Keating, a leader known for his public criticism of CBI.

This chapter, then, examines the evolving monetary policy relationship between the Bank and federal governments in the 1980s and 1990s and traces the evolution of central bank independence in Australia. The next chapter explains more fully *why* this occurred, and in chapter 7 we probe the fit (or otherwise) between CBI and democracy.

The story begins in the 1970s, when the Bank played only a policy advisory role; it was still dominated by Treasury, and the Fraser government determined key elements of monetary policy within cabinet. Slowly, and in the wake of financial market deregulation and through processes of learning, adaptation and the establishment of more trust between the Bank and the Labor government, this advisory role shifted towards a bipartite bargaining relationship in which the Bank's role was increasingly prominent. The next phase developed under Governor Bernie Fraser and this expanded independence has continued under Governor Macfarlane in the post-1996 era. Essentially, then, the RBA has asserted a more independent policy role and contemporary Australian governments have gradually (re)endorsed the concept of central bank independence.

BLACK-LETTER INTERPRETATIONS?

Most analysts, especially in the economics literature, assess the degree of a central bank's independence using 'black letter' approaches. They assess the formal legal and institutional arrangements constituting the central bank (usually in some quantitative way) to determine its independence. This is a lifeless form of institutional analysis. It misses the most important thing, human agency and the actual motives and behaviour of the key actors. The statute-reading, quantitative approach is usually part of a research agenda which, particularly in the economics literature, has typically attempted to draw links between CBI and inflation performance across countries.[6] The measures of CBI are usually proxy variables for evaluating central bank 'economic' and 'political' independence.

How does Australia measure up? In terms of economic independence, reflecting former Governor Bernie Fraser's comment that 'there is a fundamental conflict between independence and an obligation to finance the government deficit',[7] measures of economic independence have focused on the presence or absence of the requirement that central banks must finance government deficits. Central bank researchers Grilli, Masciandero and Tabellini argue that economic independence is enhanced if central bank credit to the government is non-automatic and set at market rates.[8] In Australia, various arrangements in the late 1970s and early 1980s largely freed the RBA of obligations to finance government debt and set government debt financing at market interest rates.[9] A second aspect of economic independence concerns the monetary policy instruments under the control of the central bank. If the central bank (compared to another agency, such as Treasury) does not have direct control of the cash rate, its independence is obviously impaired. In Australia it is the RBA that operates in the market to set the cash rate. A third aspect is whether a central bank has control over its own budget. In Australia the RBA has a high degree of such independence, although its accounts are scrutinised by the Auditor-General. According to such measures, then, the RBA has a relatively high degree of 'economic' independence. Indeed, in one of the major studies, Grilli *et al.* rank the RBA as having six of their seven criteria for economic independence.[10]

In terms of 'political' independence, the most common measures (following Grilli *et al.*[11]) include the degree of government control over appointments to the central bank's governing body, the length of their terms, and whether they include government representatives or fiscal authorities, whether the goal of price stability is enshrined in statute, whether the central bank is assisted in any way by legal provisions should policy conflicts with the government arise, and, finally, whether government approval for monetary policy decisions is required – arguably one of the most important measures of independence. Grilli *et al.* give the RBA a relatively low score for policy and political independence.[12] Positive factors are: the RBA Governor is appointed for a period of more than five years, the goal of price stability is enshrined in statute, and the *Reserve Bank Act* has a provision which helps strengthen the Bank's position in any dispute with the government. As we have seen, Section 11 of the Act empowers the government with final decision-making authority in relation to monetary policy in any dispute with the Bank.

On the critical issue of government involvement in monetary policy formulation, Grilli *et al.* interpret the formal, legal arrangements to conclude that government 'approval' of monetary policy is required and that this implies government activism in monetary policy and hence limited policy independence for the Bank. It is true the Act gives the government final authority, and Section 11.1 also specifies that the Bank must inform the government (in practice the Treasurer) of its policy decisions. The dispute resolution powers (to be activated in cases of policy *disagreement*) also imply the search for some form of tacit agreement between the Treasurer and the Bank over policy. Indeed, it would be surprising for the Bank's leaders not to consider the anticipated views of the Treasurer when thinking about policy.[13]

The problem with the statute-reading approach, however, is that independence (or lack of it) is constituted by the *behaviour* of the relevant actors. Institutional theory recognises that statutes and other formal or legal arrangements may shape, but can never fully determine, behaviour. The problem with statute-reading approaches is that behaviour is inferred rather than directly examined.[14] In Australia's case the relevant behaviour has changed markedly over the last two decades, but the statutes and formal arrangements have not. This suggests that the question of central bank independence is best examined through a study of actual behaviour. But monetary policy is formulated in a closed, secretive context. The critical policy relationship is between the Governor and the Treasurer, and even insiders may not know fully what has transpired (as we will see below). John Edwards, a former adviser to Paul Keating, reminds us, 'in practice the relationship between the Bank and any Treasurer is subtle'.[15] In the account below, based on inferences drawn from various policy episodes and direct accounts gained in interviews with insiders, an attempt is made to chart how this 'subtle' relationship has changed markedly in the last two decades in Australia.

1982

As we have seen, the RBA was subservient both to the Treasury and to the government from the end of World War II to the 1970s. Despite the Bank's statutory provisions, independence was not an issue. Although the Bank gained a more prominent role under the Fraser government, its function in relation to the formulation of monetary policy was still advisory. In an interview documented in a PhD thesis by Simon Guttmann dealing with monetary targeting in Australia in the 1970s and 1980s, Sir Harold Knight, the RBA's Governor from 1975 to 1982, records the Bank's views at the time about the issue of independence. The *RBA Act*, as well as the tradition of post-war practice, Knight recalled:

> Placed the government in a position of seniority, superiority, and if there had been a desire for the Bank to take actions which would be unacceptable on the part of the government, it would crystallise the availability to the government of powers of direction of the Bank and once they come into use they could very well be used as a matter of routine in ways which would came from the rather unenlightened wishes of Prime Ministers like Whitlam or Fraser. The Bank was quite clear that it should not have an attempt at a confrontation with the government. It should accept the fact that the government was in charge and the Bank was an adviser and a pusher and could do things where its authority, as accepted by the government, would allow it to work but that it had to work within the limitations of what was acceptable and achievable.[16]

A 1982 incident underlined the Bank's readiness to defend what it saw as its institutional prerogatives. In his August Budget speech, the Treasurer, John Howard, announced that the government would be requesting the Bank to make a release from the Statutory Reserve Deposits (SRDs) of the trading banks in order to increase the flow of funds for lending to housing. The context, of course, was the government's shaky position in the face of a looming federal election. Some say Howard's statement came out of the blue, without consultation with the Bank, although as Howard told the *National Times* in early 1983 he did warn the Bank.[17] Knight responded to Howard in a memo on 3 August that such a use of SRDs was an 'inappropriate mechanism and not acceptable as an element of Reserve Bank policy'.[18] Knight went on: 'the Bank staff would have severe difficulty in putting such a proposal to the Board, and the Board would be unlikely to proceed with it'. Undeterred, Howard went ahead with the announcement in the Budget. Governor Johnston, who took over at the Bank only a few days before the Budget announcement, was confronted with a government demand that was out of kilter with conventional Bank practices concerning the management of SRDs. Ian Macfarlane now recalls that it was 'one of those individual incidents where the government overstepped the mark and took us completely for granted'.[19] Johnston stood his ground and refused to make the release. As he now puts it: 'the sticking point was we would not agree to use SRDs for that purpose ... Without, you know, an overt confrontation or shaking of fists we politely made it clear that we didn't think that was a proper request.'[20] The Bank's *Annual Report* of 1982/83 spelt out the Bank's response:

> The Board was reluctant to agree to this proposal for several reasons. First, it saw difficulty in reconciling a special release from the SRD with the role which it considers those deposits must play in giving effect to monetary policy for the economy as a whole. In the immediate context, an SRD release would not have been in keeping with prevailing monetary policy. More fundamentally, a reserve asset requirement which was perceived to be subject, even in special circumstances, to selective action would very likely lose its effectiveness as an instrument of stabilisation policy.[21]

As Johnston recalls,

> these views were put to the government. In the weeks following the Budget Speech, housing finance had continued to become more readily available, partly because of improved flows of deposits to the major home lenders. There were also prospects of this trend continuing. The Board welcomed the Treasurer's announcement in November that the government had decided to defer its request.[22]

Ian Macfarlane reflects on the 1982 incident: 'that's the only thing I can remember ever resembling any form of central bank independence in those days'.[23]

JOHNSTON AND KEATING

In the monetary policy arena, the internal dynamics of power and authority in the new Labor administration, following financial deregulation, worked roughly as follows. Within the government, Treasurer Keating seized control over monetary policy, removing it from the cabinet. Keating always consulted with Prime Minister Hawke over relevant policy decisions, but Keating, along with his advisers in the RBA and the Treasury, made monetary policy. As Paul Kelly puts it, for Keating 'monetary policy was too lethal and sensitive to expose to the vagaries of cabinet discussion'.[24] The RBA had statutory responsibility for the conduct of monetary policy, but, as we have seen, this was not the convention, which had governed real decision-making in the post-war era. When Paul Keating became federal Treasurer in March 1983, he was imbued with the conventional view that the government made monetary policy, the Bank acting largely as an adviser and implementer. As Macfarlane recalls,

> when Keating came into office he clearly assumed the old rules of the game applied. The Treasurer made monetary policy on the advice of the Reserve Bank and the Treasury. I mean they were the old rules of the game. And I am sure that he came into office firmly of that view … in those days there was a very strong Treasurer and a much weaker Bank.[25]

Nevertheless, Keating and Governor Bob Johnston quickly established a good working relationship. Keating had been impressed by Johnston's and the Bank's handling of the financial deregulation decision. Also, the decision itself was, in the bureaucratic arena, a stunning victory for the Bank over an opposed Treasury. The Bank's control over the instruments of policy also rose immeasurably in the wake of financial deregulation.

The conduct of monetary policy in a deregulated environment was a steep learning curve in the 1980s, and Keating relied heavily on the Bank's advice in the new and uncertain context. Financial deregulation had left the Bank in direct control of the only remaining instrument of monetary policy, open market operations (setting the short-term official cash rate). This instrument required intimate knowledge of the markets and only the Bank had this kind of expertise. John Phillips recalls:

> All the weapons that had previously been regarded as part of monetary policy had gone, and the only weapon left was open market policy. So suddenly we were there with an instrument that Coombs had said he would love to have but that was not available to him in the sixties. And it wasn't an instrument in which there was any legislative provision for anyone else to intervene. So we had a clean sheet so far as the Act was concerned. So for the first time in history, the Bank could – provided it had the political will – determine its own policy, and then inform the government.[26]

The largest loser in the new arrangements was Treasury. The RBA had previously been dominated by Treasury, but after deregulation its role became central: it alone wielded the only remaining instrument of policy; the Bank would now deal directly with the Treasurer in policy determination. Treasury's input and advice continued, but over time its influence waned. Not only had the RBA become the lead institution in relation to monetary policy and in reading the movements in financial markets, but RBA pronouncements and research in other policy areas also gained new prominence, as did the increasing flow of speeches and the public profile of the Bank's leaders.[27]

The policy relationship between Keating and the Bank did not consist of a series of instructions from Keating to an essentially passive or subservient Bank. Keating denies that he ever made an explicit policy instruction to the Bank. 'Of course, I don't have to', he said in an interview in 1985. 'The relationship has matured. This is a relationship that has to be lubricated with a good deal of common sense. You would not want to test our respective prerogatives too much.'[28]

John Hewson – economist, policy adviser, one-time RBA employee, and later the Opposition Leader – became the most prominent sceptic of this view in the late 1980s. He became fixated with the Bank and its independence. This marked a turnaround. In 1980 Hewson had published an article in *Economic Papers*, which had defended the Bank's multiple goals and pointedly argued *against* the idea of central bank independence.[29] The revisionist Hewson, however, accused Keating of bullying the Bank, politicising monetary policy, and forcing the Bank to cut interest rates at electorally opportune times for the government. He cited the rate reductions prior to the federal elections in 1984, 1987 and 1990 as the major cases in point.[30] Most informed observers and insiders discount the latter two cases: those rate cuts were justified on economic grounds, and that argument could even apply to the 1984 case. In a long speech in 1988, Hewson gave a colourful account of the 1984 episode, alleging that Keating had pressured Governor Johnston to lower rates at a meeting in Canberra just before the August bank holiday in the lead-up to the December federal election. Hewson described the situation as the 'bank holiday massacre'.[31] In an off-the-record comment to me, one former senior Bank official confirmed that Keating did pressure the Bank. Ian Macfarlane agrees: 'In the 1980s, before I was involved, which was in 1988, there was certainly one occasion when Keating made the policy. There's no doubt about that.'[32] Drawing on inside information, Ross Gittins of the *Sydney Morning Herald* has referred to 'the ham fisted easing of policy in the run up to the 1984 election, which I now have no doubt was made under political instruction'.[33] Similarly, Alan Wood, senior economics commentator for the *Australian*, writes that:

> The only one of these [allegations of political interference] I have been able to pin down in any detail is 1984 … As I understand, what happened was that Peter Jonson and Bob Johnston both headed down to Canberra to see Paul Keating and were

treated to something they hadn't really been exposed to at all: which was a typical
New South Wales right-wing burst of aggression, an obscenity which amounted to
saying, 'Why the fucking hell are these interest rates so high?' This so disturbed
Bob Johnston that he shot back like a startled rabbit to Sydney and sort of screamed
the same thing down the phone to the market people, whereupon rates fell! No-one
was more amazed, I'm told, at the time than Paul Keating who became much more
formal in his dealings with Bob after that, I believe.

Bob Johnston has responded to these claims, saying 'categorically there was no
political element involved' and that the monetary adjustments at the time were
'wholly technical'.[34] Wood goes on to discount the other allegations of interference. He says of the 1987 and 1990 examples, 'I'm not sure about [them].
Certainly, Peter Jonson – who was there – doesn't seem to subscribe to the 1987
one, and I don't think that in the 1990s there has been a big political influence.'[35] Peter Jonson discounts the idea of political interference in monetary
policy:

> I do not believe that 'political' biases were important. To the extent that
> performance fell short of the ideal, I believe this can partly be explained by errors of
> judgement about where the economy was headed, rather than by the imposition of
> 'political judgement'. This comment is made with 1984 in mind, although it is
> intended as an overall judgement.[36]

The point in raising these claims is that, even if the 1984 incident demonstrates explicit policy bullying or interference, it stands alone. Typically, the
evolving relationship between the Bank and Treasurer Keating during the
1980s was a policy partnership based on explicit sharing of authority and regular interaction and dialogue. This occurred in the regular policy debriefings
which followed meetings of the Bank's Board, but contact was often made
informally, either in person or by phone. Bob Johnston outlined the broad
nature of the relationship in a speech during his retirement from the Bank in
1989: 'As to who makes monetary policy, I do not take issue with the descrip-
tion of arrangements in Australia as "power sharing" or "bi-partite" as
between government and central bank.' Consultation between the Bank and
Treasurer had been ongoing, Johnston pointed out. 'But consultation does not
imply domination – persuasion can cut both ways.' In response to the increasingly hubristic attacks, especially by John Hewson, Johnston went on to refute
'allegations of interest rate manipulation by the Bank for party political ends',
as 'scurrilous'.[37] This was Johnston's parting riposte against Hewson.

Johnston, of necessity, had remained largely aloof from the attacks, although they had personally wounded him.[38]

All of my respondents concurred with this 'policy partnership' model, and with the view that the Bank's policy influence increased during the 1980s. Yet although the Bank had asserted itself on the question of prerogatives in 1982 and took its statutory position seriously, it is clear that, following deregulation, the Bank did not summon up the political will to 'determine its own policy', especially in the face of an activist Treasurer like Paul Keating. Keating sees himself as the dominant partner. In interview, he declared he was 'not just in the loop' regarding monetary policy: 'I was the principal ... No policy would be made that I didn't agree with ... at no stage did the Bank have primacy in the setting of policy.' He continued:

> Let's not have any of this naivety that the person who had to stand in the marketplace to have themselves elected, and carry the ultimate responsibility for the economy, was in some way subordinate to someone he appoints to the central bank. That is not real; it's political nonsense.[39]

In rejecting the concept of CBI, Keating explained:

> In the end all relevant political authority in the country devolves to the government. Under the Reserve Bank Act this power is in a measure given to the Board of the Bank, but only on the basis that it operates cooperatively with the government. And in the final analysis the government can have its way by instruction. This makes clear that a central bank bureaucracy has a function to perform in the marketplace, but it has to perform it under the power and umbrella of the government of the day. And if people don't believe this, they believe in fairies at the bottom of the garden. In the end all the political authority in a country evolves to the government.[40]

Nevertheless, Keating did see the Bank as very important in the 'partnership' and was keen to elevate the Bank's role; not necessarily to a position of full policy 'independence', but certainly to a point where the Bank was a major policy partner. 'I was determined when I left that there stood an institution that was able to fend for itself. It could never really fend for itself against the full political authority of the government but I sought to give it some greater ability to stand there in its own right', Keating said.[41]

Legally, the Treasurer could formally instruct the Bank, but only if he informed the parliament and invoked the formal disputes procedure. For its part, the Bank could not implement a policy change without notifying the Treasurer. So the relationship had to be worked out on a more-or-less consensual basis. As Keating said during interview: 'interest rate policy was always agreed between the Treasurer and the Bank'. In a 1989 article Keating spelt out the nature of the policy relationship as he saw it. The *Reserve Bank Act*, he said:

> very clearly directs the Bank to have an independent role … The Act also requires that the Bank keeps the government informed of its policy and that the Treasurer and the Board shall endeavour to reach agreement. This requires the Treasurer and the Board to discuss matters but at the end of the day, both parties are required to be satisfied that policy is appropriate. An independent role for the Reserve Bank is therefore explicitly required by the Act. I find this entirely appropriate.[42]

For Keating, then, 'independence' did not involve complete or even substantial monetary policy delegation to the Bank (essentially the contemporary usage of the term 'independence'). Keating instead saw 'independence' as the Bank's right to be at the policy bargaining table, 'independently' putting its case, and also having the right to 'be satisfied that policy is appropriate'. This was a substantial policy role, but still some way from complete policy *delegation* and the kind of 'independence' the Bank now enjoys.

In elaborating on the nature of the policy partnership during interview, Keating added further nuance:

> People want to see these things in polarities; which is quite wrong. You've got to see this as a cooperative venture, where the Treasurer, if he or she has any sense, wants to bring the Bank along and understand their point of view … It was always better to inch everyone along … But again, when they dallied, often I'd let them as the price of getting along. It was the price of keeping the ship of state together. Because it's curtains in the markets if they think there is a major difference between the government and the Board. I used to say, this is what I think. I think rates should rise, but you don't. Let's have another look in a month. But they knew they were on a short check, right![43]

Bob Johnston describes the policy relationship with Keating from his perspective:

> I had a close and I believe constructive association with the Treasurer … By choice and by pressure of events, the style of working tended to be informal with issues, as far as possible, being worked through by discussion … This frank and business-like style and a good spirit became the norm in contacts on all issues … This did not,

however, obscure a fundamental point, namely that each recognised the statutory obligations of the other. Thus, it was the duty of the Bank to determine monetary policy and to do so solely in the light of the objectives set out in the Reserve Bank Act. At the same time the Treasurer had the right to be informed of the Bank's monetary and banking policies and to consider whether they met the tests in the Act ... And if not, should attempts to reconcile views begin?[44]

From this perspective, it is the Bank which, in the first instance at least, 'makes policy', which is then reviewed continuously with the Treasurer with a view to seeking a policy consensus. The minutes of the debriefings with the Treasurer after Board meetings during the Johnston era appear to confirm this view:

- 'On monetary policy the Treasurer expressed no difference with the Board's view that the current situation required policy to be held at about its current state of firmness.'[45]
- 'It was agreed that monetary policy should remain firm ...'[46]
- 'The Treasurer had no difficulties with the Board's position ...'[47]

For the most part, the policy relationship did reach a ready consensus. There was underlying agreement about broad aims and principles. Routine monetary policy, by its nature, is an incremental process of small adjustments to policy settings, generally not the stuff of serious conflict. The points where 'differences' arose demonstrate how the relationship worked in practice. John Edwards reports an instance in early 1986 when Keating 'was on the phone every day' arguing for a reduction in interest rates, with the Bank, for a time, resisting.[48] Paul Kelly argues that Keating did not dominate monetary policy; 'in fact the reverse was true. The conduct of monetary policy during 1986 and 1987 when the foundations of the boom were laid reflected the majority position among the family of Treasury–Reserve senior advisers.'[49] Chapter 2 explained that in early 1988 Treasurer Keating was pushing for a rise in rates but was temporarily frustrated by resistance-cum-tardiness on the part of the Bank.[50] This hardly amounted to a serious conflict, but it does show that the Bank was taking some of the initiative on policy; though perhaps on a 'short check', as Keating insists. As Bob Johnston recalls:

The Reserve Bank had decided on a tightening of monetary conditions. My recollection is that Keating preferred a rise that would deliver a sharp shock but I felt the move should start less abruptly. No precise target was settled on. It was left to the Bank to put the upward shift in interest rates into effect. But there was a delay in April, after which rates rose strongly. This was a difficult episode but was contained within the good working relationship between the Treasurer and myself. It was not a question of jurisdiction but of trying to get the right outlook. There was no thumping of tables, but the episode did reflect some difference of opinion over policy.[51]

FRASER AND KEATING

Paul Keating had appointed Bernie Fraser as Treasury Secretary in 1984, and after Bob Johnston retired from the Bank, Keating appointed Fraser to the governorship in September 1989. Fraser came from a working-class background and had risen through the bureaucratic ranks with a combination of talent and determination. The decision to appoint an 'outsider' raised eyebrows within the Bank: the much-respected John Phillips had been passed over. Many saw Fraser as a political appointment by a Treasurer keen to exert control, even as 'Keating's man'.[52] But Keating also admired Fraser's capacities. They were also close friends, they trusted each other and, besides, Keating saw Fraser as somewhat less hawkish on inflation than Phillips. Fraser had a reputation as someone wary of the power of interest rates. Yet, in one of the great ironies, it was Fraser who wielded interest rates in such a way as to ensure inflation was ground out of the system.

Fraser's appointment came at a critical juncture for the Bank. By 1989 it had raised interest rates to dizzy heights in battling the late 1980s boom. Even so, a chorus of critics saw it as soft on inflation, and Australia's comparative inflation record over the 1980s appeared, to the critics at least, to demonstrate this. The debate over central bank independence was also hotting up, with charges that the Bank lacked independence, or worse, that it did the political bidding of the government.

Keating helped fuel the debate with infamous off-hand comments in 1989 and again in 1990 that the Bank was 'in my pocket' and 'they do what I say'.[53] These gaffes reflect the intense pressure on Keating about economic policy at this time; the press and opponents were suggesting he had lost control of the policy system. In an article published in the *Sydney Morning Herald*, Keating attempted to explain and defuse the 1989 comment: 'my comments were misinterpreted', he said. 'I was rejecting [very testily] the specific notion put that the government had no control over the conduct of monetary policy.'[54] As Fraser later commented, 'the original quips were bad enough, but their repetition *ad nauseam* [by the media] in the face of denials, including by Paul Keating, was even worse in my view; it certainly did nothing to enhance the Bank's standing in financial circles'.[55] In an interview with Chris Eichbaum, Fraser commented on the 1990 'in my pocket' statement as 'unfortunate':

> He said it in a rather obscure forum – it was supposed to be a private function soon after the death of Treasury Secretary, Chris Higgins. He was boasting a bit in a way,

but he was talking more in terms of how he had got this close working relationship
with the central bank and the Treasury, and how he was on good terms with people
in the IMF and other institutions around the world, and he used this colourful turn of
phrase about having all these people in his pocket. It was unfortunate, and he
regretted it. I chastised him … he regretted it, and he never repeated it. He came
close a couple of times to more or less backing away but, being the person he was,
he couldn't bring himself to make a full apology.[56]

Keating's comments helped torpedo the Bank's credibility. For Fraser, the path
ahead would be tortuous. He did not wish to alienate Keating but, institutionally,
he felt almost compelled to assert a more authoritative, decisive role for the
Bank: its credibility and legitimacy were at stake.

Yet Fraser's first actions as Governor only fuelled the fires of criticism: in
January 1990 the Bank reduced interest rates, just before a federal election!
Although there was agreement within the Bank that rates should be cut on economic grounds, Macfarlane now recalls it was a 'very difficult time'. 'Bernie
was seen as a political appointee, and there was an election coming up in
March.' Cutting rates 'was going to be a very difficult thing to do'.[57] Fraser also
drew attention to the issue of the Bank's independence, because, as we have
seen, he openly championed the Labor government's Accord policy and was not
averse to publicly criticising the Opposition's policies. But Fraser also commented publicly about the government's policies. In 1990, for example, he suggested that some of the load could be taken off monetary policy in the fight
against inflation if the government adopted a further wage–tax trade-off under
the Accord. Keating was apparently annoyed by the contribution, but the press
welcomed it as a sign of a more assertive Bank.[58]

Other factors in 1990 were straining the relationship between Keating and
the RBA. The July statement by Deputy Governor John Phillips – that it was
'blindingly obvious' that monetary policy should not be used to deal with the
CAD and should instead be singled out to fight inflation – did not, as we have
seen, go down well with Keating. Bernie Fraser comments:

The 'blindingly obvious' episode did fracture the 'honeymoon' trust between
Keating and the Bank for a time, and it didn't help my efforts to foster the Bank's
independence which, in the early days, was conceived – necessarily I think – as
independence in partnership with government.[59]

Nevertheless, in the late 1980s and early 1990s, momentum was gathering
behind the concept of central bank independence, both in Australia and internationally. Economists had been developing various theoretical explanations as to

why governments could not supposedly be trusted to run an effective monetary policy, the implication being that the job should be given to an independent 'conservative' central bank. Economists also produced comparative empirical evidence that purported to show that CBI was associated with low inflation (see chapter 6). At a subterranean level there was the view that since the failure of monetary targeting some piece of new institutional machinery was needed in the fight against inflation; and CBI seemed to fit the bill. Things were also spurred along by the establishment of the New Zealand model in 1989, which gave pride of place to independence.

A growing chorus of critics, led by John Hewson, championed the concept of operational independence for the RBA and argued the Bank should have more of it. Relatedly, as we have seen, there was the charge that the Bank was 'politicised' and that Keating was cajoling or forcing it to manipulate interest rates to suit the government's electoral agenda.[60] On this latter charge, as outlined above, there was possibly one such episode in 1984, but otherwise the evidence is slim.[61] Nevertheless, Laura Tingle has claimed that in late 1991, when Keating was sitting on the backbench amidst a leadership struggle with Bob Hawke, the then Treasurer, John Kerin, tried to get the Bank to bring forward a decision on cutting interest rates (apparently in order to help Prime Minister Hawke confront a hostile Caucus in the midst of the recession). Soon after this Kerin (on Treasury's urging) allegedly attempted to pressure the Bank for a smaller rate cut than the Bank wanted.[62] This reflected ongoing tension between the Bank and Treasury over the pace of rate reductions. According to Tingle, the Bank prevailed, with Governor Fraser threatening to resign or to force the government to invoke the disputes procedure. Fraser confirms these events.[63] Kerin agrees that Treasury urged him to take the extraordinary step of announcing a reduction in interest rates in the August Budget speech.[64] He says he raised this with Fraser, who replied that if that was to occur, 'I'll have to give the game away.'[65] Kerin dropped the issue.

These recollections arrive at a common point and underline the growing authority of the Bank. While John Hewson and like-minded critics were attacking the Bank on the question of independence, the Bank was quietly asserting itself. It is noteworthy that both Kerin and Prime Minister Hawke were soon giving speeches which emphasised that their dealings with the Bank were based on 'due process' and respect for its prerogatives.[66]

Claims that the Bank lacked sufficient policy independence amounted to a critique of the 'partnership' model. When the Bank's chief researcher, Peter Jonson, resigned in 1988, he claimed that the partnership model muddied the waters of policy responsibility and gave too much weight to the short-run views of politicians. A serious attack on inflation would require, he thought, a more independent and forward-looking central bank.[67] Another high-profile critic was former senior bureaucrat Sir William Cole. Writing in early 1990, Cole argued that 'the degree to which the Reserve Bank is "independent" is not simply a matter of what the relevant statutes say, but the reading of them accepted within the Reserve Bank'. 'Over many years', Cole continued, 'that reading has been at the cautious end of the spectrum.' Cole lamented this, saying 'the Reserve Bank's statutory powers are formidable as are its persuasive powers *vis-à-vis* the government'. He urged the Bank to become more independent, arguing that 'the anti-inflation cause needs a champion with teeth'.[68]

In this context, one of the first speeches Bernie Fraser gave after becoming Governor was on the topic of central bank independence. Fraser argued that the Bank was not 'politicised' and that it had sufficient independence to perform its duties (at the time the RBA was running one of the highest interest rates in the world). 'The necessary authority and independence already exist', he argued.[69] Fraser also emphasised that the Bank needed to coordinate closely with the government, because an effective attack on inflation required weaving together monetary, fiscal and wages policy. 'While some critics of the macho variety might have difficulty with the notion, it is possible for the Bank to be both independent and cooperative: a willingness to cooperate in partnership [with the government] ... should not be labelled a sign of weakness.'[70] In the Bank's official view, relationships with the Treasurer took the form of 'consultative independence' (implying the bank actively consults but retains much of the decision-making prerogative). Consultation with the Treasurer, Fraser argued, 'helps avoid surprises, and the transmission of conflicting signals to the markets'.[71] In a speech in 1993, in which Fraser complained that the debate in Australia about central bank independence 'had been rendered sterile by gladiatorial notions of independence',[72] he summarised the Bank's position:

> I have said many times that the Reserve Bank does, in fact, have a high degree of political independence. We can and do pursue our statutory responsibilities without political interference. But we seek to do this in close consultation with the government – to exercise *independence with consultation*. This accords with the linkages which exist between monetary policy and other policies ... [But] cooperation and consultation are not the same as subservience.[73]

In subsequent speeches Fraser explicitly rejected the charge of 'politicisation'. 'Critics have peddled the line over the years that the Bank was "political", but no hard evidence has ever been advanced. There is none.' Citing the charge that rates were reduced prior to the March 1990 federal election, Fraser commented:

On that occasion, rates were reduced in the preceding January and February; these reductions were criticised widely as being both 'political' and inflationary – but so were several of the thirteen reductions which were made between April 1990 and July 1993. In retrospect, no objective observer could reasonably challenge the economic soundness of any of that long series of reductions.[74]

Echoing the Campbell Committee, Fraser also argued that in a deregulated financial environment overseen by increasingly powerful and vigilant financial markets, the opportunities for loose or politically manipulated monetary policy had largely disappeared:

> These days ... such manipulation will be caught out ... the financial markets in particular will see through the ruse and punish the perpetrators. Today's politicians appreciate that extended front-page reportage of a plunging exchange rate, for example, could easily outweigh any positive effects of a politically inspired cut in interest rates.[75]

In 1990, one of the Bank's critics, Sir William Cole, wrote that 'the Reserve Bank has written down its own independence. In doing so it has avoided the public identification with economic policy failures which it deserves.'[76] Two years later, in the wake of the recession, newly appointed Deputy Governor Ian Macfarlane underlined Fraser's arguments about the Bank's growing independence. Like Fraser, Macfarlane had been annoyed by the attacks on the Bank and by Keating's off-hand remark that the Bank was in his pocket. In one of his first speeches as Deputy Governor, Macfarlane appeared to respond directly to Cole's earlier criticism:

> all the decisions, all the reductions in interest rates, have occurred because they have been recommended by the Board of the Reserve Bank – the timing has been determined by the Reserve Bank and the size of the changes has been determined by the Reserve Bank. So if you don't like how monetary policy has turned out, if you think it is a terrible mess, blame us. Blame Martin Place. It would be very comfortable if every time people didn't like monetary policy they complained to Canberra. But they would be wasting their time. I think a lot of people are still thinking of the institutional arrangements as they were in the 1970s and early 1980s when Governors of the Reserve Bank had to wait patiently outside the monetary policy committee of Cabinet to get a hearing.[77]

In interview, Ian Macfarlane elaborated on what he saw as the slowly changing nature of the relationship between the Bank and Keating. Keating continued to be involved, but under Fraser the Bank made most of the running on monetary policy. As Macfarlane recalls, when Fraser first arrived at the Bank: 'he was certainly not a supporter of central bank independence'. 'He had the standard Treasury view', that the Bank's role was advisory and that the government should coordinate monetary and fiscal policy. But over time, Macfarlane argues, Fraser 'had to go through a transformation as well, which he did, slowly, at his own pace'.

> The problem was, in some sense, we had to get Bernie thinking the same way as us rather than his old Treasury view of the world. We had to get him on board ... on board at his own pace. There was no way you could bully him or anything like that. And gradually once we got him on board at his pace, he had the capacity to bring the government on board with him, which was, it turns out really terribly important.[78]

Certainly by the early 1990s, Macfarlane said in interview, things 'felt independent' within the Bank:

> We would have internal discussions here among ourselves and then we'd sort of eventually agree, let's agree to do this or that. Now, I don't know how many conversations had gone on between Bernie and Paul Keating. So for us it sounded as though we were very independent because we were giving our views to Bernie, and Bernie was either accepting ... or accepting after a bit of discussion, then they'd go to the Board ... and then would be acted on. So that clearly gave us the impression that it was being done according to the textbook. But I don't know how many conversations Bernie had had with Paul. I mean, maybe Bernie only agreed with us once he's already cleared it. So I will never know the answer to that.

Macfarlane highlights one of the tantalising problems of assessing CBI. Assuming a relatively compliant Board and senior management, the dynamics of policy-making can boil down to almost a one-to-one relationship between the Treasurer and the Governor. John Edwards writes that the Keating–Fraser relationship involved 'continuing and deepening that private line of communication between Treasurer and Reserve Bank Governor that began with Johnston and would now increase in trust, weight and understanding'.[79] But did Fraser have to clear decisions with Keating, implying subservience? Was power equally shared? Or, as seems to be the case, did Fraser take an assertive role? Fraser argues it was the latter, and adds: 'I always made a point of informing all the senior officers at the Bank of my discussions with Keating and other Treasurers.'[80]

Macfarlane thinks that the closeness of the relationship between Fraser and Keating (both as Treasurer and as Prime Minister) helped lubricate the shift towards greater CBI. Personalities matter, and Macfarlane thinks the high level of trust that existed between Fraser and Keating, and subsequent Treasurers, was an important ingredient in the Bank's move towards greater policy independence:

> Paul Keating had so much trust in Bernie, I think it meant that he did relax ... He did actually almost fall into line de facto with a relatively independent view. Because he'd put his man in charge, he trusted this guy ... it felt independent by the nineties.

Still, Macfarlane continued: 'there were little concessions that had to be made'.

> I noticed, for example, every time we'd put out a press release to say there's a change in monetary policy, we always had to say 'after consultation with the government' ... And then the government would put out its press release as well. And the government still felt that if there was any praise to be handed out because interest rates were going down, they wanted to receive it. And actually, they copped a lot of criticism when interest rates went up. So it still wasn't a clean division of responsibility. The government, I think, got the worst of both worlds in the sense that they had pretty well delegated the decision to us, but they still copped all the flak when something unpopular happened.[81]

Bernie Fraser was in no doubt about how the relationship was evolving:

> The position has evolved over the years, and certainly I would say that in the seven years I was at the Bank, there was a good deal of consultation, and I was very supportive of the need for consultation with the Treasurer ... But I think it's fair to say that over the past seven years or so, and I think that has changed from earlier times, the Board has been, as the Act says, the actual decision making body, with all sorts of input, including from Treasurers. But it's not an exaggeration to say that on the few occasions, and there were very few occasions in the last seven years, where the Bank and the Treasurer may have disagreed on the timing or the magnitude, occasionally even the direction of an interest rate change, it is no exaggeration to say that the Bank's view has prevailed. And put it down to persuasiveness or whatever, but that has been the case ... I think we've been quite persuasive in turning Treasurers around – not just Keating – but others too when they've had slightly different views on what should be done and when things should be done ... I don't believe there have been any specific instances where the Treasurer's view has resulted in a change of any significance from what the Board was intent on doing.[82]

Chapter 3 reviewed the evidence which supports Fraser's claim: the assertive role of the Bank (strongly backed by Treasury) in confronting inflation head on during the early 1990s, and convincing a reluctant Treasurer to go along with the tough approach; even to the point, according to Keating, that the Bank was going against his will and 'dragging the chain' on interest rate reductions after 1990 in the (successful) bid to exact a king-hit against inflation. There is further evidence of the Bank's growing authority. Although Keating publicly rejected the idea of using an explicit inflation target to guide monetary policy, arguing instead for an approach of greater 'dexterity',[83] the Bank, as we have seen, *uni-laterally* adopted an inflation target in 1993. Keating may have publicly criticised the idea of 'unelected officials' attempting to make monetary policy during this period, but this is largely what happened. Keating admitted as much in August 1991. On the backbench during his leadership struggle with Hawke, Keating railed in the *Sydney Morning Herald* against what he saw as the new monetary policy orthodoxy – 'the notion that interest rates should be set in a medium-term context and target inflation only' – and criticised the 'way officials on occasions go to great lengths to hem ministers in and restrict their room for manoeuvre'. Reflecting on what happened during the boom and bust, he stated:

> With regard to monetary policy there are things I would do differently with the benefit of hindsight. I would have been less accommodating in the second half of 1987 to the monetary authorities' willingness to cut interest rates … I would have also been more insistent in following my own view in 1988, to lift interest rates earlier and harder … and once we started cutting interest rates in January 1990, I should have been even more insistent than I was against Treasury and Reserve Bank advice in getting rates down more quickly … My experience with officialdom and interest rates over the past eight years is that they are too slow in lifting rates and too slow in getting them down. Too flat footed altogether.[84]

For a Treasurer who had publicly criticised the notion of central bank independence, this is a frank admission of either loss of control over policy or at least failure to exert enough pressure on his officials. Keating was clearly a significant player in the monetary policy process, but at critical junctures the officials seemed to make most of the running. This was the case under Governor Johnston in the late 1980s, and even more so under Bernie Fraser in the early 1990s.

These dynamics, however, did not amount to a contest between Keating and Fraser for policy authority. Keating was more dovish than the Bank or Treasury in the early 1990s, but so too was Fraser. True, Fraser wanted to crack inflation and pull something positive from the recession. But others within the Bank wanted to do this even more stridently. Bernie tried to temper the hawks around him, in the Bank, in the Bank's Board, in the Treasury and even in the Department of Prime Minister and Cabinet. But, as Fraser recalls, amidst the struggle, 'I felt a bit lonely at times.'[85] In dealing with policy tensions within the Bank – particularly against the hawkishness of John Phillips (Deputy Governor), and to a lesser extent Ian Macfarlane (Head of Research) and Bill Norton (Head of Financial Markets) – Fraser, by his own account, made some progress.

As part of this process, Fraser restructured the Bank's management in 1990/91, with large increases in salaries for senior staff (partly to prevent a brain drain).[86] Senior positions were thrown open and re-designated as contract positions – the Bank's senior managers were required to re-apply for their jobs. In a move that shocked senior management, Bill Norton was not reselected, and he resigned. In April 1992, John Phillips also resigned. Meanwhile, the policy battles continued on a wider front. John Edwards argues:

> Bernie was mostly fighting alone, or alone with just Kelty against the Board and the Treasury. The Department was fighting so hard that at one point [Treasury Secretary] Chris Higgins had actually argued at the Board against a recommendation to ease. Bernie was fighting in Sydney while Keating was fighting in Canberra and not least against the Department of Prime Minister and Cabinet.[87]

Like Fraser, Keating insists he made some progress in speeding up the rate reductions during this period,[88] but overall, it is clear that it was officials – especially Fraser, supported by Chris Higgins in Treasury – who were taking the initiative on policy. Chris Eichbaum's research on these issues confirms this: 'despite attempts to pressure the Bank into reducing interest rates more quickly, and the presence of a Governor who sympathized with the case, the government of the day was unable to exercise any determining influence over the central bank'.[89]

This slow transition towards greater independence continued under Fraser, reinforced by Keating's huge trust in him. The *Australian*'s Paul Kelly argues: 'just as Paul Keating's high profile obscured the Bank's essential command over interest rate policy in the late 1980s and 90s so the friendly Keating–Fraser relationship disguised the leap towards a more independent Bank which Fraser was making'.[90] But the RBA's moves against inflation were also strongly supported by Treasury, and to an extent by the Department of Prime Minister and Cabinet, especially under its post-1991 Head, Michael Keating. Keating, who had formerly been Head of the Department of Finance, moved to the top job in the department when Keating became Prime Minister in December 1991. He says that the department supported the push against inflation, especially when the depths of the recession became obvious. But he points to Treasury's significance:

> In my view the Bank did not enjoy sufficient independence at the time that it could have run an anti-inflation policy purely on its own initiative, even if it had been fully

united in this endeavour. In fact the role of Treasury was perhaps almost as critical as that of the Bank in this whole policy episode. Chris Higgins was more determined to snap inflation than Fraser.[91]

Treasury's push against inflation continued after Chris Higgins's sudden death in December 1990. Tony Cole was appointed as the new Secretary. But, as Cole commented in interview, from his perspective it was the Bank that was taking charge of monetary policy.

> The task of running monetary policy is bloody hard ... We were more and more convinced that the less politics there was in monetary policy the better ... While I was Secretary of the Treasury, I spent more and more time getting out of it [monetary policy] and letting the Bank call the shots.[92]

Bernie Fraser agrees:

> Yes, that happened. How conscious it was I'm not sure. It may have been partly that, but it was probably more that the Bank was on a bit of a roll and was making the announcements about rate changes and asserting itself and becoming much more prominent in terms of public profile and becoming the natural focus of monetary policy decisions. Treasury was left a bit in the shadows, although I still remember Tony Cole had a fair bit to say when he came along to Board meetings and there was still a fair bit of contact between the two institutions. So, I can't remember any conscious pulling back, but in a practical sense it was happening.[93]

Although Keating and subsequent Treasurers still routinely took part in monetary policy discussions and provided input, sometimes pointed, the Bank was asserting, or at least tacitly being granted, a more independent policy role. In interview, the Treasurer who followed Keating, John Kerin, broadly affirmed that the Bank made most of the running on monetary policy during his term in 1991. 'Basically, I was quite happy that that [monetary policy] was delegated pretty well to the Reserve Bank.'[94] This relative ministerial passivity was important in this critical period. It allowed the Bank (and Treasury) to make more of the running on policy. As Michael Keating points out:

> Kerin was never confident in the job. The government as a whole was conscious that its economic management credentials were vulnerable to criticism with the departure of Paul Keating to the backbench. This situation meant that the government was more inclined to conservative policy than it otherwise may have been, and more dependent on official advice.[95]

Ian Macfarlane says this pattern continued under the next Treasurer, John Dawkins: 'we were basically putting interest rates down and he was sort of agreeing'.[96] Bernie Fraser confirms this and says that Dawkins and the subsequent Treasurer, Ralph Willis, let the Bank make the running on monetary policy.[97]

By 1994, following the recession, inflationary pressures were seen to be building and the behaviour of the (overshooting) bond market indicated that the Bank was again being asked to demonstrate its policy credibility (see Figure 4.3). The Bank was more than willing to do so. Its policy response was a series of three pre-emptive rate rises, starting in August. Keating, as Prime Minister, and Treasurer Ralph Willis took part in discussions and debates about these monetary policy moves. At the first meeting Fraser wished to raise rates by a bold and unambiguous 1 per cent. Keating and Willis were hesitant. After some discussion and 'and a bit of effort' on Fraser's part,[98] there was a compromise: the first rise would be 75 basis points.[99] Significantly, however, the two subsequent rate rises were of the full 1 per cent.

Ralph Willis sums up the policy relationship during this period:

> I hear it I must say more overseas than I do in Australia, about how we don't have an independent Reserve Bank in this country, and this sits rather oddly with my experience with the way in which monetary policy has been set. All the interest rate increases that have taken place, the three that took place in late 1994, occurred on the initiative of the Reserve Bank, but with the concurrence of the government. But the initiative was the Bank's and that's properly so, that's not to say the government didn't have views about it, but it was the Bank that decided that this is what had to be done … And so in that respect I think we have a very independent central bank.[100]

Ian Macfarlane comments:

> There was still quite a lot of deference to Canberra, because at one stage we were wanting to put them up but Bernie was sort of holding back a little bit. And at one stage we said well why not do it now? And he said the Treasurer was overseas. That wouldn't happen now. You'd do it if you thought you needed to whether the Treasurer's here or not. The feeling was, I don't want to catch him by surprise. Or we ought to make sure it's at a time when the Treasurer can defend it, all that sort of stuff. So there was still a residual, still a little bit of residual deference – almost political.[101]

Fraser agrees: 'it is sometimes necessary to be a bit "political" in order to be independent; especially during the process of building that independence'.[102] Notwithstanding such manoeuvrings, it was apparent that the Bank was in the monetary policy cockpit. This became clearer during 1995–96. Early in 1995, after the three interest rate rises in late 1994, and following the Keating government's rout in a Canberra by-election, tensions surfaced over the possibility of further rate rises. Keating opposed them and publicly stated that the upcoming Budget would obviate any need for them. Fraser quickly responded in a speech, warning the government that the Budget would need to move 'much closer to balance', and that in any case, 'irrespective of any overlapping election or Budget timetable', rates would rise if the Bank thought this appropriate. 'What I would like to emphasise', Fraser said, 'is that should additional data and/or particular development lead the Bank to a judgment that more – or less – needs to be done to monetary policy, the Bank would follow through.'[103] It was a shot across Keating's bow. The *Australian*'s Alan Wood summed up: 'Fraser is making it clear the Reserve Bank will not allow monetary policy to be frozen by political funk.'[104]

Rates did not rise, but significantly they were not eased. Indeed, in contrast to what happened in the 1990 election the Bank was unwilling to jeopardise its growing but hard-won credibility. The first easing of monetary policy occurred only after the March 1996 federal election. Keating says he was not happy about this.

> The Bank thought it would be 'political' to cut rates before an election. This was really quite a shameful view. It was saying it was political to cut the rates because the Bank didn't want to look as though it was complying with the government when the government had produced the most superb set of economic conditions imaginable. If I've got any beef with the Bank through this period, it is that it should never have waited for the Coalition to be elected before it agreed to reduced rates. In other words, the Labor government never got the low rate that came from the lower underlying inflation and from falling inflationary expectations. All of these elements were put in place by the government's wages and fiscal policy and by the monetary policy tightening of 1988 and 1989, which the government had accepted responsibility for. The option for me, near a difficult election, was to have had an open brawl with the Bank and with Bernie Fraser. Further away from an election, I would have dealt with the Bank's unreasonable intransigence in much sterner and more decisive terms. The low underlying inflation rate had been with Australia from 1991. By 1995 the Bank was only hanging onto rates out of undue caution and fear of political rebuke from the Opposition. The Bank's monetary stance, then, had nothing to do with the real economy.[105]

Interviewing then Board member and head of the Australian Council of Trade Unions, Bill Kelty, Chris Eichbaum heard a similar account:

the only politics that I have ever seen in terms of my experience in the Bank, was in a perverse way ... that is to say the Bank didn't make a decision at the right time because of the sake of political considerations ... the Labor Party went into the 1996 election with higher levels of interest rates than they should have done. The rates should have reduced before the election ... but you can't be seen to be political.[106]

Asked about the impact of the electoral cycle on monetary policy, Bernie Fraser argued:

I and others in the Bank were always very aware that we were in a no-win situation with elections. To do something with an election in the wings led to accusations of being 'political', but not to do something on rates because of an election would also lead to accusations of being 'political'. That sort of thinking cemented me in the view that the Bank should act appropriately whatever the electoral cycle.[107]

MACFARLANE AND COSTELLO

The Howard government wasted no time when it gained office in 1996 and set about formalising relations with the RBA with the *Statement on the Conduct of Monetary Policy*. Besides endorsing the Bank's new-look 1990s policy framework, the *Statement*, with an eye to overseas markets, endorsed the concept of central bank independence. It was the first time in the post-war era that an Australian government had publicly endorsed and formalised CBI. The bond markets reacted positively (see Figure 4.3). Institutionally, the *Statement* marked a step beyond the Keating–Fraser regime, in which the gradual shift towards independence had been based on relationships of trust, respect and personality. Ian Macfarlane, who replaced Fraser as Governor soon after the new government was elected, worried that moves towards CBI under the previous regime might be set back if the personalities had changed.[108] Hence, for Macfarlane and others within the Bank, the Howard government's move was welcome.

At a press conference introducing the *Statement*, Treasurer Costello announced an important symbolic step: the government would not continue with the practice of putting out a press release in parallel with the Bank regarding interest rate changes, but it retained the right to comment on policy. Costello outlined the new government's approach:

I don't heavy the Reserve Bank, I can assure you of that ... when you go overseas you are still questioned 'do you have the Bank in your pocket?,' as was once claimed by one of my predecessors. That, probably regardless of the reality, probably did more damage to perceptions than any other comment. What we want to make sure is that perceptions, the statute and the reality work in harmony … Now, we emphasise in this *Statement*, what does happen is that the Reserve Bank and the government constantly talk to each other and put views. But at the end of the day the call is not made by the government … it will be the Board that will be making the decisions.[109]

The new government soon got a lesson in central bank independence; one of Bernie Fraser's last acts as Governor was to announce the first cut in interest rates in three years, two weeks before Treasurer Costello's first Budget. Costello was unimpressed but was in no position to criticise. The move signalled the Bank's assertiveness; monetary policy, not fiscal policy, would move first.[110] It also robbed Costello of the chance to claim that the Budget had established the conditions for an interest rate cut.[111]

In 1997 the Bank's Deputy Governor, Stephen Grenville, reflected on the transition to independence. 'Without confrontation, the Bank's enhanced independence emerged as a natural product of events.' He went on:

> There is a marked contrast between the current position and [previous ones]. Whereas the Treasurer used to announce M3 targets and the Bank's public profile was inconspicuous, policy changes now clearly centre around the Bank's comprehensive announcements of changes, with the decision clearly resting with the Bank's Board. The Bank's profile is reinforced by the Governor's regular appearances before a parliamentary committee, and the Bank plays a prominent role in public comment on monetary policy. While these snapshot comparisons of two different periods emphasise the extent of the change, it is less easy to identify the moment when these major shifts occurred.[112]

In one of his first speeches as Governor, Ian Macfarlane made the same point. 'It was not possible to point to the exact date when the Reserve Bank passed from being dependent to independent.' He went on, 'in my view, it has clearly been independent in the 1990s, and a good case could be made that it was largely independent in the second half of the 1980s'.[113] When interviewed, Macfarlane confirmed the gradualism and underlined the Bank's current independence under the Howard government:

> I.M.: See. I don't know where to draw the line, between [now] and when we were not independent. We certainly know now, there is no question about that.

S.B.: When did the transition occur?

I.M.: Well that's what I don't know. I don't know where to exactly draw the line. My view is that it went in phases, and the final phase was 1996 when the *Statement on the Conduct of Monetary Policy* was signed. That part is easy. That's independence from then on, there's no doubt about that.

S.B.: And Peter Costello is essentially a pretty hands-off Treasurer?

I.M.: Yes. And in fact we now have this situation where the government criticises monetary policy. And it says you shouldn't raise rates and all the rest of it. So that's a sure sign of independence.[114]

The Howard government's criticism of monetary policy came to a head, as we have seen, during 2000 and 2001. Some argued that the government should not even comment on monetary policy, following the Australian dollar's slide in January 2000 after remarks by the Prime Minister. As Treasurer Costello was quick to point out, the government had retained the right to comment on policy and Howard said: 'I can talk about the economy if I want.' Interestingly, the Treasurer stayed out of the public spat; this was a relief to the Governor.[115] The *Australian Financial Review* thoughtfully commented: 'The difficult issue facing Australia over these matters is that the culture of central bank independence is still being established, which leaves the market with little history with which to assess the recent tensions between the government and the RBA.'[116]

Meanwhile, in May 2000, in one of his twice-yearly appearances before the House of Representatives Economics Committee, Governor Macfarlane said the Bank's earlier statement about 'political' comments unsettling the dollar were not directed at the Prime Minister, but were simply 'reporting a view that developed in the markets ... we were not criticising anyone'.[117] This cautious line was also evident when Macfarlane refused, as we have seen, to link the Howard government's goods and services tax with interest rate movements.[118] For the three Labor members of the committee, such ducking and weaving on the part of the Governor prompted an extraordinary attack. Their minority report to the committee's review of the Bank's *Annual Report* for 2000 claimed that the Governor had been soft on the government, particularly in not criticising it for setting an 'expansionary' fiscal policy at odds with the RBA's tightening of monetary policy.[119] The Labor members concluded that 'the RBA had got itself caught between economic fundamentals and political pressures from the federal government', adding, 'this is not a good way to conduct monetary policy'.[120]

Subsequently, Governor Macfarlane's stance appeared to toughen slightly. In a speech in August 2000, for the first time he gently chided the government, saying 'I do have to confess a little disappointment' that the government had not produced a larger fiscal surplus in the wake of a long economic upswing. He also warned the major parties against a fiscal bidding contest in the run-up to the pending federal election and warned 'that if that were to occur, then I think there certainly would be some implications for monetary policy'.[121] The press reported that 'Mr. Macfarlane linked the Government's loose fiscal policy with higher rates.' The Bank was annoyed by this interpretation and put out a press release saying 'it was wrong to claim that rises in interest rates were due to the stance of fiscal policy' and that the Governor's comments 'in no way constituted an attack on the government's fiscal policy'.[122] This softly-softly approach did not deter Howard from returning one to the Bank. In March 2001 he criticised it for what he regarded as 'an error of judgement' over the rate rises during 2000.[123]

The Prime Minister's criticisms appear to constitute a case of what Americans call 'Fed bashing' – blame-shedding by government at the expense of the central bank.[124] In Australia, this practice has been infrequent and low-key. Paul Keating, for example, in the toughly fought 1993 election campaign did criticise the Bank, but gently. He thought there had been monetary policy mistakes that had led to the recession. He also retreated from his earlier 'they do what I say' view of the Bank. He said:

> monetary policy is not operated exclusively by the government. I would have brought the rates down much more rapidly … Now no-one in this election is imputing any blame for the unemployment to the Reserve Bank. It falls upon the Prime Minister or the Treasurer. And yet monetary policy is actually decided by an appointed Board … [To have] the government of the day bearing responsibility when responsibility is shared for these things is not good.[125]

For his part, John Howard, as just noted, lamented an 'error of judgement' on the part of the Bank and on several occasions has distanced the government from its decisions. But this is hardly serious or sustained conflict.

But is there another dynamic at work? Well-known American economist Paul Samuelson once talked about the possibility of central bankers becoming 'prisoners' of their own independence.[126] Because central bankers value independence, they may be willing to make certain concessions to government in order to retain it. Even the Bundesbank has been accused of this. As Ross Gittins suggested in interview:

> When the Governor of a central bank isn't independent – that means he doesn't have to worry about politics. But when you become independent what that means is that

you have to be your own politician because you now have something that you've got
to fight for and protect, and that is the independence of your institution.[127]

We have seen that Macfarlane appeared to pull back on the 'political comments'
issue and did not enter the political fray (as Bernie Fraser used to), not saying
much about fiscal policy, and appearing keen to avoid confrontations with the
government. This is perhaps evidence of the 'prisoner' thesis. Or it could be evidence of a tacit understanding between the government and Macfarlane that the
Bank's independence depends on staying off the government's policy turf. In
interview, Macfarlane also referred to the Bank's role in electoral dynamics. He
admitted that the 2001 federal election had some bearing on the Bank's interest
rate decisions: 'Oh, yes, well it did have some small weight in our decision. If
there was a really strong case to do something we would always do it regardless
of the election campaign. But it would have to be a pretty strong case.'[128]

On the other hand, despite occasional jibes or pointed commentary, there is
little evidence that the Bank has been under pressure from the government;
more importantly, there is even less evidence that the Bank's policy has been
influenced by what the government thinks. The Bank's policy independence is
not much doubted these days, despite the assertions of some critics like Labor's
Mark Latham. These days, the Bank has strong allies in the markets and, to an
extent, in the press. Arguably, in this context, the structure and dynamics of the
relationship with the government do not constitute a 'prison' for the Bank.

Finally, there is the question of macroeconomic policy coordination in the
context of CBI. Stephen Grenville argued in 1997 that 'the Bank is now centre-
stage on inflation control, *separate* to some extent from other arms of macro
policy, with clearly defined independence'.[129] The question is, does this kind of
separation lead to problems of coordination between fiscal and monetary policy,
and, if so is the Bank's independence worth it? There were a few instances in the
1990s when a loose fiscal policy was out of kilter with a tightening monetary
policy, creating tensions between the Bank and the government. For example,
Bernie Fraser rebuked the Keating government in 1994–95 about what the Bank
saw as loose fiscal policy and warned of potential interest rate consequences. As
we have seen, Ian Macfarlane raised this issue during 2000. Still, fiscal policy,
except perhaps for a short-term pre-election burst in 2001, has not been overly
active. Governments these days have broadly signed up to a medium-term fiscal
stance, so the coordination problem has not been a large one, although more
recently tax policies such as negative gearing have helped overheat the housing
market and created problems for monetary policy. The other thing to note is that
in the post-war era, monetary policy used to accommodate an activist fiscal

policy. But these days fiscal policy is a weaker, medium-term instrument. Hence, the earlier relationship between the two arms of policy has almost been reversed; central bankers now occasionally warn governments about the need for fiscal policy to 'accommodate' the stance of monetary policy.

CONCLUSION

This chapter has examined a shift in authority over monetary policy from politicians and Treasury bureaucrats to the RBA. Treasury lost ground first but over time politicians have also gradually given more authority and policy independence to the RBA. The transition towards CBI in Australia largely occurred under Paul Keating who, despite his beliefs, gradually ceded most of the discretion in monetary policy to the Bank. The trend was formalised by the Howard government, although without legislative change. The independence of the Bank does not constitute a formal shift in power because the government retains the legislative power; policy authority has been delegated.

The Bank's greater authority over policy has not substantially expanded its power. It operates as a relatively small player in a massive system of financial market power and control. As Ian Macfarlane put it in 1992, the Bank operates in a context in which 'the financial markets set a corridor in which monetary policy can act'.[130] Although, as Bernie Fraser argues:

> Financial markets are important but their motives and their time horizons are very different from policy-makers. So tensions and conflicts can arise, but provided their measures are soundly based and properly explained, policy-makers should not be intimidated by the markets.[131]

CHAPTER 6

RBA Independence – Why?

The only good central bank is one that can say no to politicians.

The Economist[1]

Why would successive Australian governments choose to lose routine control of a critical instrument such as monetary policy? Why did they commit themselves to monetary discipline via an independent central bank? And why, in a democracy, has much of the responsibility for monetary policy been delegated to a group of unelected officials, essentially a technocracy? Further, why did a substantial part of the slow evolution towards central bank independence in Australia occur under Paul Keating, who rejected the notion?

Chapter 5 described the events that marked the RBA's transition to independence; this chapter examines the reasons for it.

BELIEF IN NUMBER CRUNCHING?

How important are ideas in explaining the shift towards independence? Researchers such as Capie, Goodhart and Schnadt argue that 'the enthusiasm for central bank independence' is directly related to the 'power of academic ideas whose time has come'.[2] In particular, have governments and politicians been influenced by the numerous quantitative economic studies that purport to show a direct link between CBI and low inflation, or by academic theories that politicians cannot be trusted to run monetary policy?

There is some evidence that such ideas influenced the zealous central banking reforms and the move towards independence in New Zealand after 1989.[3] Australian politicians and central bankers, however, tended to be more sceptical and pragmatic, suspecting the 'power of academic ideas' in this area. The idea that granting independence to the central bank is a quick institutional fix for achieving low inflation did not catch on within the monetary policy elite.

Quantitative studies apply proxy measures for independence by coding the statutes and procedures that apply to central banks and correlating them with inflation performance across a sample of countries. The assumption is that politicians cannot be trusted to run monetary policy. They are said to be seized with 'vote calculus' motives, which lead them to crudely manipulate monetary policy for electoral ends.[4] This behaviour is modelled in literature dealing with 'political business cycles' and with the opportunistic inflation surprise strategies outlined in hypotheses dealing with the so-called 'time inconsistency problem'.[5] Sidelining governments and installing an independent and preferably 'conservative' central bank is thought to make monetary policy more credible. This in turn is thought to lower the costs of fighting inflation: wage bargainers and others will cower before the central bank and comply. As one influential study concludes, 'central bank independence leads to low inflation'. It also concludes that independence does not seem to damage GDP growth, and the authors argue that 'having an independent central bank is almost like having a free lunch: there are benefits but no apparent costs in terms of macroeconomic performance'.[6] Other studies have reached similar conclusions, while other types of quantitative research have sought to explain the origins of CBI by searching for relevant political or institutional correlates.[7]

The 'vote calculus' or 'time inconsistency' arguments, and the claim that low inflation is linked to the independence of the central bank, are not supported by evidence. It has not been proved that the behaviour that is said to drive these dynamics actually exists, or that they significantly affect monetary policy. No empirical evidence for the importance of the time inconsistency problem as a source of inflation has been found, and there is little evidence of monetary policy generated 'political business cycles' in OECD countries.[8] Moreover, the assumptions about the behaviour of politicians are often misleading. Ian Macfarlane has pointed out that the operation of monetary policy in Australia had traditionally been 'politicised' in the sense that governments often had difficulties, particularly with interest rate rises, which were sometimes either abrupt or delayed amidst controversy.[9] But the wider claim raised in the economic models of CBI is whether politicians' behaviour is determined by a crudely opportunistic vote calculus. The answer, these days at least, is generally not, especially in the monetary arena. Politicians certainly want votes but, as argued more fully below, the vote-calculus model of monetary policy is too crude. In Australia, chapter 5 found *perhaps* one instance of attempted political manipulation of monetary policy in the early 1980s, but generally Treasurers have not attempted to manipulate the RBA. From the late 1980s the Bank rather than the government was taking most of the initiative on policy, and this is significant because central bankers themselves do not condone the sort of shenanigans implied by models such as the time inconsistency hypothesis. Stephen Grenville has commented: 'The simple version of the [time inconsistency] problem has never appealed to central bankers who believe their reputation is at stake.'[10]

A range of quantitative studies have challenged the connection between independence of the central bank and low inflation.[11] One well-known researcher, Adam Posen, argues that both outcomes are caused by a third variable, the strength of financial sector interests.[12] Posen has sought to directly test the alleged causal connection between CBI and low inflation via the idea that a tough and credible central bank will help lower the costs of disinflation (i.e. reduce the 'sacrifice ratio').[13] In a survey of several countries he finds no relationship between measures of CBI and credibility, as measured by relative disinflation costs.[14] Alan Blinder, an economist and former Vice-Chairman of the Federal Reserve Board, also doubts the 'credibility hypothesis': despite 'much fascinating theory to the contrary, I do not know a shred of evidence that supports it'. He writes, 'it seems to be one of those hypotheses that sounds plausible but turns out on careful examination to be false ... illustrating once again the power of wishful thinking'.[15] Other studies have reached similar conclusions.[16] Recent empirical work by Blinder suggests that it is not institutional parameters (such as independence) but the central bank's *reputation* as an inflation fighter, established over time, which is the most important ingredient of credibility.[17]

Of course, correlation can never confirm causation.[18] The developments we have witnessed regarding low inflation and CBI may simply be parallel movements with no causal relation. Indeed, both developments may have a common source, such as the growing strength of financial sector interests or a strengthening anti-inflation culture.[19] The correlation studies tend to be sensitive to model specification and sample type.[20] Additionally, and more seriously, the use of proxy measures – especially for central bank independence – introduces measurement problems that raise fundamental questions about the value of quantitative approaches. The proxy measures for independence rely on analysis of the black-letter statutes and formal institutional arrangements. Typically, the bank's formal mandate and goals – terms of appointment of leaders, the composition of the Board, the financial relationship with government – are all proxied to assess independence.[21]

Such formal approaches have been severely criticised.[22] The process of identifying the factors in any composite measure and assigning relative weights to them are necessarily subjective.[23] A more serious problem is that the formal measures of independence are not the real thing. The focus of enquiry needs to be on behaviour, not statutes. As one critic, James Forder, puts it: 'statute reading measures of independence make no effort to measure behaviour'; 'reading statutes does not measure independence, passing them does not create it', mainly because independence is a type of *behaviour*, not a statute or institu-tion.[24] Eijffinger and De Haan (who use the quantitative method) admit:

> It is difficult to measure the degree of legal independence central banks have, let
> alone the degree of their actual independence from government … Actual as
> opposed to formal independence hinges not only on legislation, but on a myriad of
> other factors as well, such as informal arrangements with government, the quality of
> the bank personnel, and the personal characteristics of the key individuals at the
> bank … factors such as these are virtually impossible to quantify.[25]

Hence, the formal arrangements of central banking do not necessarily predict behaviour. In Germany, for example, the government has on occasion overruled the institutionally strong Bundesbank! Lohmann reports, 'The Bundesbank's formal status remained unchanged from 1957 to 1992. Yet the degree to which German monetary policy was vulnerable to political pressures fluctuated con-siderably over this time period.'[26] In Australia, institutional arrangements have hardly changed since 1945, yet as we have seen, the RBA has gone from relative dependence to relative autonomy. This suggests that the role of institutional arrangements is context-specific and variable. Governments and central bankers are not passive in the face of institutional arrangements. Their strategy and behaviour depend not only on context but also on their own motives.

Alan Blinder concludes that the results of studies that link CBI with low inflation are 'not very robust',[27] another leading scholar, Charles Goodhart, of the Bank of England, admits the results are 'pretty feeble stuff on which to base a policy campaign' for greater central bank independence.[28] Michael King con-curs: 'these challenges raise the possibility that the orthodoxy underpinning central bank independence may one day fall apart'.[29] For his part, Bernie Fraser also poured cold water on the studies linking CBI with low inflation. In 1994 he argued, like all 'free lunches … this one is too good to be true'. He noted the problems of measuring independence, arguing that quantitative measures 'can be downright misleading'. He also thought that low-inflation outcomes were driven by a range of factors. Arrangements such as CBI, he thought, were unlikely to buy much in the way of policy credibility: 'credibility has to be earned', he said.[30] Paul Keating also concurred. As the Opposition-led campaign for CBI was intensifying in the late 1980s, he declared that institutional fixes such as an inflation-only goal or CBI would not in themselves do much to bring inflation down. He suggested that the independent Bundesbank was not the prime cause of Germany's low-inflation record. The real cause, he said, was Germany's rock-solid culture of low inflation. Making statutory changes or 'amending the *Reserve Bank Act* and thinking inflation will disappear in a relatively painless way is the height of naivety or straight quackery'.[31]

EXPERTISE?

If Australian monetary policy elites, including Treasurer Keating, were not swayed by the findings of quantitative research, were they more inclined to endorse CBI because they thought central bank 'experts' should run monetary policy?

Monetary policy is complex, requiring expertise in monetary affairs and a sensitive reading of the markets. The RBA's expertise and capacity substantially boosted its policy clout in the wake of financial deregulation and the shift to market-based policy instruments. The commercial sensitivity of monetary policy also suggests the need for a relatively closed policy forum. Parliament is probably not the place to make monetary policy, or at least routine monetary policy adjustments. Indeed, as we have seen, Treasurer Keating thought monetary policy too demanding and sensitive even to trust to cabinet. But nor did Keating believe in technocracy, in allowing 'unelected officials' to make policy. He preferred the 'partnership' model: experts should be on tap, not on top. Stanley Fischer, formerly of the IMF, argued that central bankers, 'shielded as they are from public opinion, cocooned within an anti-inflation temple', could all too easily become too hawkish and 'develop a deflationary bias'. It was important, Fischer thought, 'to expose central bankers to elected officials'.[32] This was Keating's view, and the statutory provisions of Australian central banking insisted on communication between the Bank and the Treasurer and, ultimately, on some form of tacit agreement over policy. Keating, as both Treasurer and Prime Minister, clearly thought he had the expertise and backing to engage with the Bank as a policy partner. We have seen that some of Keating's policy calls may have been superior to those of the Bank during the late 1980s and early 1990s. On the other hand, despite some disagreements, Keating worked well with the Bank and generally respected its 'expert' input. So, the claims for policy authority based on 'expertise' should not be wholly discounted. Nevertheless, in the light of Keating's general endorsement of the 'partnership' approach, they do not help us fully explain Australia's transition towards CBI.

INSTITUTIONS?

Paul Keating took institution-building and institutional prerogatives seriously. In chapter 5 we saw that he understood and respected the formal 'prerogatives of the Bank'. The 1959 Act had granted formal policy independence to the Bank, so Australia's 're-commitment' to its independence could occur without statutory change. Given this institutional foundation, if the Bank was of a mind to increasingly assert its independence, as it was in the 1980s and especially the 1990s, a Treasurer could not ignore or easily abrogate this. The transition towards CBI in Australia was in part a process of the Bank asserting its formal statutory rights; in this sense statutory independence mattered, or at least helped. After financial deregulation the Bank was able to exert direct control over the key instruments of monetary policy. Yet the formal institutional arrangements remained unchanged, and the Act was not altered. Although the formal arrangements could accommodate change, they did not cause change.

What mattered more in this respect were informal institutional accommodations and the way in which the volitions of the key players and institutional arrangements combined to produce change. Critically, the Bank's leaders were keen to assert a new institutional role and Treasurer Keating was prepared to acquiesce. For these and other reasons, Keating wanted to develop a cooperative relationship with the Bank and understood the need to make concessions as part of the 'price of getting along'.

Does the wider pattern of institutional interaction help us explain Australia's transition to CBI? Writers such as Hall and Franzese have argued that the presence of an effective, coordinated system of wage bargaining is likely to reduce the costs of disinflation by promoting coordination between monetary and wages policy. This, they argue, potentially reduces the costs of a tough monetary policy, and thus promotes a favourable environment for central bank independence.

There are two problems with such an explanation in the Australian context. First, although Labor's Accord-based wage bargaining system did help to moderate inflation, it failed to avert the policy-induced recession of the early 1990s that flowed from the RBA's disinflationary stance. This is hardly an example of successful policy or institutional coordination, of the kind likely to create benign views about central bank independence. Second, the gradually increasing levels of commitment to central bank independence in Australia, especially in the 1990s, occurred when the Accord was *losing* its potency for centralised wages coordination, as the wages system moved towards more deregulated forms of 'enterprise bargaining' and as inflation was declining. Additionally, in 1996, just when the Howard government formally endorsed central bank independence, it jettisoned the Accord; hardly an action in line with the institutional logic outlined by Hall and Franzese. Therefore, the interaction between wage bargaining systems and central bank independence does not provide a convincing explanation in this case. We might argue that, as the Accord's power against inflation was waning in the 1990s, governments saw CBI as a substitute device to control inflation, but as we have seen, Australia's monetary policy elite did not really believe in the link between CBI and low inflation.[33]

DOMESTIC PARTISAN POLITICS?

Another explanation for central bank independence focuses on the distributional aspects of monetary policy and the outcomes of domestic political machinations and coalitional politics.[34]

As we have seen, the Liberal Party in Opposition under John Hewson made most of the running on central bank independence, with Labor publicly opposed. Ian Macfarlane has commented:

> Almost from day one, it got caught up in politics, with one party putting a rather doctrinaire version of it straight into its platform, and another party professing to see no value in it at all. This kept accusations of a lack of independence in the news, and it also made it difficult to have a calm and rational discussion of the subject.[35]

Beyond such contests, egged on by the media, was there a groundswell either way?

The literature assumes that the protagonists are the financial sector, industry, labour and, in some cases, agriculture. For scholars such as Epstein, 'central bank policy will depend on the relative power of finance, industry and labour'.[36] In terms of policy preferences, the financial sector is assumed to favour 'sound finance', restrictionist policy and an independent central bank.[37] Labour interests are assumed to prefer an expansionary policy and a subservient central bank. Industry's stance is thought to resemble labour's, but it depends on the level of inflationary concern in industry and on the strength of ties between industry and the inflation-averse financial sector.

Does this help us with the Australian case? Have expansionary interests challenged financial interests and deflationary policies, leading to, first, marked conflict over monetary policy and, second, to a winning coalition led by the finance sector favouring CBI?

Broadly, the answer to the first question is: 'not particularly'. Neither the Australian Labor Party nor the unions have much criticised the commitment to low inflation. Indeed, the former ACTU secretary, Bill Kelty, was a relatively cooperative member of the RBA Board throughout much of the period in question.[38] The RBA's introduction of a 2–3 per cent inflation target in 1993 and its subsequent development did not spark a partisan political contest. In 1995, as

part of Accord Mark VIII, the ACTU committed itself to the RBA's formal inflation target. Organised labour appears almost an ally of the RBA.

Industry, especially manufacturing industry, has little political clout and
weak links with the financial sector. Industry has endorsed the need to reduce
inflation, and industrialists are aware that deflationary policies have helped discipline labour and reform the labour market, a cause they have championed.
Industrialists' complaints about monetary policy have been ad hoc. In the late
1970s, for example, the Victorian Chamber of Manufactures complained about
the costs of fighting inflation, and more recently the Australian Chamber of
Commerce and Industry has criticised the 'phantom concern about inflation'.
But industry, and other sectors such as the retailers or construction, complain
only sporadically about interest rates,[39] and have not engaged in a detailed,
research-based debate with the proponents of 'sound money'. The agricultural
sector has also complained about interest rates but, led by the National Farmers
Federation, it has broadly endorsed an orthodox monetary position and has certainly not challenged the concept of RBA independence.

And, of course, nor have financial interests. The rapid growth of the financial
sector, its growing policy clout, and the support given to this sector and to issues
such as low inflation and central bank independence by the media, are all important issues when analysing the coalitional politics surrounding the RBA's
independence. Hence, in answer to the second question above, yes, a finance-
dominated coalition has obviously encouraged independence. Yet a dominant
'sound finance' coalition is a necessary but not a sufficient condition for central
bank independence. The political context also mattered.

Although the politics of monetary policy in Australia was not exactly 'low
voltage', especially during the policy-induced recession of the early 1990s, it
has not generally been the stuff of major partisan conflicts. Support for low
inflation has been bipartisan, and the debate over CBI in the late 1980s and early
1990s was polite, as the Bank slowly evolved without fanfare. Significantly,
voters have over time come to favour low inflation, and slowly, a low-inflation
political economy has been established in Australia (see chapter 4). Almost
immediately following the early 1990s recession, the RBA established a (low)
inflation target. The move was broadly welcomed, the main criticism being that
it was not bold enough. Further moves towards independence, and particularly
the formal endorsement of it by the Howard government, were widely approved.
Some writers have advanced a 'public preference explanation' for low inflation
and CBI.[40] The example of Germany's low-inflation culture as a major driver of
CBI in this respect is often cited. In Australia, however, the development of the
public preference for low inflation and CBI followed, rather than led, the key

developments. It was not the public that drove the changes but policy elites, in government and especially in the RBA.

THE ROLE OF CENTRAL BANKERS AND POLITICIANS

Australian central bankers have increasingly championed independence. The reasons are straightforward. Central banks work with and through financial markets, and the markets clearly prefer an independent central bank. As the economist Gerald Epstein comments, 'central bank control over financial conditions depends more and more on their ability to affect market expectations', and such expectations are more easily managed if central banks have the ability to 'impose policies unfettered by the democratic process'.[41] Central bankers also champion independence because it frees them from detailed policy bargaining with government, simplifying the monetary policy process. Moreover, as bureaucratic theories of central banker preferences point out, independence strengthens the institutional position of the bank so that it can more effectively deploy or cultivate its key resources of monetary expertise, control over information, an aura of 'soundness' and public service, and even a degree of 'mystique' regarding monetary techniques.[42] Australian central bankers may have doubted that independence would automatically produce low inflation via some kind of 'credibility dividend', but they still wanted to boost the Bank's credibility. Not only was there a credibility crisis in the late 1980s and early 1990s, but credibility was also thought to help lower long-term interest rate premiums. At a more abstract level, credibility is seen as a badge of professional legitimacy among central bankers.

The preferences of politicians are more complicated. Central bank analysts, such as John Goodman, assume that politicians favour an expansionary policy. 'Politicians ... are not unaware of the importance of price stability, but they tend to be less willing than central banks to subordinate other goals such as growth and employment, to the fight against inflation.' He concludes that 'conflicts between politicians and central banks are therefore likely'.[43] Politicians are typically assumed to desire policy control and policy discretion, and hence are said to be averse to central bank independence.[44] Goodman argues that this aversion might be overcome if, reflecting political instability, politicians believe they will soon lose office and wish to tie the hands of their successors. Political leaders who have a sure grip on government will wish to maintain a high degree of policy discretion. 'By contrast, political leaders who expect to be in office only for a short period of time (and return to a long period of Opposition) may be willing to bind their own hands in order to bind the hands of their successors.'[45]

Does this logic apply in the Australian case? Broadly, no. The critical test was in 1996 when the Howard government won a huge election victory and was clearly destined for at least two terms in office, but signed up to CBI. Much the same applies to the British case under the newly elected Blair government in 1997.

What of Bernhard's argument that governments adopt CBI as a means of diffusing internal party conflicts over monetary policy?[46] Again, this is not helpful in the Australian case. Monetary policy and the institutional arrangements pertaining to it were worked out, as we have seen, at the elite level: cabinets and the party room did not determine, or even debate monetary policy.

For a rounded account of the evolution of CBI in Australia we must specify, first, the policy agenda of political leaders, and second, the institutional arrangements that broadly accord with such an agenda.

In contrast to most deductive *a priori* reasoning about the policy preferences of politicians found in much of the literature, it is clear that political leaders such as Keating did become committed to a low-inflation agenda, at least after the early 1990s recession. The last thing politicians wanted to do was throw away hard-won gains on the inflation front. Beyond this, in a difficult macroeconomic context, politicians have learnt that low inflation can actually be achieved. Australia's relatively high-inflation economy of the 1980s was spectacularly turned around in the 1990s. It was a major policy win, and it meant that politicians had converged with central bankers on a broadly common agenda.

The view that politicians will reject or water down a low-inflation policy in the name of expansionary goals misunderstands the mindset of political leaders and central bankers and the discourse of monetary policy. The RBA and politicians have moved beyond the standard debate about short-term restriction versus an expansionist policy, arguing since the early 1990s that a low-inflation policy is the best way of *sustaining* an expansionary economy cycle. This argument is borne out by the Australian experience: since the recession the RBA has at times slowed the economy, but the general trend has been expansionary.

Nor, as argued above, do politicians manipulate monetary policy for crude political ends. If anything, especially these days, governments go out of their way to refute the perception of such activity. In the monetary arena, politicians have focused instead on a subtle set of rationalities associated with 'risk management' in new and highly uncertain environments. In pursuing financial deregulation, governments have created a world of swirling capital flows and extreme financial vulnerability. In this context, off-loading monetary policy to an independent central bank, as part of a wider strategy to manage risk and avoid blame, makes political sense. As we have seen, Paul Keating lamented that the government, not the RBA, was blamed for the early 1990s recession, and this experience encouraged the evolution of CBI in Australia. In fact, Keating was taken aback by the recession. It shook his faith in the mechanistic workings of policy instruments and levers to shape the economy. The idea of off-loading, or even partly off-loading, monetary policy began to look more attractive. As Paul Kelly writes, 'independence was a gift under duress from the politicians who felt, post recession, that distance from the interest rate levels wasn't such a bad option'.[47]

Such a preference is not predicted by theories which assume that politicians will seek to maintain control of monetary policy in order to pursue votes. Governments choose to give up direct control of a critical policy arena because an independent central bank is a handy political buffer and because monetary policy is seen as technical and highly risky.[48] For politicians, the pay-offs from controlling monetary policy are too lopsided. A good monetary policy may be rewarded, but the benefits of low inflation or sound economic growth are often diffuse and the electorate may not even see the link with monetary policy. On the other hand, there are obvious electoral disadvantages for a government wielding a tough monetary policy. In short, governments have recognised that direct control over monetary policy is a political liability. Of course, moving monetary policy to an independent central bank does not 'depoliticise' it (especially given its distributional impacts), but it takes the heat off the government. Prime Minister Howard, for one, has demonstrated a willingness to scapegoat the Bank. And at the very least, an independent central bank frees politicians from the obligation to constantly defend or explain interest rate levels.

Risk management by politicians, however, is not the whole story, at least in Australia. The RBA's independence emerged in a context where politicians, especially Treasurers, trusted their central bank Governors. They respected their expertise and believed the Bank would not deliberately jeopardise the government. This belief survived the searing experience of the recession, with the RBA becoming more (not less) independent after the recession. The evolving relationship was constructed on existing statutory foundations, lubricated by personalities and by trust. It developed under Keating and Johnston, was cemented under Keating and Fraser, and has continued under Costello and Macfarlane. Trust should not be underestimated. The kind of CBI that developed in Australia could not have occurred without it, especially in the Keating era.

CREDIBILITY AND FINANCIAL MARKETS?

Thus far we have focused on domestic political factors in which the volitions and strategic choices of politicians and central bankers loom large. We should also look at the broader context surrounding state elites and monetary policy networks, especially domestic and international financial markets. Here we return to the issue of policy 'credibility'.

A standard argument in the literature is that international monetary integration and the growing power and policy preferences of financial markets are now major factors shaping the goals and capacities of governments and monetary policy-makers around the world. This has reconstituted the politics of monetary policy. The markets exert a strong *disciplinary* impact; policy discretion in the monetary arena has undergone a secular narrowing, limiting the room for 'political' intervention. As one writer has put it, 'Those pushing for more independent central banks are well aware of these pressures. Making central banks more independent is now an act of self-preservation in the face of dangerous, volatile and potentially punishing markets.'[49] Financial markets can set the value of currencies, alter the cost of credit and debt, or inflict damage via capital flight. This does not necessarily amount to a loss of policy sovereignty,[50] but global policy convergence is striking, especially in the monetary arena. Most countries follow policies of 'sound finance', low inflation, and central bank independence in an apparent bid to boost monetary policy credibility and win financial market confidence. Sylvia Maxfield and others have argued that contemporary moves towards central bank independence can partly be seen as a device by which governments and central banks signal credibility and credit-worthiness to financial markets and investors. Maxfield says, 'foreign investors read central bank independence as a signal of the strength of domestic proponents of sound money, both within government and among domestic social groups'.[51] Berman and McNamara argue: 'concerns about credibility drove the decision to make the European Central Bank the most independent central bank in the world … to reassure financial and business elites that price stability would trump other economic goals'.[52] Charles Goodhart gives a party-political twist to this argument by suggesting that even left-wing governments have an incentive to appease markets and potentially reduce long-term interest rates by adopting CBI. Labour governments promoted CBI in New Zealand in 1989, in France in 1994, and in Britain in 1997.

Australia, with its relatively high dependence on foreign debt, its heavily traded currency, its commodity-dependent export structure, and its poor savings and investment profile, is exposed to financial market sentiment, suggesting that the arguments above also resonate with local experience. Indeed, we know that the bond market insisted on an interest rate premium in Australia in the 1980s and the first part of the 1990s in the light of relatively high inflation and/or associated monetary policy credibility problems. Australian policy-makers recognised the power of the markets and the changed context of monetary policy following financial deregulation. As we saw in chapter 5, Bernie Fraser thought political tampering with monetary policy would incur the wrath of the markets. Keating agreed: conflict between the government and the Bank, he thought, would be 'curtains in the markets'.

This account, however, does not show how such concerns encouraged Keating to delegate monetary policy to the RBA, or at least to acquiesce as the Bank asserted authority. Significantly, from the 'signalling' perspective, Keating publicly refused to endorse the concept of CBI and often criticised the notion. This is hardly kowtowing to the markets. It is consistent, however, with the view outlined above, that Australian policy-makers such as Keating and Fraser were not impressed with the argument that CBI would buy policy credibility, or that credibility by itself would bring down inflation. Fraser, an ex-footballer, no doubt thought the hard yards would have to be made where they counted most – on the inflation front itself.

This argument from policy pragmatism, however, does not explain the Howard government's 1996 decision to publicly commit to independence for the RBA in the *Statement on the Conduct of Monetary Policy*. Clearly, the new government thought there was something to be gained by the action. The bond market seemed to agree, judging by the downward movement in the long-term interest rate at the time. The government was seeking to boost the Bank's credibility and to reassure the markets about its intentions regarding the Bank and monetary policy. Treasurer Costello explicitly stated this in a press conference: 'The purpose of this *Statement* is not only for Australia but internationally.'[53] Perhaps the new government even believed the theory that CBI was linked to low inflation. Perhaps it was partly a matter of style or fashion. The Howard government, like the Blair government in Britain, clearly thought that CBI's time had come, was happy to say so and to clear the air on the issue. So was the RBA. As Macfarlane has said: 'The *Statement* ... at the time of my appointment was a means of clearing up any remaining ambiguity about the relationship between the government and the Reserve Bank.'[54]

CONCLUSION

Behaviour and trust have combined with the institutional setting to shape central bank independence in Australia. Political leaders will attempt to shape their institutional context for strategic reasons, although some of the explanations advanced at this level – such as vote-calculus models or Goodman's argument about the electoral time horizons of politicians – do not apply in this case. Successive governments off-loaded responsibility because politicians saw the

RBA as having the necessary expertise, because they trusted the RBA, and because they found monetary policy was getting too hot to handle.

This is ironic, given the Bank's policy errors associated with the recession of the early 1990s. But the recession also encouraged politicians to delegate responsibility for a tough and dangerous policy arena. Monetary policy operates in the context of financial markets which generate institutional expectations and incentives. These pressures are not ironclad imperatives – witness Keating's public refusal to endorse CBI – but they do offer rewards for 'appropriate' monetary and institutional settings. It is striking to witness the degree of monetary policy convergence that has occurred in recent decades around the world.

In a paper published in 1997, Stephen Grenville, the Bank's Deputy Governor, summed up his views about what drove the transition to CBI in Australia:

> The shift from regulation to market-based policies (with the Bank having the technical expertise in these) was clearly an important on-going force. Just as clearly, personalities (the Treasurer and the Governor) have been an important part of the story. The increasingly prominent role given, world wide, to central bank independence – and the enhanced role of central banks in most OECD countries – was also important in shaping people's views on what was normal for central bank/government relations. The academic debate [quantitative studies, etc.] was not prominent, but it worked in the same direction.[55]

CHAPTER 7

Should the RBA Be Independent?

The newly enshrined authority of the Reserve Bank has changed economic power in ways to which our political culture has not yet adapted.

Paul Kelly[1]

With greater independence and policy clout, central banks have been forced to shed their earlier mystique and confront the 'democratic deficit' which independence implies. The *Australian Financial Review* has said that an independent central bank 'occupies an unusual place in a democracy',[2] largely because independence devolves substantial policy authority to unelected officials. In Europe there has been a debate about the 'democratic deficit' created by the highly independent European Central Bank.[3] It is time for a similar debate in Australia.

As we have seen, central bank independence in Australia in the 1990s was worked out incrementally by a process of *elite* interaction and accommodation, and the idea was never fully debated in public. In fact, to most people it was not clear who was running monetary policy. By 1996, the incoming Howard government announced the independence of the Reserve Bank as a *fait accompli*. Yet, as the *Australian Financial Review* suggests: 'While central bank independence has become an accepted part of the landscape in modern democracies, the idea deserves a lot more scrutiny because it really still is a work in progress.'[4]

UNPACKING CBI

An independent central bank can be seen as an example of 'new governance', which emphasises government policy devolution and power-sharing with other institutions.[5] CBI can also be seen as recourse to institutional arrangements involving 'non-majoritarian' forms of governance, involving, for example, court rulings, devolving policy-making to independent regulatory agencies, or even passing policy up to supranational institutions. Governments have adopted such arrangements because, according to the standard arguments, they believe that policy effectiveness might be enhanced, because independent institutions are seen as better able to harness expertise or quicker to make decisions, because they are shielded from the hurly-burly of partisan politics, or because they are better placed to take a long-term view of policy.[6]

In a democracy, however, central bank independence is always a relative concept. There is no such thing as 'full' independence. The government retains legislative power over the central bank and monitors its performance. The government typically appoints the central bank's leaders and scrutinises the bank's finances. Many governments – including Australia's – have a statutory provision which enables the government, *in extremis*, to instruct the central bank on policy and override its authority. Governments typically set the broad, and sometimes the specific, policy goals for the central bank.

As we have seen, it is possible to distinguish between 'goal' and 'instrument' independence. As Alan Blinder, formerly of the US Federal Reserve, says, in a democracy 'it seems not just appropriate, but virtually obligatory, that the political authorities set the goals ... giving the bank such authority to set the goals would be an excessive grant of power to a bunch of unelected technocrats'.[7] But if independence means anything, central banks should have discretion over how they wield their policy instruments to achieve the goals set by government – in other words, 'instrument independence'. In some cases governments set relatively broad goals. The RBA is charged to pursue low inflation, full employment, and 'the prosperity and welfare of the Australian people'. The goals of the US Federal Reserve are similarly broad. But in New Zealand, for example, low inflation is the only formal goal; the Finance Minister and the Governor of the Bank negotiate an inflation target in periodic Policy Target Agreements. A similar process, following the Blair government's moves in 1997/98, establishes a policy Remit to the Bank of England, again focused on low inflation. The RBA has more room to manoeuvre in relation to its goals, and is therefore more independent than its counterparts in New Zealand or Britain. As we have seen, in the early 1990s the RBA arrived more or less 'independently' at the initial decision to shift priorities and fight inflation head on.

DEMOCRATICALLY JUSTIFYING CBI?

Democratic legitimacy implies that elected governments have a popular mandate and thus they (and not some other body) are legitimised to control public policy. Accordingly, Alan Blinder wonders whether CBI might not be 'profoundly undemocratic'.[8] A key question is how much tension there is between the policy effectiveness and market 'credibility' supposedly garnered by CBI, on the one hand, and democratic legitimacy, on the other?

Perhaps the tension is not severe. After all, liberals have long argued that governments should not monopolise all power and authority. The doctrine of the separation of powers, or contemporary arguments for devolving authority under the banner of 'new governance', align with such liberal ideas. As former Treasury Secretary Ted Evans says, 'it is quite common for parliaments to delegate matters to other bodies'.[9] There is also the 'dirty little secret' of Westminster government: unelected officials and advisers have always wielded influence if not authority.[10] Nevertheless, the extent of the *policy-making* authority being devolved to central banks arguably raises these issues to a new level.[11]

Proponents of non-majoritarian governance (and CBI) argue that any such tensions can be resolved through rigorous forms of accountability. It is argued that accountable institutions can be developed that help promote the kind of policy effectiveness that governments wish to achieve. In this view, governments trade some of their direct democratic authority for greater policy effectiveness; it's the choice of a democratically elected government! As Verdun argues, 'normal democratic governance', where power holders are directly accountable to the electorate, could be complemented by 'non-majoritarian modes of governance', and 'properly accountable, non-majoritarian modes of governance can be fully legitimate'.[12]

Central banks around the world have worked to overcome their earlier secrecy and improve their accountability and disclosure. Besides establishing more explicit and transparent monetary policy regimes, they have provided more information, commentary and justification for their actions. In New Zealand, for example, the Policy Target Agreement between the central bank and the government requires the RBNZ to explain any failure to achieve the set inflation target and to outline steps to be taken to achieve the target. The Bank of England legislation of 1998 contains similar provisions. Regular appearances of central bank leaders before parliamentary committees charged with probing the central bank's activities and performance are now widespread, including in Australia. Central banks now make more effort to signal their policy moves and to publish commentary on the economy and the rationales for policy decisions. Such disclosure not only aids accountability, but also assists the markets to understand the central bank's thinking.

A Bank of England survey reports evidence of moves towards greater accountability and disclosure. For example, 88 per cent of the 94 central banks surveyed had explicit targets against which to measure policy performance; 75 per cent were subject to formal monitoring by the legislature; 81 per cent provided explanations for policy changes on the day of the change, while 78 per cent explained policy decisions in standard bulletins and reports.[13]

In advancing the case for CBI, Alan Blinder presents five answers to the question; 'how can an independent central bank be rationalised within the context of democratic government?'[14] First, CBI can be thought of as a piece of 'constitutional' engineering designed by governments. Governments choose to delegate policy authority because they believe it will help them attain *their* goals more effectively. Also, making a central bank independent is a governmental or legislative choice and at least in principle is reversible. Second, the bank's leaders should be politically appointed and have their authority formally delegated by elected representatives. Third, governments should set the bank's goals. Fourth, governments should be able to override the central bank in extreme cases. Fifth, central banks must transform themselves and become open, accountable and transparent: 'public accountability is the moral corollary of central bank independence'.

ACCOUNTABILITY AT THE RBA?

The first three of Blinder's principles have always applied to the RBA: its independence amounts to a formal delegation of authority from the government, the RBA's leaders are politically appointed, and the government has set the Bank's goals (though only broadly). The fourth principle, the override provision, was added by the Chifley government in the 1940s, while the fifth principle slowly emerged, especially in the 1990s, as the RBA became more open and accountable.

The shift towards openness and accountability marks a new chapter in the development of central banking. Traditionally, central banks shrouded their activities with a protective, authoritative mystique, born of their arcane skills and knowledge and their close links with governments and the financial community.[15] As the financial journalist Edna Carew has written, the RBA 'long had a reputation as a gratuitously secretive organisation, given to speaking in obscure bureaucratic language and unwilling to divulge its motives or intentions to the market'.[16] Former Governor Bob Johnston says that the traditional central banker's view was to 'never justify and never explain the Bank's activities'.[17] As we have seen, even in the late 1980s, the RBA did not announce interest rate changes, leaving the markets to second-guess them. The post-war RBA Governor, H. C. Coombs, summed up the traditional mystique of central banking:

> Central banking is a strange profession little understood by the members of the public whose interests it exists to protect, by governments with which it shares responsibilities, or by financial institutions whose activities it to some degree controls. Those who practice it often feel themselves to be members of an

international freemasonry, a kind of 'mystery' in the medieval sense of a group who possess exclusive knowledge or skill, and indeed there has always been an element of mystery in the contemporary world about what central bankers do.[18]

Over time, the mystique is receding. But what in the contemporary context does 'accountability' imply for central banks? Arguably, there are three factors: the bank's goals should be explicitly defined and clearly ranked; it should be clear who bears final responsibility for policy; and the bank's policy-making should be transparent.[19]

The goals of monetary policy were clouded with uncertainty in the 1980s in Australia; inflation, employment and the current account all seemed to be competing for attention. In the teeth of the early 1990s recession, the Bank assertively pursued a stronger anti-inflation policy (although it soon reached a consensus on goals with the government). The Bank also shifted its focus to the medium term in pursuing its goals. Again, the Bank was making the running, and this helped short-circuit the argument about a trade-off between inflation and employment. Its strategy has been to present itself not just as opposing inflation but as committed to the goals of growth *and* employment. Former Governor Bernie Fraser argued: 'Community support for low inflation is likely to dissipate unless the Bank can help to deliver some gains in employment and living standards.'[20] Ian Macfarlane, in the context of the long expansion since the 1990s, repeatedly argued that low inflation is the best way of producing *sustainable* economic growth and hence (by subtly shifting to a medium-term policy frame) that the goals of low inflation and employment growth do not conflict. This clarification of the goal framework was eventually formalised in the Howard government's 1996 *Statement on the Conduct of Monetary Policy*. Significantly, the dual goals that had received much criticism from the neo-liberal right were maintained. A positive stance on employment was seen to help legitimise the Bank. Nor was it a good idea to (re)endorse independence for the Bank (as the *Statement* did) and at the same time drop the employment goal.

Successive governments and the RBA have resisted calls to enhance the Bank's accountability by having a single, easily measured goal of low inflation. The potential ambiguity of the dual goals has been resolved in part by adopting a medium-term policy framework and by prioritising low inflation. As we have seen, the RBA tentatively announced an inflation target in 1993, and gradually the target has become a key aspect of the Bank's strategy. The target helps the government, the public and others understand what the Bank is trying to achieve and how it operates on the inflation front. Also, as the 1996 *Statement* pointed out, the explicit target helps to shape inflation expectations. More recently, however, the Bank's tentative efforts to move beyond its inflation-targeting frame-

work and use interest rates to try to reel in the overheated housing sector have
raised important new questions about the Bank's strategy, an issue we return to
in chapter 9.

Second, on the question of who bears final responsibility for monetary
policy, the government claimed this in the Chifley override provision of 1945.
However, routine authority for policy lies with the Bank, or more precisely, with
the Bank's Board. As the 1959 *Reserve Bank Act* says, 'the Board has the power
to determine the policy of the Bank'.[21]

Third, the RBA has improved its performance in terms of openness and
transparency. The flow of information from the Bank is now voluminous as it
explains and justifies its policies. In the 1980s, for example, the number of
speeches given by the Governor and senior staff increased and the *Reserve Bank
of Australia Bulletin* and the Bank's *Annual Reports* became more open about
the Bank's operations. Writing in 1988, Peter Jonson noted that 'performance
has been lifted in recent years. Speeches by Governors have become more frequent and informative. Relations with the media have become more professional. The Bank's monthly *Bulletin* and its *Annual Reports* have been much
improved.'[22] All this was for the good, Jonson added: 'the discipline of having to
explain itself more thoroughly is likely to lead to better standards of analysis
within the Bank'.[23] Significant also was Governor Fraser's move in 1990 to publicly announce and explain interest rate changes in press releases. In 1998, Alan
Blinder applauded this as a model which other countries should follow; and
many have since done so.[24] We have also seen how the Bank, in 1992, accepted
responsibility when Deputy Governor Macfarlane announced to critics that they
should not blame the government but 'Blame us, blame Martin Place' for any
perceived policy failures of the early 1990s. More broadly, the responsibility for
public disclosure has been carried by the Governor and also by other senior staff
in an increasing flow of press releases, public speeches and articles. Also significant are the Bank's detailed quarterly *Statements on Monetary Policy*.[25]

Governor Macfarlane thinks the Bank is now transparent. The majority of
the House of Representatives Economics Committee, which regularly questions
the Bank, concurs: 'While the media, academia and some financial market commentators will always want more information, the Committee considers the present distribution of information is effective.'[26] The *Australian Financial Review*
agrees:

> The RBA rightly argues that it is already among the most transparent of the world's
> central banks. It gives a great deal of immediate information about the reasons for
> its monetary policy decisions. And it provides detailed analysis of the economy in
> the form of quarterly surveys of the economy and testimony before parliament.[27]

Reflecting on these changes, Governor Fraser announced in 1995 that 'we certainly put a lot of effort into describing and explaining our activities these days', and in 1996 he declared 'the Bank has come a long way in this regard, and much further than most other central banks'.[28] Fraser also defended the Bank's legitimacy and accountability by stressing that, although independent, it valued close consultation with government and the active coordination of monetary policy with other arms of policy: a model that Fraser named '*consultative* independence'. 'The Bank does not operate in a vacuum and cooperation between the Bank and the government of the day befits our democratic society and the interdependence of economic policy objectives.'[29]

In December 1992 Governor Fraser commenced appearing annually before the House of Representatives Standing Committee on Banking, Finance and Public Administration in order to explain the RBA's operations and policy decisions. These appearances were part of a wider process of reviewing the annual reports of departments and statutory authorities. Compared to today, the media took little notice. The incoming Howard government, in its 1996 *Statement*, raised the profile of the Governor's appearances before the House Committee and doubled their frequency. Governor Macfarlane regards these hearings, in which the Governor and several senior staff are questioned for three to four hours, as a central accountability mechanism for the Bank.

Although the committee is briefed and coached by senior economists and monetary policy experts before such encounters, the transcripts show that its members lack monetary policy expertise; they sometimes ask tentative or ill-informed questions; and they do not seem to have the capacity to pin down the Bank on technical issues. The committee's chair, David Hawker, admits that this is a problem but says the hearings help in 'providing training for MPs to become more skilled in this area'.[30] Some committee members have complained that the Governor does not always answer their questions fully.[31] In a *Minority Report* in June 2000, three Labor members of the committee claimed that the Governor was 'evasive' and had 'refused to answer questions' on matters such as alleged disagreements on the Board, issues of fiscal policy and their bearing on monetary policy, and Prime Minister Howard's comments on monetary policy.[32] The current operations of the committee suggest the need to review its capacities. At the very least, it requires a stronger and more expert secretariat and some of the members need more 'training'.

MORE ACCOUNTABILITY AT THE RBA?

Observers of the politics of central bank independence in the United Sates have noted that calls for reform or greater accountability tend to come in cycles that match periods of economic stress induced by monetary policy.[33] There has been less time to observe these dynamics in Australia, but it is noteworthy that, after a dream run, the RBA came under fire as soon as it commenced a series of policy tightenings in late 1999, the first in almost five years. On several occasions Prime Minister Howard publicly doubted the need for interest rate rises and called on the Bank to explain its policies better.[34]

Others made similar calls during this period of heightened Bank scrutiny. For example, after a surprise 0.5 per cent rate hike in February 2000, business leaders and associations, the Labor Opposition and the Australian Democrats argued that the Bank's policy deliberations were still too opaque.[35] The critics argued that the Bank's 600-word press release was too brief, that Board deliberations and decision-making should be reviewed, and that minutes of Board meetings should be published (as is the case for the Federal Reserve and the Bank of England). These calls were echoed in June 2000 in the *Minority Report* of the House of Representatives Economics Committee. More recently, there have been calls for the Bank to explain and defend its policy rationale in the wake of the interest rate increases in late 2003; moves which in part were intended to constrain credit growth and property prices but which stray beyond the Bank's formal mandate to fight only CPI inflation.

Governor Macfarlane used to give private briefings to finance sector representatives (say, a visiting delegation of investment bankers), but this practice raised concerns among those excluded and inevitably second- or third-hand information appeared the press.[36] It has now been discontinued. The Governor does not give interviews, although journalists can question the Governor or other senior staff at speaking engagements. Not surprisingly, there have been calls for the Governor to follow the European Central Bank model and hold press conferences to explain the Bank's policy decisions.[37] However, both the Bank and the government realised that press conferences would expose the Governor to awkward questions, for example, about fiscal policy (and, at the time this idea was raised, about the impact of the government's GST and associated tax cuts on monetary policy).[38] Unlike Bernie Fraser, Governor Macfarlane has remained fairly quiet on the fiscal policy front. He will not provoke the government if he can avoid it.

The Bank uses the media strategically. It sometimes leaks information to selected journalists who act as its mouthpiece when it wants to put information about in the market. As one former Bank official commented: 'The Bank uses newspapers to manage expectations. It's a game the Bank manages very well. Senior people talk to a small handful of the economics writers from the major papers on a strictly non-attributable basis.'[39]

The Bank and the government have also resisted the calls to publish Board minutes. This is typical of a wider pattern among central banks. In the Bank of

England survey noted above, only 18 per cent of the 94 central banks published their minutes and only six published the voting patterns of their Board or monetary policy committee.[40] The RBA once kept only the briefest notes about what happened at Board meetings. Starting in late 1997, partly in anticipation of further pressure for their release, it began preparing more detailed minutes; they now run to four or five pages. Questioned by the media about publication, Treasurer Costello ruled it out, saying it would restrict Boardroom discussion.[41] In his day, Bernie Fraser argued much the same.[42] Others say, probably rightly, that the publication of minutes is a secondary issue and that in any case the Bank would sanitise them.[43]

Ian Macfarlane, when questioned by the House Committee, rebutted the idea of publication of the minutes, although he also said he would 'not die in a ditch' over the issue. He suggested that the media had a vested interest in raking over the minutes of Board meetings in order to generate stories. More importantly, he argues that minutes take time to prepare and would delay the Board's message – 'in the case of the United States about six weeks, in the case of the Bank of England, it's up to a fortnight later'.[44] Second, the process would inevitably turn into a negotiation among Board members over content and produce a 'committee document'. 'The problem', Macfarlane says, 'is the very nature of minutes.'

> You have the meeting and someone has the job of writing up the minutes. They cannot write everything that happened. They have got to try to work out what they think is important and what is not. Then they have to distribute that to the members of the Board, who have to have an opportunity to say, 'No, you've got that wrong,' or 'No, we spent more time on this,' and then they have to come back with their comments. There are going to be conflicts there – someone says one thing, someone says the opposite – and you have to go through a negotiating procedure to try to sort that out.[45]

Third, Macfarlane discounts the value of minutes: 'I find in the countries, particularly the United States, which has the longest tradition of putting minutes out that when the minutes go out they do not really have much influence at all on public debate.'[46] Fourth, he argues that the Board members themselves do not want the minutes published.[47] The *Australian Financial Review* agrees: 'The question of publishing the minutes of the voting record of the Board may not be as simple as it appears. After all, not all independent Board members will be prepared to accept the publicity that follows the disclosure of their votes on controversial decisions.'[48] Bernie Fraser says: 'My concern about the publication of minutes was that this would risk making Board members performers in media serials, rather that participants in policy debates.'[49]

Finally, Macfarlane thinks the RBA's current practice of issuing a press release to accompany and explain policy changes is the best approach. 'The stuff we do put out when we change policy is very important information. This is real-time information.' He also suggests that publishing the minutes would be 'actually easier'.

> It gives the people who are putting the minutes together the benefit of hindsight. When you are deciding which things you really want to emphasise, you know what has happened, you know how the market has reacted. You know what the press has said, and you know what the politicians have said. It is not the same discipline as having to say honestly what you think at the time before you have seen what the reaction is. My view is that what we do is actually more valuable and there is a bigger discipline on us.[50]

In what the journalist Paul Cleary calls a 'little-known triumph of trans-parency',[51] the Bank's quarterly *Statement on Monetary Policy* is now reason-ably comprehensive, providing detailed information on the Bank's analysis of the economy, the inflation outlook, and the Bank's policy thinking; although, again, the Bank's recent rate decisions partly aimed at the housing sector need more justification. Also, as Deputy Governor Glenn Stevens has pointed out, the content of the *Statement* generally resembles the material provided to the Board when making policy deliberations:

> The analytical and descriptive material in the *Statement* bears a rather strong resemblance to that in the Board papers. In other words, the analysis available to the Board that month [i.e. when the *Statement* is released] is for the most part in the public domain within days of the meeting … Since the themes in the economy tend to evolve gradually most of the time, moreover, the analysis is usually not that different to what was said to the Board in the previous month or two. The material in the *Statement* on the policy considerations behind recent decisions is also very similar, as you would expect, to the arguments put in the Board papers.[52]

Should the Governor give more speeches? This was put to Macfarlane by the House Committee in May 2000, and he replied:

> I make speeches when I have something to say. I think this [i.e. the House Committee] is a very important forum. This is really the best forum of the lot. But I also make speeches if I have some particular thing I want to say. I do not really feel that I want to be up there every week or fortnight making statements, because there

are too many people going through the entrails and saying, 'He used the word
"strong" this time, now he has used the word "solid",' and all the textual criticism
that goes on. I think too many speeches would probably be destabilising, but we do
quite a few.[53]

The current practice is to issue a press release only for a change of policy, but
some in the Labor Opposition, for example, have called for press releases when
the Board's decision is to make no change. This issue was raised again in early
July 2003. The Governor's comments before the House Committee in June 2003
on the balance of risks in monetary policy suggested to some that a rate cut
might be in prospect. Subsequently, the Bank decided not to cut (on the basis of
a slightly upgraded economic assessment of the international situation), it
issued no explanation. But some commentators were miffed. David Bassanese,
writing in the *Australian Financial Review*, suggested for 'purely public relations alone the days of the RBA not issuing statements after policy meetings
might be numbered'.[54] Macfarlane, however, rejects the idea.

> You could make a case that it was a good idea, but I do not think it is. We already
> put out the most detailed account of any central bank when we do make a change.
> We put much more into it than anyone else does because we have got something
> pretty constructive to say. If every time we did not make a change, we had to say
> something, it would be a real burden to try and find 50 different ways of saying:
> Nothing has changed, therefore we are not changing[55] ... sometimes you can go for
> 18 months without making a move, and, if at every meeting you have to give an
> explanation, you run the risk that everyone will compare what you said this month
> with last month. It concentrates everyone on short-term monthly data. That is the
> bit that worries me ... the people who are most interested and most informed are
> people whose jobs depend on picking the day of a particular change and for who
> the difference between a half and a quarter is phenomenally important in terms of
> what happens to the money market that day, whereas to understand the economy
> and the role of monetary policy, you have got to look at a much longer horizon. But
> there are not many people out there who can be paid for taking a longer horizon
> view.[56]

In late July 2003, at a press conference announcing that Ian Macfarlane had
been reappointed as Governor, Treasurer Costello broadly agreed with
Macfarlane's views: 'I think the tendency to issue statements explaining why
you haven't done something can sometimes cloud the issue. I have watched this
with the Federal Reserve in the United States.'[57]

DEMOCRATISE THE RBA?

Arguably, the RBA is more open and accountable. It could perhaps do more, but any gains on this front from more speeches, press conferences or the release of Board minutes would be quite limited compared to the large steps the Bank has already taken. Nevertheless, it could do more to explain its broader policy stance, especially now that it appears to have targeted asset inflation in the housing sector and strayed beyond its formal mandate. Has Australia reached an acceptable equilibrium between central bank independence and accountability, and should we accept the current model as close to central bank 'best practice' in a democratic setting? Some would say yes. Despite calls for more disclosure during monetary policy hot-spots, there have been no demands to revisit the notion of CBI itself. Even the Labor critics of the Bank in the House Committee have moved beyond Labor's traditional concerns about CBI and have called for *more*, not less, independence.[58]

Still, if an independent central bank is held to be legitimate in a democracy, does this not imply some notion of popular understanding and consent for the idea? Contemporary theorists of deliberative democracy argue that it requires informed and unconstrained deliberation and consent by those subject to the decision.[59] But the theory of democratic elitism (or relatedly, the normative theory of technocracy)[60] holds that the average citizen is unwilling or perhaps unable to understand the complexities of rarefied policy arenas (such as monetary policy) and is willing to defer to elites and experts, provided they are accountable. Elite rule is held to be more efficient, more effective, or perhaps all we can hope for in a complex society, where many people prefer to watch television and leave the difficult stuff to others. In this elitist view, the role of 'democracy' is limited to notions of a popular mandate which confirms or replaces elites at periodic elections. This version of democratic theory is most in sync with CBI. In this kind of world, democratic institutions become the arenas in which elites aligned with the central bank (and perhaps the financial sector) seek to legitimise and defend its independence.[61]

On the other hand, if we embrace theories of democracy that emphasise the active representation of citizen views or citizen participation in government, an independent bank looks more problematic. This is especially so if citizens have not comprehended or have not given active or informed consent to the notion of independence. In Australia it seems that the comprehension and 'consent' come mainly from elites in government, the markets and the media. Indeed, former Treasury Secretary Ted Evans has suggested that the Australian public has not yet fully recognised that 'it is the Bank, not the Government, that determines when their mortgage rates will increase or decrease'.[62] Paul Kelly is probably right when he suggests that our political culture has not caught up with the idea of independence for the central bank. It is not clear that the average punter understands or accepts what has happened regarding independence, partly because the relevant survey research has never been conducted in Australia.

Evidence from the United States shows that citizens do not like the idea of unelected officials having substantial policy authority. Indeed, 69 per cent of respondents to a 1998 Gallup Democratic Process Survey objected to the idea of leaving policy decisions to unelected experts.[63] Such findings suggest that Australia should openly debate the idea of CBI and assess the views of citizens. One model is the Bank of England Inflation Attitude Survey, which asks citizens about their views on inflation, and about their knowledge of monetary policy, the monetary policy process, and the performance of the central bank.

An informed debate could elicit calls to 'democratise' monetary policy. One means to achieve this might be a re-endorsement of Australia's unusual practice of having the Treasury Secretary on the RBA Board. Re-endorsement is hardly a radical step, but at least it is a link between the government and the Board (although it is not clear to whom the Treasury Secretary is responsible when on the RBA Board; see chapter 8).

Democratic scrutiny could be applied to the appointment of the RBA's leaders by a joint parliamentary committee that questions potential applicants and advises the government. At present the appointment process is closed and is controlled by the Treasurer. Scrutiny would most likely 'politicise' the process, which, at its best, might open up debate about the priorities and processes of monetary policy.

Australia could also follow the British and New Zealand approach and further 'democratise' the setting of the central bank's goals. A Policy Target Agreement makes it easier for the government to alter the Bank's policy goals in a routine manner.

We could also debate the status of the *Statement on the Conduct of Monetary Policy*, particularly with regard to a future change of government. The Bank obviously thinks that the policy framework it evolved in the 1990s, together with the *Statement* which endorses that framework, are the products of its own work. Ian Macfarlane clearly thinks (or at least hopes) the *Statement* will stand and that the Bank's mandate will not be formally revisited. Interviewed after the 2001 federal election, he commented:

> My understanding is if this election had have had a different outcome ... [Labor leaders] Crean and Beazley would have basically accepted that. There is no way

they were going to come in and tear it up ... So my guess is that the minimum fuss way of doing it is just to say somewhere in a speech or something – 'and of course we will continue this relationship as embodied in that document'.[64]

Interestingly, on his reappointment as Governor in July 2003, Ian Macfarlane asked the Howard government to re-endorse the 1996 *Statement*, which it did.

The *Australian Financial Review* asks whether the Bank's mandate should be debated and delegated under new terms by each new government.[65] This would certainly be a more open process than currently prevails. Implementation of the advice of the Labor members of the House Economics Committee – writing the provisions of the 1996 *Statement* (or some variation of it) into the RBA legislation – would also ensure debate and scrutiny.[66]

Finally, and more radically, we could return to the post-war model of government dominance of the Bank, or to the Keating model of an active policy partnership between the Bank and the Treasurer. As Keating saw it, the RBA would offer 'independent' policy advice and jointly formulate policy with the Treasurer (although, as chapter 5 explains, this model – even under Keating – was overtaken by the Bank's increasing independence in the 1990s). Parliament is not expert or speedy enough to formulate monetary policy, but a return to bipartite policy-making would make monetary policy more directly 'democratic' by including the Treasurer.

WILL IT HAPPEN?

Barring some policy catastrophe, any significant steps towards democratising monetary policy – and especially moving back towards a bipartite policy model – are unlikely. As we saw in chapters 5 and 6, government leaders have endorsed CBI for strategic political reasons. Even Paul Keating gave the RBA its head. With an independent central bank, governments can distance themselves from interest rate decisions and can blame the bank if monetary policy goes wrong. Still, monetary policy cannot really be 'depoliticised' – governments will still suffer for poor macroeconomic performance. Some writers refer to a 'complex reciprocity' between the government and the central bank.[67] The government can off-load responsibility for monetary policy and shed at least some blame (if need be) onto the Bank – so-called Fed bashing. In turn, the Bank accedes to such treatment in order to gain or preserve much-prized independence.

A second rationale for the independence of the central bank is that financial markets like it. The need to please financial markets clearly constrains governments. As we have seen, the markets reacted negatively when Prime Minister

Howard commented on monetary policy in early 2000. A similar pattern of constraint is discussed by the economist Joseph Stiglitz, an adviser to the Clinton administration:

> Early on ... we adopted a policy of not commenting on Fed policy, not because we did not have strong views – at certain critical stages, many in the Administration thought their policies were seriously misguided – but because we thought public debate would be counterproductive. We thought the Fed would not listen, the newspapers would love the controversy, and the markets, worried by the uncertainty that such controversy generates, would add a risk premium to long-term rates, thereby increasing those rates, which is precisely what we did not want to happen.[68]

Another example of such market constraint is the reluctance to publish the minutes of the Board. If the minutes reveal disagreements they could impact negatively on market sentiment (although revelations of differences of opinion between the Bank's leaders and the Treasury Secretary in recent years did not produce much market reaction). A further example of market constraint relates to the government's power to override the RBA. It is supposed to give the government the whip hand, if needed, and was an important aspect of the Chifley government's 'democratisation' of the Bank. But it has never been used and governments today would be reluctant to exert it for fear of negative market reaction. All this suggests that democracy has limited power in the monetary arena in the face of the markets.

Is there a way out? Should governments – or indeed central banks – deliberately attempt to counter the power of the markets and free the political space surrounding monetary policy? Central bankers such as Alan Blinder and Bernie Fraser have made this case. Blinder argues that central bankers need some autonomy from the short-termism and skittishness of the markets. As he was leaving the RBA in 1996, Fraser anticipated Blinder's arguments and also thought the markets were too hawkish on inflation.[69] Fraser's response was to defend the Bank's institutional machinery: the 'bank's best protection against being swayed unduly by the financial markets' was to be found in the sort of central banking practice he had championed. 'Of special significance in this connection are the multiple objectives of the Bank.'[70]

Can governments counter the markets? They could try ignoring or revising their perceptions of market constraint. What if, for example, a government 'democratised' monetary policy, say, by establishing a bipartite policy relation between the Bank and the Treasurer, and still managed to run a low-inflation economy? The markets would react negatively at first, but they might get used to the new arrangement. This outcome is not inconceivable, although the heightened uncertainty would be a negative for the markets. Short of popular clamour for such an experiment, however, governments would not willingly encounter such risks.

CONCLUSION

Milton Friedman once argued that 'monetary policy is too important to be left to central bankers'.[71] Governments should play a more active role in the monetary arena, but the political winds are not favourable. The Business Council of Australia, representing the corporate sector, has suggested a new form of independent fiscal policy to help overcome political gridlock and policy inflexibility. Following suggestions from Alan Blinder, the BCA proposed applying the model of independent monetary policy by establishing an independent fiscal policy board with discretionary control over certain taxation levels.[72] When the House Economics Committee asked Governor Macfarlane about this in November 1999, he had a bob each way:

> I could certainly imagine circumstances where I would like an arrangement like that to be in place ... On the other hand, it is a very big step to take fiscal policy – the taxation system – out of the democratic process. It is a much bigger step than taking monetary policy out. Monetary policy does not have the distributional consequences that fiscal policy has ... I cannot imagine that a democratic society would be able to handle that as comfortably as they can with monetary policy.[73]

In the meantime, whatever the merits of Friedman's argument, central bank independence seems to have arrived; the task now is to minimise the 'democratic deficit' in such arrangements. At present it appears that greater central bank accountability is the official cure. The RBA's current practices have substantially improved the accountability and transparency of monetary policy. Although there is room for improvement, compared to the vagaries and closure of the past, attentive observers now have a clearer idea of what the key monetary policy instruments and targets are, and where, how and why policy decisions are being made. The recent caveat here is the Bank's yet-to-be-adequately-explained foray into attempting to douse the property sector by means of higher interest rates.

What of the future of central bank independence? How will tensions between central bank technocracy and wider democratic impulses pan out? Although the Bank has held formal statutory independence since 1911, never before has it experienced the current combination of autonomy and policy clout.

The tensions during 2000 between the Bank and the Howard government underline this new political dynamic.

A critical test of course will be economic management. The Bank got off lightly for the monetary policy errors of the late 1980s and the subsequent recession – partly because of incipient public perceptions about the Bank's role, and partly because Treasurer Keating manfully claimed ownership of the recession with his infamous comment about 'the recession Australia had to have'. Since then Australian macroeconomic performance has featured low inflation and comparatively good growth, so during the 1990s the RBA cemented its independence under the watchful eye of the markets. Recent tensions between the government and the Bank are more about political posturing and blame-shedding rather than any serious revision of the RBA's independence. But as Ian Macfarlane says, independence 'can be taken away if we do not handle it properly'. Paul Kelly also reminds us that ultimately it is 'performance which sanctions independence'.[74]

CHAPTER 8

Internal Governance and the Board

Board members, who in earlier years might have been prepared to be quite passive, are now more prepared to argue their own views … an evolution has occurred in the way the Board has viewed its responsibilities.

Governor Ian Macfarlane[1]

We have already seen how the RBA has dealt with its external environment, both in monetary policy and in its relations with government. This chapter looks at the internal processes of formulating monetary policy. The RBA Board is unusual in that the Secretary of the Treasury is a voting member and it has a majority of lay, part-time members. We outline the debate about possible reforms. The main suggestion is that the system does not need much fixing, although changes to encourage a more robust policy debate on the Board should be pursued.

THE INTERNAL POLICY PROCESS

Policy processes within the Bank have traditionally been shrouded in secrecy. Minutes of Board meetings are not released, even to the Treasurer. Board members take an oath not to reveal Board matters, and there is a 15-year moratorium on access to the Bank's archives.[2] Nevertheless, the Bank's decision-making procedures are becoming known. The Bank points out that its deliberations are based on publicly available data, and in the last decade it has made a considerable effort to clarify its monetary policy framework and has presented comprehensive assessments of the economy and policy in its quarterly *Statements on Monetary Policy*.

A speech by Deputy Governor Glenn Stevens in late 2001 outlined the Bank's internal policy procedures.[3] The rhythm is set by the Board meetings, which are held on the first Tuesday morning of each month (except January).[4] In the preceding weeks, the Bank's Economic Group assembles data on a wide range of trends and prepares documents for the Board's deliberations. Most of the data comes from official statistics. The Bank has better research capacity than any government department, including the Treasury. The Bank tends to attract capable staff and has (with some exceptions) a good record in reading the economy. Particularly since the early 1990s recession, the Bank pays attention to anecdotal information, both from the lay Board members and from the markets. The Bank deploys officers in capital cities who are in constant liaison with business leaders, state governments, industry groups and academics.

About twelve days before a Board meeting the Bank's Economic Group meets to review the most recent information and assess trends. It evaluates information in the light of the current level of short-term interest rates, and against several Taylor type-rule calculations – which provide a benchmark for interest rates against two measures, output relative to estimated potential output, and inflation relative to target inflation. The group uses various monetary conditions indexes (which combine interest rates and the exchange rate), though it has some reservations about how much weight to give them. The group runs various simulations on a macroeconomic model to inform its judgements.

The Bank's Financial Markets Group follows a similar process. When the two groups have formulated their preliminary views, their senior members compare notes. The Bank considers this an important meeting, which allows an appropriate melding of economic analysis with an assessment of market conditions and expectations. Then each group drafts a paper dealing respectively with the economy and market developments. These draft papers are discussed in a meeting convened by the Policy Discussion Group, made up of the Governor, Deputy Governor and other senior managers. The papers are finalised and sent to Board members several days before the Board meets. If the Governor thinks that the policy decision before the Board is clear-cut, the papers contain a policy recommendation. If things are murky, the papers contain options, with a recommendation left until the Board meets. Either way, the Board normally receives a clear recommendation from management.

The Bank keeps the Treasury and the Treasurer informed. The Treasury Secretary, of course, receives the Board papers and so knows the policy recommendations. In Bernie Fraser's day, the Governor often spoke directly to the Treasurer prior to Board meetings: 'I might talk to the Treasurer if something was going to happen ... I would talk to the Treasurer beforehand and say look this is what we're proposing to do. This is the recommendation to the Board.'[5] Governor Macfarlane has continued this practice. In making monetary policy, he said,

> You'd decide what you wanted to do. Normally, you write a Board paper. And in between writing the paper and having the Board meeting you talk to the Treasurer – as a courtesy – and you say this is the recommendation we are bringing to the Board. And he can argue vigorously against it if he wishes to, and if he were to

come up with some brilliant arguments I hadn't thought of, maybe they would have some influence. But by and large, well, he can't say, no don't do that.[6]

THE BOARD AND BOARD MEETINGS

The *Reserve Bank Act* specifies that the Bank's Board shall be composed of the Governor and the Deputy Governor, the Secretary of the Treasury and six part-time members.[7] The Governor and Deputy Governor serve seven years while the part-time members serve five years. All positions are subject to reappointment at the discretion of the government. The part-time members are generally drawn from the business sector, along with an academic economist and perhaps a trade unionist (at least under a Labor government). The composition includes a mix of expertise in monetary policy and finance drawn from the official family, as well as practical experience and a wider perspective. The 1937 Royal Commission into money and banking thought the Board should be composed of persons with a 'breadth of outlook'. The *Reserve Bank Act* effectively bans appointments from the financial sector, a provision inserted to prevent conflicts of interest. Section 17 (1) declares, 'a person who is a director, officer or employee of a corporation (other than the Reserve Bank) the business of which is wholly or mainly that of banking is not capable of appointment'.

At the time of writing the members of the Board include: Ian Macfarlane (Governor); his Deputy, Glenn Stevens; Treasury Secretary, Ken Henry; Professor Warwick McKibbin of the Australian National University; Jillian Broadbent, a company director with a background in finance; R.G. Gerard, Chairman of Gerard Industries, a manufacturing firm; from the retail sector Frank Lowy, Chairman of Westfield Holdings; from the rural sector Donald McGauchie, chairman and director of various companies; and from the mining sector Hugh Morgan, CEO, First Charnock Pty Ltd.

Board meetings are held at Martin Place and last three or four hours from about 9.30 am. Under Governor Johnston the meetings lasted almost a day. In the post-war era, they lasted almost two days (although then the Bank's responsibilities were broader). Bernie Fraser cut the meetings to the current length. For the most part, the meetings are described as fairly relaxed affairs. Presentations by the Bank's Assistant Governors (Economic, and Financial Markets) explain the contents of the Board papers. Separate papers might also be presented on issues of topical interest. After discussion and questions, the Board considers the policy recommendation of the Governor. The recommendation is usually to move interest rates up or down by a small amount (usually 25 basis points) or to hold. The Board is described as 'collegial' and the meetings relatively 'informal'. Bernie

Fraser, a fan of the lay Board, implied that in his day a bit of yeast was needed at times. The Board members

> would make comments about how the stories that were being presented on domestic economic or international developments compared with their own experiences or their own observations ... There'd be a bit of exchange, not always as much exchange as I would have liked. I think some of the Board members were a bit over-awed by it all. But over time that tends to break down and there is a bit more discussion and exchange.[8]

The Governor chairs the meetings. Although Section 21 (3) and (4) of the *Reserve Bank Act* specifies that the Board is to vote, decisions are usually arrived by consensus, with the Governor reading the mood of the meeting. When the decision is difficult or contentious, a vote may be taken; this has been rare, but in recent years it has become more common. Reflecting on his time on the Board between 1985 and 1995, Australian National University economist Bob Gregory said, 'In my time, the Board did not vote ... It was mainly a consensus arrangement, and if a consensus could not be reached, then the status quo prevailed.'[9] If a vote does occur, a Board member can request that their dissenting vote be recorded in the Board minutes. The Governor and the other members of the official family could theoretically be exposed to the unseemly situation of being voted down by the Board's lay members, who have six votes.

After the meeting the members are often entertained by a speaker at luncheon. Bernie Fraser recalled that 'there's a view that having got to a consensus decision everyone then would be behind that. And in my experience Board members are very good in operating in that way and not going out and intimating that maybe they didn't support a particular recommendation ... That didn't occur.'[10] If the decision is to alter rates, the afternoon is spent drafting a press release. The process of writing up the Board minutes also commences. The decision is announced at 9.30 am on the Wednesday following the Board meeting. Observers and the markets have come to expect this level of transparency. But in earlier years, rate decisions were sometimes announced between Board meetings, although the Board was always formally consulted. In some cases a Board meeting would give conditional approval for a rate change (for instance, pending the arrival of new data), which would be announced when it was made. Ian Macfarlane says the discretion to alter the timing of policy announcements is still there but 'we have not used that for quite a while'. These days, 'the emphasis on transparency means that would be difficult, unless circumstances were exceptional, to have a meeting, agree to do something and then not do it for two weeks'.[11]

Before policy is announced, the Governor informs the Treasurer of the Bank's decision, usually by phone. During Bernie Fraser's term, the Bank and the Treasurer would both put out press releases about the Board's decision, with the contents worked out between the Bank and the Treasurer's office. The joint press releases were terminated in 1996 by the incoming Governor, Ian Macfarlane, and Treasurer Costello. The outgoing Governor, Bernie Fraser, commented:

> It was more a perceptions thing, I think. There was a view that because the Treasurer was announcing or commenting upon the rate change at the time it was being announced, there was still this perception that the Treasurer was somehow influencing it. And earlier Treasurers, encouraged by Treasury, may have and no doubt did want to keep that perception alive. But Costello was persuaded that there was no need for him to virtually repeat what the Bank was saying … Let the Bank take the flak for any rate increases. But of course they wanted to get some kudos for rate reductions. It's been a hard process. How long it will persist I don't know.[12]

Since the 1970s, a formal monetary policy debriefing session has followed the monthly Board meetings. It is held in the Bank's offices in Martin Place or in Canberra, with the Bank's Governor and Deputy Governor, the Treasurer and relevant advisers. The Bank describes them as 'our meetings' and sees them as an opportunity to explain policy and to brief the Treasurer on general monetary issues. When Paul Keating was Treasurer, and particularly when Bernie Fraser was Governor, the meetings were informal. Just before his retirement, Fraser noted that consultations between the Bank and the Treasurer 'have become more structured in recent times under Treasurers Willis and Costello'.[13]

WHO REALLY RUNS THINGS?

The Bank broadly likes the current set-up. The consensus among RBA watchers, and informally from the Bank itself, is that the Bank's leaders, especially the Governor, are by far the most influential players at Board meetings. Governor Macfarlane and the Bank team have always prevailed, even during tensions over rate decisions during 2000 and 2003. The Prime Minister has complained on several occasions about monetary policy, and Treasury Secretaries Ted Evans and Ken Henry and others have opposed the Bank's moves in recent years to raise or hold up rates, but the Bank's team and its supporters on the Board have been dominant.

As the journalist Peter Hartcher comments, 'the Bank has a powerful home advantage'.[14] First, the Bank's leaders are the policy experts in the monetary arena and they analyse the data and work on the issues full-time. Second, they carry the institutional imprimatur of the Bank's leadership team. Third, the Bank's policy experts control the flow of information going to the Board. Fourth, the Bank sets the agenda of the meetings and structures debate around a formal policy proposal that it has formulated. Fifth, the Bank's leaders establish the intellectual framework and discursive environment for Board debate. A former head of the British Treasury and Secretary of Cabinet, Robert Armstrong, suggests one way in which this subliminal pattern can work.

> Obviously I had great influence. The biggest and most pervasive influence is in setting the framework within which questions of policy are raised ... We set the questions which we asked ministers to decide arising out of that framework and it would have been enormously difficult for any minister to change the framework, so to that extent we had great power.[15]

Bernie Fraser broadly agrees that the Bank's professionals were dominant.

> Within the management of the Bank we would get to a view that we should be increasing or reducing interest rates, and a recommendation of that kind would go into the Board papers ... The Board would consider the recommendation and in my experience we were quite persuasive. The Board tended to accept the recommendations.[16]

Former Treasury Secretary Tony Cole agreed that 'the technicians tended to dominate the development of policy'.[17] So did Paul Keating: 'Most Boards are reasonably malleable to the Governor's interests, mostly. But again, Governors have got to earn regard. And once they have, they find their supporters on the Board.'[18] John Phillips painted a picture of a reasonably compliant Board, dismissing the fear that the government can stack the Board. He recalls Paul Keating saying:

> He didn't know what the devil we did to people he put on the Bank Board. He put on the Bank Board people he thought would be sympathetic to his point of view and after the first meeting they were singing the Reserve Bank's songs.[19]

Similarly, the *Australian*'s Alan Wood has said: 'The private responses of insiders to critics is that the Board is only there to provide insight into various sectors of the economy, and that on monetary policy it does what it is told by the Bank's professionals.'[20]

But Bob Johnston claimed that the Bank's professionals were not in the habit of railroading the lay members, adding, 'it was not good policy-making to go against the diametrically opposed view of two or three members of the Board'.[21] Although he did not elaborate, John Phillips said there was the rare occasion 'when the *consensus* of the Board was different to what was put forward from the Executive'.[22] Bernie Fraser also thought Wood had 'much too simplistic a view of the way the Board operates'.[23] In a speech on his retirement in 1996, Fraser defended a 'good Board' as one of the four pillars of the RBA's institutional model.[24] Similarly, in his day Coombs defended the utility of the Board, suggesting that 'the existence of a Board to whom executive decisions have to be submitted forces them to consider the reasons for the action they recommend and to justify their recommendations'.[25] Bernie Fraser commented that the lay Board members 'take their responsibilities very seriously, and they work hard at them – notwithstanding the occasional cheap shot in the media that they merely rubber stamp the Bank's views'.[26] In an interview with Chris Eichbaum in 1997, Fraser said the lay members were 'not the sort of people who sit around rubber-stamping what is put in front of them, [they] have their own view of things and aren't lightly persuaded to a viewpoint'.[27] Still, as above, Fraser thought the Bank was 'persuasive'.

In interview, Fraser said, 'there's only been one occasion in my experience when there was a vote'. Interestingly, John Phillips said, 'there was never a formal vote in my time'.[28] Neither would elaborate, but the implication is that the blow-up occurred after Phillips left the Bank in 1992.

In his retirement speech, Fraser said that the Board 'helps keeps the Bank team honest, it brings a "real world" dimension to policy discussions'.[29] The Bank, he said, valued the experience and the up-to-date anecdotal information of the part-time members. This was one of the strengths of the Australian system, Fraser thought. The official statistical information the Bank considers is always out of date; anecdotal input from the business world can be useful, especially at turning points in the economic cycle.[30] Tony Cole agreed, speaking of the need to 'harvest the anecdotes'; 'the role of telling us what's going on from the businessman's perspective is very important'.[31] John Phillips commented that a part-time member who stays on the Board after retiring from business is 'nowhere near as valuable'.[32] According to Fraser:

> Board members, if they've done their homework – and many of them do work hard and come armed with these kinds of anecdotal materials – can make a worthwhile input. Good people ask good questions about why *we're* doing things. And if they

are good people ... they can also add authority to the decision. It's not just the management of the Bank, it's not just a few bloody bureaucrats up there who are putting up interest rates, it's the Board.[33]

Note that Fraser says that 'many' rather than 'all' the members work hard. But the function of the Board in deflecting sole responsibility from the 'few bloody bureaucrats' should not be underestimated. The Board's composition is as much about politics as about running the economy. The presence of wider representation helps legitimise the Board and makes the Bank look more 'democratic', at least compared with a narrow technocracy in which the Bank's professionals have complete authority.[34] A lay Board also makes life easier for the Bank because its professionals are not confronted with too many 'experts' when putting forward policy.

There is also a historical dimension. The Board's operations have not remained static. In the light of recent developments, Ian Macfarlane cautions against seeing the Board as easily dominated. In earlier years when the Bank had little independence and played a passive policy role, the Board tended to be compliant. Policy discussions were couched in vague language (to 'tighten' monetary conditions, etc.) promoting consensus. As the Bank has become more independent and the policy decisions more precise, the Board has become more assertive. Heightened awareness of the role and responsibilities of directors has also played a role. As Macfarlane puts it: 'Board members, who in earlier years might have been prepared to be quite passive, are now more prepared to argue their own views ... an evolution has occurred in the way the Board has viewed its responsibilities.'[35]

Moreover, news about arguments and divisions on the Board has leaked into the public arena and is speculated on by the press and the markets. For example, it became public knowledge that Treasury Secretary Ted Evans apparently voted against all the interest rate increases of late 1999 and 2000.[36] When retiring from the Board in early 2001, Professor Adrian Pagan publicly commented on proceedings and revealed splits on the Board.[37] Leaks during 2003 are discussed below. Under questioning by the House of Representatives Economics Committee, the Governor has admitted that leaks have occurred and that the Board has become more assertive.

Hence, the Bank's leaders largely dominate the Board but are not all-powerful. The Bank's professionals usually carry the day, although the Board's divisions and assertiveness are clearly increasing. The Board's outside experts – the Treasury Secretary and an academic economist – can, at least in theory, counterbalance the Bank team. Tony Cole argued that Bob Gregory played this role well: 'he would challenge the Bank, he'd challenge the orthodoxy all the time'.[38]

BOARD COMPOSITION?

The composition of the Board has over the years attracted considerable commentary and criticism and is the main issue on the reform agenda that periodically surfaces. The bones of contention are the presence of part-time or lay Board members, the ban on persons from the banking or financial sector, and the inclusion of the Treasury Secretary.

Is the lay Board up to the complex job of setting monetary policy? Speaking in the early 1990s, Sir William Cole thought not.

> There are a number of problems with the present structure which relate to the non ex-officio members. Most of these directors, typically, are very busy people in their outside activities. Their reputations do not depend, for good or ill, on the performance of the Reserve Bank, but on their other activities. Many, although eminent in their own fields, may not be well qualified to handle, on a part-time basis, the complex issues of national importance that come before the Board. Moreover, the part-time directors may not feel themselves equipped to stand up to the 'professionals' on the Board.[39]

Does the Board need more outside experts who can challenge the views of the Bank's professionals, and even bring their own analysis and proposals to the Board? Cole argued that the part-time members should be replaced with three full-time experts in monetary affairs. Professor Warwick McKibbin, economics professor at the Australian National University, interviewed before taking up his position on the Board, said, 'I think questions should be asked of the people running monetary policy. What are they doing, why they are doing it. You could balance it with more expert input.'[40]

In January 2001, the same view was expressed by a retiring Board member, Professor Adrian Pagan, another ANU economist. The current Board, he thought, was largely 'supervisory' and tended to be 'reactive': 'it is there really to examine the cases that are actually being made by the persons who are in charge of the institution ... There's just not enough internal dissent. I think it's very hard to dissent against the Governor.'[41] A stronger, more proactive Board could challenge the Bank's professionals, as the lay Board members could not. 'Perhaps the external Board members should not only review policy proposals but also be capable of initiating them ... it is desirable that the Board should have before it a range of well argued proposals, not all of which emanate from the RBA.'[42] Pagan suggested that two or three of the outside members should be monetary experts and serve on the Board full-time. Since he objected to representation of the financial sector on the Board, he presumably favoured more academics. Pagan wanted the RBA Board to become a bit more like the Monetary Policy Committee of the Bank of England, but without going all the way. That committee is made up of the Bank's leaders and other professional economists. Pagan clearly valued the lay members' input: 'I think the businessmen do a good job, they do ask questions, they treat it quite seriously. The only question you'd want to ask is whether we just want to be going another step. For that, you'd want to appoint two people who are more macro-policy experts than businessmen.'[43]

Mark Latham, a vocal former member of the House Economics Committee, and one of the authors of a Minority Report in 2000, supports these calls. In parliament he urged 'the government to urgently revise the membership of the Board and appoint a far higher proportion of monetary policy experts. The stakes are too high to ignore this problem.'[44]

But the Bank clearly likes the current arrangements. Bernie Fraser entered the recent debate, declaring Pagan's views 'mostly hogwash'.[45] During interview, Bob Johnston defended the lay members:

> The Board is strengthened by its make-up. I think it's got a lot of virtue in having people from different walks of life and different areas of the economy, who don't profess to bring high theory to the Board, but know whether something will fly or whether it won't.[46]

Ian Macfarlane comments:

> I have actually come to appreciate and favour [the lay Board] now, although I used to be a strong opponent of it. I think it's better to have a lay Board than another group of monetary economists at the Board, which is the British model, which is the one everybody loves at the moment. Bernie Fraser was a very strong advocate of a lay Board ... we are unusual, very unusual, in that respect.[47]

The Bank argues that its Board is not just a star chamber of narrow technical expertise, but benefits from the presence of a cross-section of members (although drawn mainly from the business community). Former Treasury Secretary Ted Evans, in a speech defending central bank independence, argued in 2000 that the Board should not be comprised only of technical experts: 'at least at this stage of Australia's economic development, monetary policy has become independent partly because the Bank Board is not so comprised'.[48]

The second point of contention regarding the Board's composition is the ban on finance sector representatives because they are thought to be subject to

potential conflicts of interest. Board members routinely receive inside information about the price of money in the short-term market. They are also privy to
other important information and may be tempted to push for rate decisions
likely to benefit their own sectoral interests. As John Phillips sees it: 'Everybody
on the Board has conflicts. It's a necessary part of the structure we've got.'[49]

The framers of the original *Reserve Bank Act* banned financial sector representatives from sitting on the Board but, formally, the matter has proceeded no
further. It seems that potential conflicts of interest are a price worth paying to get
broad representation on the Board. The Bank itself appears sanguine about the
issue. Bernie Fraser said during interview, 'Board members should be appointed
for their ability to take the national view and to forget about their sectional interests. And I think, in my experience, that they've been able to do that pretty
well.'[50] John Phillips concurred: 'You know, it can work quite well, as long as
the people put on the Board ... have a high ethical standard.' The part-time
Board members, he said,

> seem to be able to sit down, listen to debate, and bring a national perspective to bear
> on it ... It's quite interesting to watch how they will often bring forward arguments
> that would be totally opposed to what their constituents would want them to bring
> forward ... It's quite staggering, and it's not easy for people to understand who
> haven't sat through it.[51]

Periodically, however, the Bank is shaken by the issue. A former RBA director,
Brian Quinn, was found to have defrauded his company, Coles Myer. In mid-
1997 the Bank's apparent confidence in an 'ethical fix' was questioned when it
was revealed that Western Mining Corporation had quadrupled its forward sales
of gold at the same time as the RBA was secretly selling two-thirds of its gold
reserves. Hugh Morgan, the CEO, was a member of the Bank's Board at the
time.[52] He did not, and was not required to, absent himself from the Board meetings which dealt with the gold sales. The Bank says the Board would become
unworkable if those with potential conflicts of interest had to absent themselves
from Board meetings.

The old distinction between the financial sector and other sectors of business
is increasingly meaningless. All large corporations (and many small ones) now
deal extensively in foreign exchange and money markets, and the business
world is becoming 'financialised'. So why continue to make the distinction on
the Board between financial sector and non-financial sector leaders?

The third point of contention regarding the Board's composition is the inclusion of the Secretary of the Treasury. Australia is unusual in having a Treasury

Secretary as a full voting member on its central bank board. Britain and Germany have Treasury or Finance Secretaries on their central bank boards, but they advise and do not vote. The only other country besides Australia to have a voting Treasury Secretary on its Board is Fiji. In May 2000, questioned by the House Committee about the presence of the Treasury Secretary on the Board, Governor Macfarlane said: 'You are opening up the great issue of the *Reserve Bank Act* ... which I do not particularly want. I am comfortable with the current arrangements we have. They may not be perfect, but I am comfortable.' He added that present arrangements had not impaired the Bank's decision-making, and noted pointedly that the presence of the Secretary had not 'deflected' the Board.[53]

The critics, however, see several problems in Australia's arrangements. The *Australian Financial Review*, pursuing its case for the release of Board minutes, argues that a necessary corollary is that the 'Secretary to the Treasury should no longer remain a voting member of the Board. The potential consequences for the Australian dollar of having a public disagreement between the Treasury and the RBA are too damaging.'[54] This is not a strong argument. In the past, Board disputes were kept in-house. In May 2000, for example, Ian Macfarlane replied to a question by the House Economics Committee about disunity on the Board: 'No, I am not able to comment on that.'[55] Now they are in the open. Press reports have claimed that Treasury's Ken Henry, as well as Donald McGauchie, favoured lower rates.[56] In response to questioning, the Governor told the House Committee in June 2003, 'I'm not denying there was a difference of opinion between the Reserve Bank and Treasury – it's actually quite common. The only thing that's different this time is that someone thought it important enough to call up a journalist and talk about it.'[57] He thought such leaks – made, he assumed, by an 'over-energetic official somewhere in the bureaucracy who has tried to blunder into the debate' – were 'rather irritating'.

This is an interesting comment. First, the Bank seems to be more relaxed about divulging what happens on the Board and does not fear that internal differences of opinion will unsettle the markets. It has been proved right on this. Second, the Board is no longer watertight. How and why is it leaking? Some in the press and the markets think that the Treasurer's office is leaking the Secretary's Board debriefings, but public admission that your Secretary is losing boardroom debates does not seem like a great idea. More plausibly, the aim is to put public pressure on the Bank or to distance the government from the Bank's decisions. Another possibility is implicit in Macfarlane's comments – the 'over-energetic official' is almost certainly within Treasury. Perhaps Board information is discussed in the upper reaches of the Treasury and someone is passing it on. This suggests individual action rather than a conspiracy to challenge the Bank.

Critics argue that current Board arrangements confront the Secretary with conflicting loyalties; does he or she serve the Bank, the Treasurer, or the Treasury? If it's either of the latter two, this would potentially compromise the Secretary and reduce the Bank's independence. In 2000, the Labor *Minority Report* of the House Economics Committee said: 'The RBA Board should be made fully independent of the federal government by removing the Secretary of the Treasury.'[58]

There are two assumptions at work here: that the Bank's independence is sacrosanct; and that the Secretary's loyalties, when on the Board, are to the Treasurer. This second assumption is flawed because it is not clear whom the Secretary serves when on the Board. The central bank legislation of the Chifley era conceived of the Secretary as the government's watchdog (although Chifley abolished the Bank's Board and replaced it with an advisory committee headed by the Secretary).[59] The 1959 *Reserve Bank Act* does not specify any loyalties for the Secretary.

In interview, Ian Macfarlane said that 'no one has ever understood whether the Treasury Secretary speaks for the Treasury or the Treasurer, and I still don't know the answer to that'.[60] Probably the best answer is that the Secretary is relatively independent of the Treasurer, and acts as an individual 'policy professional', though perhaps broadly reflecting the Treasury line. Bob Johnston recalled that, in his opinion, the Secretary was definitely not on the Board to present the Treasurer's position.[61] In 1990 Secretary Chris Higgins graphically illustrated this by going against his minister's wishes. Johnston commented, 'I was surprised that it wasn't kept in, in-club, really... But [the Treasury Secretary] is not there to argue the Treasurer's position on things.'[62] Macfarlane pointed out: 'The only time the question has been put to the test it was clear that the Secretary was representing the views of the Treasury and not the Treasurer.'[63] So the Treasury Secretary, it seems, has substantial autonomy from the Treasurer while on the Board. In an interview with Chris Eichbaum, Bernie Fraser broadly concurred with this view: 'it has often been the case that there is a Treasury position that goes on irrespective of what the Treasurer is suggesting'. Fraser also recalled that when he was Treasury Secretary he was never provided with any 'guidance' from the Treasurer prior to Board meetings and thought that the Secretary's role, at least on the Board, was to serve both the Treasury *and* the Bank. 'On occasions I happily went along with decisions that would have been regarded as quite contrary to Treasury positions.'[64]

In an interview with Chris Eichbaum, former Labor Treasurer Ralph Willis admitted that the role of the Secretary was a 'grey area'.[65] Under Westminster conventions, the Secretary's role in acting independently of the Treasurer, and even of the Treasury, is extraordinary. True, the Treasury Secretary is not bound by the Board's secrecy provisions when dealing with the Treasurer, but more broadly it seems that the doctrine of central bank independence has filtered into the Treasury and now shapes the behaviour of the Secretary while on the RBA Board.[66]

REFORMS?

The environment in which the RBA operates has been transformed since the *Reserve Bank Act* was drawn up. The economic environment is complex and the Bank itself now has far more authority and independence. Do we need, therefore, to revamp the Bank's internal governance? In particular, does the Board need fixing, or is there room for improvement?

The Board's increasing activism is a good thing if it is evidence of robust policy debate at the Board level. It seems desirable to move further in this direction, towards a governance system which is even more open, contested and 'democratic', in which more voices and input are heard. If, for argument's sake, we adopt such a value framework, we can then examine questions of 'reform'.

First, Australia could adopt, say, the New Zealand model (or return to the Chifley model) – abolish the Board's decision-making powers, give policy authority to the Governor, and leave the Board with an oversight role.[67] This would sharpen accountability – only one person is making the decisions. But clearly it would diminish the voices heard during decision-making. Nor does it conform to wider trends in central banking to dilute the power of governors and give monetary committees or central bank boards more clout.[68] Adrian Pagan, for example, thinks the RBA should not follow New Zealand's example. He worries that the RBA's professionals might be too close to the markets and considers a more diverse Board appropriate: 'I argued against this [the New Zealand model] on the grounds that there was always a danger that the RBA could become "Sydney-centric", in the sense of being too close to the financial markets.'[69]

Second, should we remove the Treasury Secretary from the Board or remove the Secretary's vote on the Board? Probably, no to both. Again, the Secretary adds to the input on the Board and can quiz and challenge the Bank's experts (though perhaps not prevail). The presence of the Secretary should also aid the coordination of monetary and fiscal policy. John Phillips, for one, values the fiscal policy perspective: 'The Treasury tends to look at problems through fiscal eyes rather than through monetary eyes. And it's not bad for the Board, I think, to have that kind of perspective brought to bear when policy is debated.'[70] The Campbell Committee endorsed the continued presence of the Secretary on the Board.[71]

As to whether the Secretary compromises the Bank's independence, as Labor's Mark Latham claims, this depends on whether the Secretary does the government's bidding. The evidence suggests not, at least not in any crude sense. Plus, is it worth sacrificing voices, input and expertise for more 'independence'?

Third, if all the outside Board members (at least those in business) have financial interests and are potentially compromised, should we remove them? Not necessarily. They bring opinions, practical knowledge, a broad perspective and a wider legitimacy to the Board. Should we admit people from the financial sector? They would add monetary expertise and could quiz and (perhaps) challenge the Bank's professionals. Moreover, now that 'financialisation' is blurring the distinction between finance and the wider business sector, there seems no reason to exclude financial sector representation from the Board. On the other hand, it can be argued that the Bank is already close enough to the markets, and we should not move further in this direction. For Pagan, 'that's another reason why you'd not want to appoint people from the financial markets'.[72]

Fourth, do we need a more expert Board? The answer is probably yes. The Howard government seemed to agree when it appointed Jillian Broadbent to the Board in 1998. She had extensive experience in the finance sector and was well acquainted with monetary policy issues (although, as required by the Act, she resigned from her financial sector position before joining the Bank). It is desirable to have more experts on the Board who can keep the Bank's professionals on their toes.

Should we go further, like the Bank of England, and adopt a fully expert Board stacked with professional economists? Again, a wide diversity of voices and experience on the Board is preferable. A good compromise is Pagan's suggestion to appoint two extra macroeconomists with access to Bank research and resources. They could be appointed as half-time members. This would promote robust input into the Board, but also allow some escape from the Bank environment: otherwise there is a risk that they might become clones of the Bank's professionals.

Ian Macfarlane rejects Pagan's model as too much like the Bank of England.

Professor Pagan's views on the appropriate governance arrangements for a central bank are very heavily influenced by the Bank of England ... I think we have to be a little sceptical at this stage on the Bank of England model for several reasons. We must remember that the UK was the last country to adopt the principle of central bank independence. Being the last one to do it, they have come up with a model which I think shows the usual zealousness of the recent convert. The Bank of England model has a board which basically consists of professors of economics, so it is not at all surprising that a professor of economics is very much in favour of that model ... There are some strengths in such a model in that it does mean that the board members are going to be well-educated in monetary economics. The argument against it, from broad democratic principles, is that it means you have a board which is not really representative of the country – it does not represent a whole lot of different experiences or approaches. It basically means that you add another four monetary economists to the three monetary economists who are already on the board. So you have more expertise but you have it drawn from a very narrow range of possible disciplines.[73]

We should aim for a slightly larger and more diverse Board. The suggestion is not radical; it reflects the current strengths of the Board. The debate at the technical level would be widened by the addition of, say, two extra monetary experts to the Board. This would help keep the Bank's professionals on their toes and counter tendencies towards 'Bank think'.

CONCLUSION

The Reserve Bank is simultaneously open and secret. Openness and accountability have developed over the last two decades, especially in the 1990s, but the Bank still has a relatively secretive chamber, the Board. Nevertheless, its procedures and the Bank's internal policy processes are slowly yielding to greater disclosure.

Would a different Board produce substantially different or better policy? It's a moot point. John Phillips is happy with the current set-up.

I don't see any evidence that [other countries] have got it more right than we have. I'm a great believer in this thing that you don't change things just to change them … I look at the US system, and theirs is bureaucratic in the extreme. It's political in the extreme. And the Bank of England system is a different one entirely. And I look at the New Zealand one and the Canadian one, and, you know, I haven't been able to convince myself that any of these models have produced an outcome which is superior to what we've had.[74]

In New Zealand and Canada, where the Governor is in sole control, large errors in policy have occurred. In the final analysis, the most appropriate changes for Australia are minor. If we value a diverse Board, with more voices and input and a greater dispersion of expertise, we should follow Adrian Pagan's suggestion and add more monetary expertise to the Board. In order to maintain a buffer between the Bank and the financial sector, despite the 'financialisation' noted above, the current ban on financial sector representatives should stay in place.

CHAPTER 9

New Challenges in a World of Asset Inflation

If we had a lot of bad experiences, and we go through another cycle, we might seek some very clearly thought out regulations.

RBA Governor Ian Macfarlane[1]

Central bankers have helped quell CPI inflation and won a measure of market credibility and institutional independence, but they face new challenges. One is the threat that e-money and electronic commerce pose to the operation of monetary policy; this is probably overrated, largely because the cash to GDP ratio has been surprisingly stable or is declining only slowly in most countries.[2]

The most significant new threat is asset price inflation and associated financial instability. Just as the battle against consumer price inflation seems to have been won, a different form of inflation is rampant in equity and property markets. The challenge, it seems, has shifted from instability in the monetary system to wider forms of financial instability. The typical pattern is large upswings in asset prices leading to over-valuation, followed by sharp corrections and associated financial stress or collapse. Individual financial institutions become overextended during the boom, and their failure creates difficulties for the rest of the system via contagion. Increasingly, however, the financial distress being encountered is systemic, affecting a wide gamut of institutions; the knock-on effects may lead to a recession or even debt deflation. In other words, the dynamics of the financial system and the health of the real economy have become more closely connected. And this connection is intensified by the sharp increase in business and household debt in recent years and the mass entry of pension funds and small investors into equity and property markets.

Since the 1970s, in successive cycles, many economies – Japan, East Asia, Australia, Britain, the Nordic countries of Europe, Mexico, parts of Latin America, and most recently the United States – have experienced acute bouts of systemic financial instability. Steeply rising debt levels, 'irrational exuberance' in property and equity markets and soaring asset prices have been followed by inevitable corrections and crashes. These asset bubbles and subsequent financial collapses have had severe effects on the wider economy.

Across a range of countries, the cost of dealing with banking crises (bailouts and recapitalisation) has ranged from 5 per cent to 40 per cent of GDP, with even larger effects in terms of lost output.[3] Japan's bubble economy collapsed in the early 1990s and was followed by prolonged economic stagnation; the more recent collapse of US equity markets saw market values drop by almost $7 trillion, twice the nominal cost to the United States of World War II.

The financial liberalisation of the last three decades marks an unprecedented transformation from a heavily regulated financial system to an increasingly free, market-led system. This has unleashed an almost infinite supply of credit in an environment where monetary stability and investor exuberance have driven asset markets sky-high. Financial liberalisation and low CPI inflation are clearly linked to current financial instability.

These are challenges that central bankers have been afraid to seriously confront. So far, the debate has focused on making asset price stability a potential target of monetary policy, either in its own right or as a signal of incipient consumer price inflation. They have also considered a possible role for prudential policy.

This chapter contends that these forms of intervention are logically inconsistent with the deregulated framework of monetary policy that has emerged from the breakdown of the tight system of controls, sometimes referred to as 'financial repression', introduced to aid financial stability in the aftermath of World War II. In the deregulated framework, as it was consolidated in the 1990s, central banks have used interest rates to target stable rates of CPI inflation and (directly or indirectly) stable rates of output growth. Prudential regulators sought to protect bank depositors and other consumers of financial services from unsound behaviour – such as the maintenance of inadequate reserves – by individual financial institutions.

In a deregulated system, the task of allocating investment capital and consumer credit among individuals, firms and nations is left to financial markets. One justification of this approach is the efficient markets hypothesis. In its strongest form this states that all relevant information in any financial transaction is contained in the relevant price, and hence that markets contain the best estimate of the value of any asset, including equities. Modified versions admit to limited adjustment periods or information gaps (of the kind that might justify the work of professional market analysts), but these are seen as minor; the implication is that equity markets, for example, cannot become substantially over- or under-valued. A less doctrinaire version of the hypothesis is that markets are more efficient and effective in allocating capital and credit than any regulatory regime.

The existence of asset price bubbles contradicts the efficient markets hypothesis. In a policy framework based on any version of this hypothesis it is necessary to accept fluctuations in asset price. There may be room for marginal interventions when asset prices seem clearly out of line with fundamentals, as in the case of 'dirty floats', but not for systematic intervention.

If asset price bubbles are seen as a serious economic problem, any feasible response must return to policies of financial repression. The most straightforward responses include qualitative controls restricting the allocation of credit for investments in assets that are seen as subject to overpricing, and restrictions on financial innovations that derive their supposed value from unsound speculative arrangements which boost asset prices. There is no suggestion here that policy-makers are about to abandon the current policy regime, although, if cycles of financial instability become larger and more extreme, a fundamental rethinking of policy may be needed.

ASSET PRICE BUBBLES AND ASSET PRICE VOLATILITY

A study by Borio and Lowe at the Bank of International Settlements assembled data on trends in asset markets across a range of countries since the early 1970s.[4] They looked at the main asset classes – equities, commercial and residential property – and combined them into a weighted aggregate measure of asset prices (Figure 9.1).

Borio and Lowe discern several trends. First, equity prices tend to lead asset price upswings and are also the most volatile, followed, respectively, by commercial and residential property. Second, the aggregate asset data reveal three broad cycles of asset inflation since the early 1970s – roughly, the early to mid-1970s, the mid-1980s to the early 1990s, and the mid-1990s to the present. Third, the amplitude and length of the cycles appear to be growing, with the latest upswing being driven mainly by equity markets. Similar patterns of instability and volatility have occurred in exchange rate markets in the wake of deregulation.

Borio and Lowe and others point to one cause, or at least facilitator, of the new instability: credit growth.[5] In most industries, as supply increases, prices and profits are squeezed, thus limiting expansion. This is not necessarily true of the financial sector. Once under way, a credit expansion tends to boost output and push up asset values through leveraged acquisitions, thus promoting *further* credit expansion.[6] As Figure 9.2 indicates, since the 1970s surging credit growth has tended to be accompanied by upswings in asset prices.[7]

Liberalisation and easy credit have been matched with a new competitive urgency among banks and an increasing array of lending institutions. They all

Figure 9.1   Real aggregate asset prices, various advanced economies, 1970 to 2000 (1980 = 100)

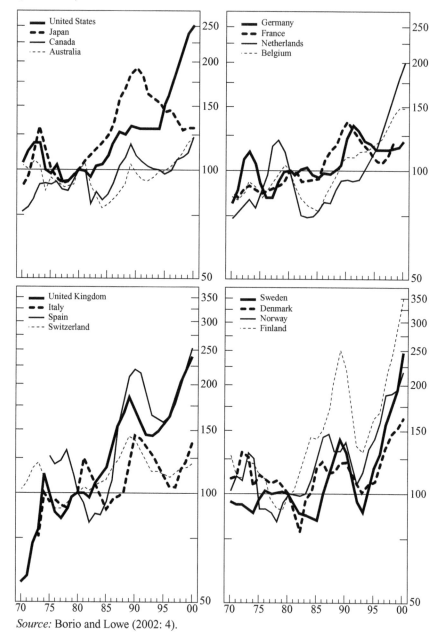

Source: Borio and Lowe (2002: 4).

Figure 9.2   Real aggregate asset prices compared with credit, various advanced economies, 1970 to 2000

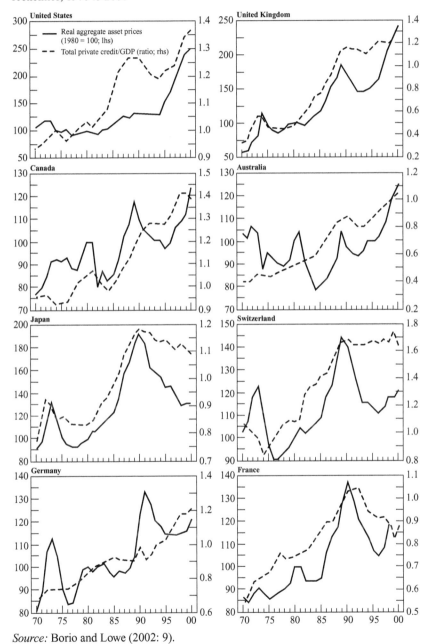

Source: Borio and Lowe (2002: 9).

Figure 9.3   Household debt as a percentage of household disposable income, various advanced economies, 1981 to 2002

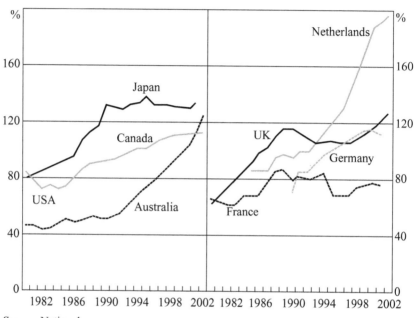

Source: National sources.

chase market share with competitive rates, new financial products and often a relaxation of lending standards, aimed at enticing borrowers. As the Bank of International Settlements argued in its 2001 *Annual Report*:

> Financial factors have long played a role in shaping business cycles. However, as domestic financial systems and international capital flows have been liberalised, this role has grown. Developments in credit and asset markets are having a more profound effect on the dynamics of the typical business cycle than was the case a few decades ago, and have also contributed to the increased frequency of banking system crises.[8]

Although the broad link between credit growth and asset inflation is clear, the exact dynamics of the relationship are still poorly understood. Borio and Lowe argue that lack of research prevents us from answering many questions: when should credit growth be considered 'excessive', what might be the cumulative

Figure 9.4 Debt-servicing ratio: household interest paid as a percentage of household disposable income, Australia, 1977 to 2002

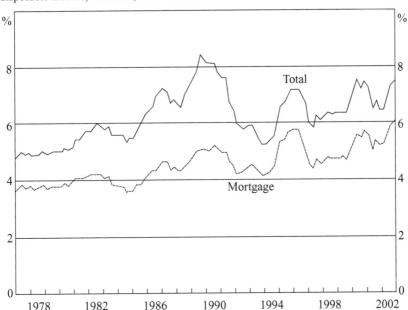

Sources: Australian Bureau of Statistics; Reserve Bank of Australia.

effects of credit expansions, how might credit booms interact with other financial imbalances.[9]

On the demand side, borrowers have been eager to increase their gearing as the price of credit has fallen. The achievement of low inflation in many countries in the 1980s and 1990s steeply reduced interest rates and the cost of borrowing. Although debt-to-income levels among firms and households have climbed steeply in many countries (Figure 9.3), debt-servicing ratios, or the interest-to-income ratio, have risen only modestly, as the data for Australia indicate (Figure 9.4). Lower interest rates have made debt more affordable and encouraged higher borrowing. The wealth effect of rising asset prices has also encouraged higher borrowing.

Monetary stability – low inflation – plays another role in asset inflation. Conventional wisdom holds that sharp fluctuations in inflation help destabilise the financial system because the cost of debt increases if inflation suddenly falls. Similarly, high inflation tends to encourage debt-based asset acquisitions and other forms of speculative behaviour. Hence, although monetary stability and financial stability have been seen as complementary, they are not mutually exclusive. After all, three of the biggest asset bubbles in the twentieth century – the United States' in the 1920s and 1990s, and Japan's in the late 1980s – occurred in a low-inflation context (in Japan in the late 1980s CPI inflation remained at close to zero while equity prices almost tripled and commercial property in Tokyo more than tripled). In East Asia and many other countries, including Australia, inflation has been low or has fallen to low levels in the last two decades, but financial instability has only increased.

Revisionist thinking suggests that monetary stability promotes expectations that there will not be a policy-induced downturn, and encourages investor optimism and risk-taking. The animal spirits of investors have helped spur surging asset prices. As the BIS argues:

> At the root cause of these [financial] cycles typically lies a wave of optimism generated by favorable developments in the real economy. This optimism contributes to the underestimation of risk, overextension of credit, excessive increases in asset prices, over-investment in physical capital and, in some cases, overly buoyant consumer expenditures.[10]

Part of the reason why financial and asset markets are subject to such mood swings is that the fundamental value of assets is very hard if not impossible to assess. Market participants rely heavily on gut feelings, favourable but impressionistic interpretations of the available data, and hearsay. The problem is compounded by inadequate risk-management techniques, short-termism, pressures for strong bottom-line returns, and investment strategies which extrapolate current conditions into the future.[11] This helps explain why markets sometimes undergo significant shifts even in the absence of significant new data. Optimism and surging markets have also been driven by technology-inspired 'new economy' expectations and by strong productivity growth and corporate restructuring, all of which have lowered inflation and boosted profits. In such a context rising asset prices are warranted, but the line between sustainable and unsustainable expansion is difficult to pick. Optimism encourages investors to stay with the market in the expectation of ever-higher returns, leading to what the Keynesian-inspired theorist Hyman Minsky called the 'euphoric economy'.[12] In 1996, the Federal Reserve's Alan Greenspan famously described the US economy as experiencing 'irrational exuberance'.[13] Familiar stories about market faddishness and herd behaviour are relevant here. Very quickly, however, the herd can turn, startled by some event or piece of bad news, and optimism may quickly turn to pessimism and a frenzy of selling and collapsing prices.

THE POLICY DEBATE

Neither the state of economic theory nor relevant policy history encourages optimism about potential policy responses to asset inflation.

At present, economic theory is still grappling with asset inflation. Some modified Keynesian accounts offer promise, but so far, adequate theoretical accounts of asset inflation, and especially asset bubbles, are yet to be developed.[14] Although it seems obvious in the light of historical experience that asset price bubbles occur, mainstream economic theory does not universally accept their existence. In particular, so-called New Classical accounts rule out the phenomena discussed in this chapter. The overriding assumptions are that markets are flexible, that information is close to perfect, and that markets reach equilibrium and clear virtually continuously. This is the basis of the efficient markets hypothesis noted above. Temporary disequilibrium might arise due to some kind of external or exogenous shock, but flexible markets are assumed to quickly revert to equilibrium. In such a world the miscalculations and over- or undervaluations that characterise bubbles and crashes are assumed to be impossible: financial markets are efficient not irrational, and price movements are a 'random walk' generated by the arrival of new information.

Neither is history encouraging in relation to policy solutions. No policy regime has yet succeeded in achieving monetary *and* financial stability in a liberalised system.[15] The Gold Standard era, which combined a liberalised financial system with gold as the monetary anchor, achieved monetary but not financial stability. The interwar years saw the emergence of fiat money regimes, but this helped loosen constraints on credit expansion and the system was marked by high levels of financial instability and the collapse of the 1930s Depression. Following World War II, the Bretton Woods system of 'financial repression' was an illiberal policy response to the instability of earlier liberal financial systems. It featured exchange controls and regulated exchange rates, and focused on heavily regulated monetary and credit aggregates. For a period it all but eliminated financial instability. But the system was abandoned in the 1970s amidst difficulties in dealing with stagflation and regulatory evasion. The current return to a liberalised system (after a period of drift in the 1970s) has used tight monetary policy to achieve monetary stability. But the liberalisation of the credit system, policy inattention to asset inflation and, to some extent, lax prudential standards, have helped fuel the current cycles of financial instability.

Although asset prices have fluctuated widely since the financial liberalisation of the 1970s, there has been little support for intervention to stabilise asset prices, with the partial exception of exchange rates. Economic theory predicted that speculation would ensure that asset prices remained close to fundamental values, so fluctuations in asset prices, including exchange rates, were initially seen as teething difficulties. This view was taken, in particular, with respect to the housing price boom and slump experienced in Australia, Britain and the Nordic countries in the late 1980s. When asset price volatility persisted into the 1990s, it was generally seen as the price of liberalisation, more than offset by the benefits of free capital movements. Asset price volatility provides substantial profit opportunities for participants in capital markets, which doubtless eased this acceptance.

In the 1990s, however, countries with recently liberalised financial markets (Mexico, Russia, Argentina) experienced financial crises which could be analysed in terms of capital market volatility. The greatest such event was the Asian crisis of 1997–98, which affected most of the economies of East and Southeast Asia. The Japanese bubble and bust of the 1980s and 1990s, previously seen as an isolated instance reflecting the exceptional nature of the Japanese economy, came to be seen as a model for asset price boom and slump.

In this context, the policies of the US Federal Reserve, and particularly its Chairman, Alan Greenspan, have come under increasing criticism. The central point is that, having warned of 'irrational exuberance' in 1996, Greenspan should have sought to constrain the growth in equity prices through tighter monetary policy or, at a minimum, through continued warnings regarding the unsustainability of the boom. Instead, in the eyes of critics, Greenspan effectively recanted his 1996 scepticism and became an influential advocate of the 'new economy' thesis underlying the boom. Subsequently he gave the market the green light by lowering interest rates and talking up the 'new economy'.[16] The general reluctance of central banks to restrain asset inflation has created the impression that they will stand on the sidelines and then try to mop up the bust, thus creating problems of moral hazard.[17] This belief was referred to in the late 1990s as the 'Greenspan put'. If the US economy makes a reasonable recovery from the current recession, Greenspan's hands-off approach will be (or seen to be) partly vindicated, and concern over asset price bubbles will diminish, at least until the next major cycle.

Policy responses to the problems of asset price inflation have focused on the possibility of preventing or controlling asset price booms, particularly through monetary policy. The first problem, however, is to identify a bubble. As Greenspan observes: 'If we could find a way to prevent or deflate emerging bubbles we would be better off. Identifying a bubble in the process of inflation may be among the most formidable challenges confronting a central bank.'[18]

Although the existence of a bubble in Japanese land prices in the 1980s and US equity markets in the 1990s was widely recognised, policy authorities typically have difficulty answering crucial questions: is there a bubble; if so, how big is it; will it decline or collapse; if the latter, how damaging will this be? As the Bank of International Settlements points out, authorities must make a judgement about potential market gyrations that is superior to the judgement of millions of investors who have put their money on the line: 'such a judgement would require a high level of proof'.[19] After studying experiences in thirty-four countries since the 1960s, Borio and Lowe conclude that identifying bubbles is fraught with difficulties. They suggest instead that a combination of rapidly growing debt and asset prices provides a reasonable guide to troubles ahead, and recommend:

> [a] slightly modified policy regime, under which the central bank responds not only to short-term inflation pressures but also, at least occasionally, to financial imbalances. Under such a regime, the central bank might opt for higher interest rates than are justified on the basis of the short-term inflation outlook.[20]

A related argument is that an inflation-targeting regime could be extended to a longer-term, more flexible stance. This was recently put by Charles Bean of the Bank of England at a 2003 RBA conference on asset inflation and monetary policy. A forward-looking, flexible, inflation-targeting central bank, Bean argues, 'should bear in mind those longer-term consequences of asset price bubbles and financial imbalances in the setting of current interest rates'.[21] The proposal that price indexes should incorporate asset prices, first put forward by Alchian and Klein, was revived by Goodhart in the context of the current debate about asset price bubbles.[22] This proposal has received limited support, however, because the price of assets is determined by a range of factors, including risk attitudes and expectations of future productivity.[23] Central bankers and monetary economists have been more sympathetic to the idea of taking some account of asset prices if these are seen as likely to boost spending (through wealth effects) and hence spill over into general inflation.[24] However, the dynamics are difficult to fathom, and they raise the uncertainty surrounding policy calculations to daunting levels. The problem is compounded if the timeframe of an inflation-targeting regime is extended, because long-term forecasting is inevitably very imprecise. These difficulties, combined with the lags associated with monetary tightening, raise daunting issues for monetary authorities.

The use of monetary policy to fight asset inflation has also been subject to the standard argument that a policy with a single instrument – short-term interest rates – should be directed towards a single target – CPI inflation. The introduction of additional targets is likely to blur the policy focus and raise uncertainties about the policy authorities' priorities. Indeed, the 1990s regimes that targeted CPI inflation were partly designed to overcome this problem. In the absence of clear evidence that asset price inflation leads to future CPI inflation, tinkering with the CPI measure of inflation raises the danger of adopting a multi-objective policy without explicit acknowledgement of the fact. Financial markets, in particular, do not want any diminution in their capacity to read the policy authorities' intentions.

A third criticism sees interest rate policy as a weak tool for moderating asset price inflation. In a major speech defending the actions of the Fed, Greenspan argues that interest rate policy is a blunt instrument and that the link between interest rates and asset prices is highly uncertain.[25] A rise in interest rates amidst the euphoria of a boom may have little effect. Greenspan cites the US rate rises of 1989, 1994 and 1999, none of which did anything to stem the market. A small rate rise might even backfire if it reassures investors about the inflation outlook and spurs optimism about the future. A large rise might work, but if it is big enough to pop an exuberant bubble it could damage the wider economy. Greenspan is emphatic:

> It seems reasonable to generalise from our recent experience that no low-risk, low-cost, incremental policy tightening exists that can reliably deflate a bubble. But is there policy that can limit the size of a bubble and, hence, its destructive fall out? From the evidence to date, the answer appears to be no.[26]

Asset inflation also raises an important political problem for central banks. Easy credit and asset booms are popular, providing a sense of opportunity and economic well-being. Any policy intervention that produces a slowdown in activity is likely to be unpopular. Also, the central bank may be unable to convincingly demonstrate, even *ex post*, that a policy tightening was necessary.[27] In the event that a misjudged policy response produces a significant slowdown or a recession, the political consequences are likely to be far more severe than in the converse case, where a boom is allowed to run on excessively. Borio and Lowe comment: 'it takes a brave central bank to raise interest rates in the absence of obvious inflationary pressures'.[28] Central bankers have worked hard in the fight against CPI inflation to win market credibility and institutional legitimacy and do not wish to jeopardise these achievements.

Discussions at the RBA conference mentioned above summarised the current state of the debate.[29] Most participants agreed in principle with the desirability of managing bubbles, but doubted that there was sufficient information on which to formulate policy in most cases. The consensus was close to the position put by Glenn Stevens:

We don't know enough about the behaviour of asset prices, much less about their linkages to the economy through the financial sector, to make forecasts with any confidence. Nor do we know much about how the dynamics might respond to monetary policy ... A case *might* be made on rare occasions, to adopt a policy of 'least regret' so far as asset prices are concerned, if financial and macroeconomic stability were thought to be at risk. To do so would probably require an acceptance of a longer time horizon for inflation targets, and an acceptance of a bit more short-term deviation from the central point of the target [original emphasis].[30]

Pointedly, Stevens adds that 'these issues remain unresolved among theorists and practitioners of monetary policy'. Andrew Crockett, formerly of the BIS, admits the difficulties for central bankers, but says 'it seems a counsel of despair to say that nothing can be done'.[31] Greenspan is not hopeful. And when asked about what central bankers should do about asset inflation, the RBA's Ian Macfarlane simply stated, 'I don't know the answer ... that is a huge problem.'[32]

This inconclusiveness reflects an air of artificiality about the entire debate. Concerns about the dangers of asset price booms and debt deflation are complex and wide-ranging; they cannot easily be fitted into an analytical framework based on a single variable, such as a measure of inflation.

PRUDENTIAL POLICY

Can prudential policy provide an answer? Its use to control asset price volatility, leaving monetary policy focused on traditional inflation targets, seems to have considerable promise. As Borio and Lowe note, this allocation of responsibility seems to meet the famous Tinbergen criterion of assigning one instrument for each target.[33]

This is, however, a misperception. In the policy framework arising from liberalisation, the justification for prudential regulation is based on the principal–agent problem. This emerges when financial institutions manage the assets of depositors, or other customers, who are not in a position to monitor their activities closely. That is, prudential policy tries to ensure that individual financial institutions act honestly and manage risks appropriately. The typical instrument of prudential regulation is an examination of an institution's capital adequacy ratios and other measures of the riskiness of its portfolio. These measures depend on market asset values. Thus prudential regulation, properly applied, can ensure that institutions do not respond inappropriately to market signals, but it cannot deal adequately with market prices that are themselves distorted by bubbles or busts. Borio and Lowe say: 'It is *distortions* in perceptions of asset values and risk – the very raw material on which prudential regulation operates – that generate financial instability.'[34] Hence, 'If excessive optimism and biases in risk assessment are widespread, supervisors may find it difficult to establish with sufficient clarity that lending is inappropriate.'[35]

This point is put clearly by Carmichael and Esho of the Australian Prudential Regulation Authority (APRA).[36] Responding to the suggestion of Schwartz[37] that prudential authorities should link portfolio composition to capital requirements or deposit premiums, thereby penalising banks that lend on bubble assets where prices are subject to bubbles, they argue that the proposed policy:

> requires regulators to form judgements about the optimal structure of the real sector – an area in which their expertise would have to be questioned. Second, it involves substituting the judgement of regulators for the judgement of bank management – something that runs counter to the risk-based philosophy that has been emerging in banking regulation in recent decades … While we accept that shifts in portfolio composition can play an important role in facilitating the development of asset price bubbles, introducing a system of benchmark portfolio weights and penalising deviations from those benchmarks would be an extremely costly and inefficient way of dealing with the problem. *It would also be a retrograde step in the evolution of regulatory philosophy away from directives that substitute the commercial judgements of regulators for those of bank management* [emphasis added].[38]

Critically, the modern framework of monetary policy implicitly relies on a three-fold division of responsibility. Central banks, using short-term interest rates as their primary instrument, are responsible for stabilising the inflation rate at a low target level. Prudential regulators are responsible for ensuring that individual financial institutions maintain an appropriate balance of risk and reserves. The task of determining asset prices or, equivalently, the volume and allocation of aggregate investment, is left to capital markets.

RECENT AUSTRALIAN POLICY EXPERIENCE

The RBA's response to rising debt and asset price inflation appears to be opening a fascinating new chapter in monetary policy, and it has raised tensions between the Bank and the government to new highs. Credit growth for housing has increased rapidly, as have housing prices. Credit growth for investment housing reached almost 30 per cent per annum during 2002 and 2003. The RBA is worried about the build-up of household debt, in part because highly geared borrowers are vulnerable to the effects of any economic downturn.[39] It also fears that surging house prices are raising issues of inter-generational equity. 'We have been disturbed by the speculative excesses that have been occurring in the housing sector. There is no doubt about that,' says Governor Macfarlane. 'All this adds an extra degree of complexity to the making of monetary policy.'[40] The Bank hopes that its 'open mouth' policy of warning about potential price declines, especially in investment houses and apartments, will see a gradual unwinding of the current pressures. Macfarlane has also admitted the Bank is not confident that higher, or even much higher, interest rates would cool the overheated property market; a point he made to the House of Representatives Economics Committee in 2003.[41] We can assume that the Bank has no wish to re-run the policy experiment of the late 1980s. In the run-up to the next federal election, the Howard government does not want the RBA to get too adventurous with monetary policy. Nor has the RBA *formally* factored asset prices in to a new inflation-targeting framework. The re-released 2003 *Statement on the Conduct of Monetary Policy* says nothing about debt or asset inflation, or a revised inflation-targeting regime, or the inclusion of asset prices in the Bank's 'price stability' mandate.

Nevertheless, the Bank raised interest rates in November and December 2003 and hinted at more rate rises to come. The rises produced a storm of criticism, especially from the rural sector and exporters hard hit by a strongly rebounding dollar. After the December rise, the government went public: Deputy Prime Minister John Anderson said 'enough is enough', while Prime Minister Howard worried that the economy would be 'clobbered to death' by further rate rises. The government is clearly not happy. Even Treasurer Costello, usually low key on monetary policy, questioned the Bank's move and thought that inflation was set to decline over 2004 and 2005. He also reiterated the government's position that interest rates should never be directed at the housing sector: 'you don't set interest rates to try and get some kind of level of house prices'. [42] The rate rises occurred in the face of the RBA's own forecast which points to an expected fall in underlying CPI inflation for 2004 and a rise to around 2.5 per cent by the latter part of 2005; in other words a relatively benign inflation outlook.[43] In its November *Statement on Monetary Policy*, the Bank spoke of the need to shift policy to a less 'expansionary' setting, although why, given the inflation forecast, was not altogether clear. In justifying raising interest rates, the Bank also said, 'A separate, but no less important issue … is the rapid run-up in household debt.'[44] Since dealing with debt and asset inflation is not part of any formal policy mandate, the Bank appears to be entering uncharted discretionary territory. One assumes that the Bank does not want to revisit its discredited, ad hoc 'checklist' approach of the 1980s, but it appears to be moving incrementally in this direction. Alan Mitchell of the *Australian Financial Review* writes of the RBA's 'shift in policy'.[45] But the Bank has not formally justified this altered approach. Indeed, doing so explicitly would almost certainly invite a confrontation with the government. Policy transparency and the earlier rigour of the Bank's inflation-targeting framework have thus far been partial casualties. Amidst the current storm of criticism, one government backbencher has called for the Bank's Board to be sacked.

ALTERNATIVES

As the discussion above suggests, the current policy debate on asset price inflation has reached an unsatisfactory point. On the one hand, it is generally agreed that asset price inflation now occurs more regularly, and that the bursting of asset bubbles can damage the financial system and the macroeconomy, as well as individual investors. On the other hand, there are powerful objections to any plausible policy response that might be considered within the current policy framework, which assumes that markets handle the task of allocating financial assets better than regulators do.[46] In the light of the speculative bubble that dominated the world's best-developed and most sophisticated capital markets in the 1990s, few economists or central bankers now endorse the strongest forms of the efficient markets hypothesis. Nevertheless, in a policy framework which leaves responsibility for asset price determination to markets, excessive volatility in asset prices, along with asset price bubbles, is *inevitable*.

With the arguable exception of 'jawboning' or 'open mouth' policy, the current policy framework admits no response to control asset price volatility. Either we accept volatility in asset prices, including bubbles, as part of the price of liberalisation, or we reconsider the entire policy framework. If damaging bubbles are an inevitable consequence of financial liberalisation, some measures of financial repression may be needed to reduce their frequency and severity. A return to more detailed and intrusive regulation would completely reverse the policy developments of the 1980s and 1990s.

There is no room here for a detailed analysis of options. The central element of the post-war policy of financial repression was 'qualitative control', that is, directions to financial institutions to reduce lending to sectors seen as 'overheated' while maintaining or even increasing lending in other areas. In modern terms one way to proceed is perhaps to more sharply define the system of deposit protection provided by government. Financial institutions that chose to operate within this system (most, presumably) would, as a quid pro quo, submit to qualitative controls on the composition of their loan portfolios, with a view to reducing credit flows to 'overheated' sectors.

CONCLUSION

Asset price volatility is an inevitable consequence of financial market liberalisation, and, in extreme cases, inevitably generates asset price bubbles, the bursting of which imposes substantial economic and social costs. Yet all conceivable policy responses within the existing liberalised financial system face daunting levels of uncertainty and risk. Recent efforts to develop lead indicators of financial instability are commendable but do not (and probably cannot) go far enough in reducing the uncertainty confronting policy-makers.[47] The calibration of instruments, such as interest rates, in dealing with overheated asset markets is also highly uncertain. Both sets of problems constrain the options open to policy-makers and highlight the economic and political risks associated with policy adventurism or, worse still, policy errors. This suggests that policy-makers will remain nervously on the sidelines of financial market gyrations or at most make small, tentative adjustments to interest rates in attempts to constrain markets. This has been the stance of recent monetary policy moves in Australia in the face of overheated housing prices; although the moves still await a formal, articulated rationale.

Given the pattern of increasing debt and asset market volatility, the future looks uncertain. Another significant cycle of asset price movements, especially in one of the major economies, could see a fundamental revision of thinking about the costs and benefits of liberalised financial systems. Arguably, the only alternative in the monetary policy arena is a return to some degree of financial repression. As Ian Macfarlane observes:

> I think the really fundamental answer is, if they can't sort them [financial crises] out, then the only ultimate answer is some form of re-regulation. I'm not for a minute thinking it's going to happen in the next decade. But I would not rule out the possibility that in twenty-five years, if we had a lot of bad experiences, and we go through another cycle, we might seek some very clearly thought out regulations.[48]

More could also be done via fiscal policy. As in the late 1980s, Australia still has a tax system that encourages speculation in assets such as property. An increase in capital gains taxation (substantially reduced by the Howard government in 2000) would be a good start. Reducing or eliminating negative gearing in the investment housing market would also help, though some compensating changes would need to be made in the rental housing market.

Conclusion

This book has charted the changing role and clout of the RBA. The Bank emerged from its post-war condition of relative obscurity in the early 1980s when deregulation had wiped the monetary policy slate almost clean, leaving only the manipulation of short-term interest rates, an instrument controlled by the Bank. This form of monetary control would become the key 'swing' instrument of macroeconomic policy and a major weapon against inflation. The RBA and monetary policy moved to centre stage.

The RBA, and monetary policy, focused on achieving and sustaining low inflation after the early 1990s recession. By the mid-1990s the Bank had achieved low inflation and an unprecedented level of credibility – the stuff of orthodox central banking.

However, the Bank resisted the ultra-orthodox New Zealand model and persisted with its more flexible approach. It presided over low inflation and began to chart a new policy orthodoxy by achieving comparatively strong growth performance. This can be seen either as a new 1990s approach to monetary policy and central banking practice or, in the Australian context, as a partial return to the views of the 1980s, which also emphasised growth. Of course, despite strong growth performance, unemployment (properly measured) and labour market insecurity still remain major problems, one facet of the new political economy of low inflation.[1] Politicians have come to realise that low inflation is electorally popular, not least because debt-exposed voters do not want the central bank to raise interest rates in the face of an upsurge in inflation.

The RBA has changed in many important ways, but the Bank's statutory provisions have not. This suggests that informal institutions and arrangements matter a great deal. The Bank operates in an invisible force field of institutional incentives and disincentives. It needs credibility in the markets and elsewhere to operate effectively, and the search for credibility has preoccupied it. But as its clout and independence have risen, so has its need to achieve wider community and democratic legitimacy. This credibility–legitimacy frame, and the search for balance between the two, is a good way to describe the key institutional dynamics that enmesh and shape the RBA.

What also stands out is the odd texture of Australian democracy (perhaps any Western democracy). None of the major changes in this story were widely debated in public. The low-inflation agenda of the early 1990s, inflation targeting and central bank independence were worked out behind closed doors at the elite level. It may be dawning on the informed public that, nowadays, the Bank runs monetary policy, but few know the details of how, why or when this massive shift in authority occurred.

NEW CHALLENGES

Financial deregulation posed major challenges to monetary policy and the Bank in the 1980s and the subsequent recession, and the liberalised financial system is still throwing up new challenges to central bankers world-wide. The current problems of burgeoning debt and asset price inflation (in Australia, in housing) can be seen as a partial re-run of the late 1980s. It marks a new chapter in the continuing dilemma of controlling credit and asset prices in a deregulated environment. The response is at present distorting domestic monetary policy as the Bank aims for 'least regret' and adjusts interest rates at a higher level than otherwise necessary. The Bank's adventurism on this front marks a departure from the CPI inflation-targeting framework of the 1990s; the move has angered the Howard government.

The tentative addition of asset inflation to the list of factors to consider when setting interest rates has raised the conventional uncertainties surrounding monetary policy to new levels.

The new political economy of inflation makes use of the structural and institutional parameters of the new political economy of inflation, and these have been manifested mainly through microeconomic price disciplines and restraints imposed by competition, productivity growth and wages moderation (i.e. labour market discipline is imposed through substantial levels of unemployment and labour market insecurity). In other words, the 1980s strategy of working down inflation on several policy fronts – including microeconomic reform – has finally come into its own, and a new political economy of inflation has emerged. It is these factors, more so than what Paul Keating calls 'a bit of shifty management at the top of Martin Place', that are now sustaining low inflation. Monetary policy, just as it was in the 1980s (though under different circumstances), is now back playing a supportive role.

Beyond this, there are questions about the sorts of conditions and outcomes that will be required to sustain central bank independence. These questions will be highlighted if central bankers stray too far beyond their mandate to fight CPI inflation. Once more, central bankers – or at least at the RBA – appear to be entering uncharted waters, posing interesting questions about their future role.

Notes

Introduction
1 Alan Blinder, former Vice-Chairman of the Federal Reserve Board (1996: 5).
2 Coombs (1981: 141).
3 The *Australian* (26 June 1990).

1 Slowly Building the Reserve Bank
1 Schedvin (1992: 45).
2 de Kock (1974).
3 Goodhart (1990).
4 See Broz (1998: 231).
5 Broz (1998: 239).
6 Broz (1998: 242).
7 Gollan (1968); Love (1984).
8 Gollan (1968: 16–17).
9 Fischer and Kent (1999).
10 Coombs (1931: 35).
11 Beazley (1963); Schedvin (1992: 47).
12 Love (1984: 51).
13 Gollan (1968: 107).
14 Fitzpatrick ([1941] 1969: 305).
15 Cited in Gollan (1968: 103).
16 Quoted in Coombs (1931: 35).
17 Schedvin (1992: 48).
18 See *Commonwealth Parliamentary Debates*, 21 November 1911: 2906, and 22 November 1911: 3022, 3027.
19 Maxfield (1997: 29–30).
20 Gollan (1968: 101).
21 *Commonwealth Parliamentary Debates*, 15 November 1911: 2646.
22 Coombs (1931: 76–8).
23 Coleman (1999).
24 *Commonwealth Parliamentary Debates*, 1924: 1506; Love (1984: 87).

25 Giblin (1951: 352).
26 Coombs (1981: 108).
27 Coombs (1981: 109).
28 Schedvin (1992: 59, 61).
29 May (1968); Coombs (1981: 115–17).
30 Coombs (1981: 112). See also Rowse (2002: 189).
31 Love (1984: 165).
32 *Commonwealth Parliamentary Debates*, 1945, Vol. 181: 546.
33 Schedvin (1992: 311).
34 Bean (1999: 32, 67).
35 Butlin (1983: 104–5).
36 See Whitwell (1994); Cornish (1992); Macfarlane (1997a); Nevile (2000).
37 Chifley, *Commonwealth Parliamentary Debates*, 1945, Vol. 181: 547.
38 Schedvin (1992: 89).
39 Crisp (1977: 179).
40 Coombs (1981: 111).
41 Butlin (1983: 100–1); Schedvin (1992: 71–3).
42 *The Economist*, 24 February 1945.
43 *Bulletin*, Sydney, 31 January 1945.
44 Giblin (1951: 347).
45 Crisp (1977: 182).
46 Block (1977).
47 See Coombs (1981: 114–15).
48 May (1968).
49 Rowse (2002: 208, 211).
50 Whitwell (1986: 104–5).
51 Rowse (2002: 232–330).
52 Schedvin (1992: 152).
53 Eichbaum (1999: 127–8).
54 Jones (2001).
55 *Sydney Morning Herald*, 14 October 1954.
56 Rowse (2002: 216).
57 Coombs (1981: 137–9).
58 Rowse (2002: 84).
59 Butlin (1983: 115).
60 Interview, Sydney (August 2001).
61 Schedvin (1992: 543).
62 Interview, Sydney (August 2001). See also Rowse (2002: 289).
63 Interview, Sydney (August 2001).
64 Schedvin (1992: 205).
65 Quoted in Rowse (2002: 289).
66 Coombs (1981: 110).
67 Weller (1989: 128).
68 Personal communication, 13 May 2003.
69 As outlined in Love (2001: 57).
70 Schedvin (1992: 337).

71 Interview, Sydney (August 2001).
72 Love (2001: 5–59); Wallace (1993: 121–3).
73 Eichbaum (1999: 200).
74 Campbell Committee (1981: 26).
75 Campbell Committee (1981: 19).
76 Campbell Committee (1981: 20).
77 Campbell Committee (1981: 21).
78 Campbell Committee (1981: 20).
79 Campbell Committee (1981: 19).
80 Pauly (1988); Glynn (1992).
81 Weller (1989: 376–82).
82 Marr (1983: 9).
83 Reserve Bank (1979).
84 Schedvin (1992: 544–5).
85 Phone interview, November 2002.
86 Interview, Sydney (October 2002).
87 For a more detailed account of Johnston see Edwards (1996: 209–14) and Marr (1983).
88 Marr (1983: 8).
89 Quoted in Marr (1983: 9).
90 Treasury's submission to the Campbell Committee strongly makes this argument. See Treasury (1981).
91 Kelly (1992: 83–6).
92 Interview, Brisbane (August 2001).
93 Interview, Sydney (November 2001).
94 Rowse (2002: 247).
95 Quoted in Kelly (1992: 86).
96 Interview, Sydney (October 2002).
97 Macfarlane (1998: 16; 1996: 34).
98 *Australian Financial Review*, 26 August 1983.

2 Into the Monetary Policy Wilderness

 1 Written communication, 7 March 2003.
 2 Bell (1997: ch. 5).
 3 See John Button (1998: 326).
 4 Macfarlane (1998: 17).
 5 Macfarlane (1998: 17).
 6 Block (1977a); Gowa (1984).
 7 Hirsch (1978).
 8 Heilbroner (1979).
 9 Kalecki (1943).
10 At least in the absence of an incomes policy aimed at moderating wages.
11 Fraser (1994a: 19).
12 Hughes (1980); Battin (1997); Bell (1997).
13 Macfarlane (1998: 9).
14 Macfarlane (1998: 9).

15 McCallum (2000).
16 Friedman (1968).
17 M3 is measured via the total volume of cash, bank deposits and liquid securities.
18 Guttmann (2003).
19 Grenville (1997: 128); see also Jones (1983).
20 Goodhart (1992: 314).
21 The RBA emphasised its 'flexible' approach to monetary targeting and this reflected underlying concerns within the Bank about how well such a system could be made to work. See Guttmann (2003).
22 Guttmann (2003: 109).
23 Battin (1997); Bell (1997).
24 Brash (1997).
25 Reserve Bank (1993: 2).
26 Grenville (1996: 37).
27 For critiques see J. Galbraith (1997) and Eisner (1995) and *The Economist* (1997). For critiques of the idea that unemployment is mainly a supply-side problem, see relevant chapters in Bell (2000) and Mitchell and Carlson (2002). For a more general critique of monetarism, see Kaldor (1982).
28 Guttmann (2003: 334).
29 Budget Paper, No. 1 (1982: 35).
30 Guttmann (2003: 222).
31 Guttmann (2003: 175, 330).
32 VCM (1977).
33 Eichbaum (1999: 207).
34 Reserve Bank of Australia, *Annual Report* (1979: 7).
35 RBA, *Annual Report* (1983: 5).
36 Keating (1989).
37 Stilwell (1986); Singleton (1990).
38 This supportive role also applied to other policy fronts, including later attempts to deal with Australia's current account problems. The Bank's former Deputy Governor, Stephen Grenville (1997: 131), says, 'The overriding impression, looking back on this period, is of monetary policy being used as a stop-gap measure to buy time while other policies were put in place to handle more deep-seated problems.'
39 Hughes (1997: 162).
40 Grenville (1997: 136, 153).
41 See Moore (1992: 28).
42 RBA, *Annual Report* (1983: 8).
43 See, for example, Moore (1992).
44 A strong defence from senior officers in the Department of Finance can be found in Keating and Dixon (1989).
45 Guttmann (2003: 233).
46 Harper (1988); Grenville (1990).
47 Macfarlane (1998: 7).
48 Indeed, by the late 1980s credit aggregates were rising fast as inflation was falling!
49 RBA, *Annual Report* (1985).
50 Macfarlane (1998: 10).

51 Grenville (1997: 135).
52 Guttmann (2003: 268).
53 Guttmann (2003: 274-6; 342-4).
54 Guttmann (2003: 335, 342-44).
55 Phone interview, November 2002.
56 See also Edwards (1996: 293-5).
57 The exchange rate has a direct effect on inflation via the price of imports and exports and also via its influence on economic activity.
58 Johnston (1987: 8).
59 RBA, *Annual Report* (1987: 6); Grenville (1997: 134).
60 Interview, Sydney (October 2002).
61 RBA, *Annual Report* (1986: 13).
62 Guttmann (2003: 338 ff).
63 RBA, *Annual Report* (1986: 5).
64 Jonson (1988: 38).
65 Macfarlane (1998).
66 Written personal communication, 9 October 2002.
67 RBA, *Annual Report* (1987: 12).
68 The RBA engaged in net sales of $1.2 billion during July and August 1986, for example, with a similar sale in January 1987.
69 RBA, *Reserve Bank Bulletin* (February 1986: 10).
70 RBA, *Annual Report* (1987: 12).
71 Written communication, 23 March 2003.
72 Written personal communication, 9 October 2002.
73 Interview, Sydney (October 2002).
74 Macfarlane (1998: 10, 11).
75 Interview, Sydney (November 2001).
76 Kelly (1992: 370).
77 Kelly (1992: 369).
78 Grenville (1997: 139).
79 Quoted in Love (2001: 80).
80 Interview, Sydney (October 2002).
81 Suich (1991: 16).
82 RBA, *Annual Report* (1990: 33).
83 See P. Walsh (1995), *Confessions of a Failed Finance Minister*, Random House Australia, Sydney.
84 RBA, *Annual Report* (1988: 14).
85 The J-curve became a mantra during this period. It implied that a falling currency would reduce imports and boost exports and thus help correct the current account problems.
86 Macfarlane (1991: 190).
87 Edwards (1996: 339).
88 Interview, Sydney (August 2001); see also Edwards (1996: 327-9).
89 Written communication, 7 March 2003.
90 Interview, Sydney (November 2001). See also Edwards (1996: 328).
91 Quoted in Tingle (1994: 27).

92 See Figure 2 in Love (1995). Opposition Leader John Hewson claimed it was an example of 'political interference', *Australian,* 17–18 November 1990.
93 Interview, Sydney (November 2001).
94 Quoted in Love (2001: 293).
95 Grenville (1997: fn 8).
96 Edwards (1996: 329).
97 Tingle (1994: 28, 335).
98 Hughes (1997: 162).
99 Quoted in Kelly (1992: 489).
100 Interview, Sydney (August 2001).
101 Quoted in Kelly (1992: 489).
102 Interview, Sydney (August 2001).
103 Kelly (1992: 492).
104 Written communication, 9 October 2002. Johnston's emphasis.
105 Grenville (1997: 147).
106 Grenville (1997: 152).
107 Interview, Sydney (August 2001).
108 Underlying inflation is the CPI rate, net housing mortgage costs.
109 Hughes (1997: 160).
110 Written communication, 23 March 2003.
111 Written communication, 7 March 2003.
112 Macfarlane (1998: 11).

3 Snapping the Stick of Inflation

1 *Australian* (26 June 1990).
2 *Australian Financial Review* (16 July 1997).
3 For example, one of the Blair government's first acts was to make the Bank of England independent of the government in order to appease the financial markets and improve the Bank's (and the government's) market credibility.
4 Aybar and Harris (1998).
5 Fraser (1994a: 23).
6 The leading economies, or OECD 7, are Japan, Britain, the United States, Canada, Italy, France, Germany.
7 See Eichbaum (1999); Kirchner (1997).
8 Interview, Canberra (February 1997).
9 Macfarlane (1996: 35).
10 See the sympathetic critique in Walsh (1989a).
11 Tingle (1994: 71).
12 For example, see 'Reserve Chief attacks GST', *Sydney Morning Herald,* 23 November 1991; 'Labor Goes on Warpath: Reserve Chief Blames Hewson for fall in A$', *Australian,* 3 February 1993. Fraser also attacked the Opposition's plans for restructuring the RBA (see chapter 4). For attacks by Fraser on the Opposition Leader, John Howard, see 'Reserve Chief Slates Howard', *Australian,* 12 July 1995, and 'Opposition Furious Over Fraser's Remarks', *Australian Financial Review,* 13 July 1995.
13 Interview, Canberra (February 1997).

14 This issue is taken up in chapter 5.
15 Macfarlane (1998: 14).
16 *Commonwealth Parliamentary Debates*, 1 March 1989.
17 Edwards (1996: 376).
18 The letter is now posted at: http://www.henrythornton.com/article.asp?article_id =1333.
19 For example, see the reports from Stutchbury (1989) and Cleary (1989) and the analysis in Carew (1992: 254–6).
20 Button (1998: 329).
21 Quoted in Edwards (1996: 380).
22 Pitchford (1989).
23 Gittins (1990a).
24 Phillips (1990). As Gittins (1990) points out, the Bank had been making this argument for some time prior to Phillips's 'front page' presentation.
25 Cleary (1990).
26 Gittins (1990).
27 Interview, Sydney (November 2001). Phillips also says: 'it was interesting because during all of the period, and right up until the present day, Keating has never said anything about that issue to me'.
28 *Australian* (26 June 1990).
29 Quoted in Burrell (1990).
30 Fraser (1990: 13).
31 Fraser (1990: 15).
32 Written communication, 2 September 2003.
33 Quoted in Edwards (1996: 381).
34 Grenville (1997: 140).
35 Edwards (1996: 378).
36 Interview, Sydney (November 2001).
37 Cockburn (1990).
38 Quoted in Tingle (1994: 94).
39 Edwards (1996: 378).
40 Edwards (1996: 380).
41 Edwards (1996: 407).
42 Fraser (1994a).
43 Watson (2002: 82).
44 Button (1998: 337).
45 Macfarlane (1992a: 5).
46 Fraser (1984: 231).
47 As Michael Stutchbury wrote in August 1990: 'The most pathetic part of the monetary policy puzzle is the sight of highly paid Melbourne bankers … complaining about high interest rates. The leaders of the finance sector, usually the most hairy chested on the need to attack inflation, have wimped out as the monetary policy screws increase the price of the reckless lending of the mid-to-late 1980s': *Australian Financial Review*, 1 August 1990.
48 Phillips (1993: 341).
49 Fraser (1990a: 20).

50 Stutchbury (1989a).
51 Grenville (1997: 140).
52 Written communication, 2 September 2003.
53 Macfarlane (1998: 11).
54 Jonson (1988; 1990).
55 Jonson (1988: 50).
56 Jonson (1988: 43).
57 Jonson (1990: 2, 4).
58 Written communication, 23 March 2003.
59 Fraser, Interview (Brisbane, 8 October 2003).
60 Phone interview, November 2002.
61 Fraser (1990a).
62 Gittins (1990a).
63 'Bank Targets Inflation – and Cops Out', *Australian*, 21–22 April 1990.
64 White (1992: 16).
65 Grenville (1997: 141–2).
66 Interview, Sydney (November 2001).
67 Interview, Sydney (February 1997).
68 Grenville (1997: 152, 141), my emphasis.
69 Quoted in Kelly (1992: 495).
70 Written communication, 2 September 2003.
71 Quoted in *Decisions* magazine (1990), Vol. 2: 8, my emphasis.
72 Fraser (1991: 1), my emphasis.
73 *Australian* (7–8 September 1991).
74 Interview, Sydney (November 2001).
75 Quoted in the *Australian*, 22 May 1992.
76 Written communication, 2 September 2003.
77 RBA, *Annual Report* (1992: 3), my emphasis.
78 Written communication, 2 September 2003.
79 Macfarlane (1992: 16).
80 Grenville (1997: 144).
81 RBA (1993a: 25).
82 Tingle (1994: 316).
83 Edwards (1996: 405).
84 Reserve Bank of Australia, *Annual Report* (1991: 4).
85 See the account of this in Edwards (1996: 405).
86 Quoted in the *Australian* 23 February 1991.
87 Interview, Sydney (October 2002).
88 Edwards (1996: 378).
89 Interview, Sydney (November 2001).
90 Interview, Sydney (November 2001).
91 'Coalition Will Review Fraser's Job', *Age*, 24 November 1991.
92 *Sydney Morning Herald*, 23 November 1991.
93 Interview, Brisbane (8 October 2003).
94 Tingle (1994: 72–3).
95 Quoted in Kelly (1992: 495).

96 Quiggin (1997: 177).
97 Nevile (2000). The economist, Barry Hughes (1997: 163), puts this down to the priorities of the Bank and to the wider 'money club', one which 'puts a higher premium on avoiding inflation over other matters than most in society'.
98 Fraser (1992: 7).
99 Fraser (1993: 3).
100 Fraser (1990a: 24).
101 Bell (2002).
102 Chapman and Kapuscinski (2000).
103 Reserve Bank of Australia (1993a).
104 See Eichbaum (1993).
105 Phillips (1992: 16).
106 Interview, Sydney (November 2001).
107 Fraser (1996: 17).
108 Fischer (1995).
109 Fraser (1996: 16).
110 Macfarlane (1998: 13).
111 Interview, Canberra (January 1997). See also Eichbaum (1999: 306).
112 Written communication, 2 September 2003.
113 Eichbaum (1999: 299–301).
114 Stevens (1999: 48), original emphasis.
115 Coleman (1991); Eichbaum (1999).
116 Fraser (1996: 19).
117 Grenville (1996: 33, 37).
118 The criticism here goes to questions of excessive hawkishness on the part of central banks and also to criticisms of orthodox understandings of unemployment, involving, for example, the supply-side focus on unemployment and the NAIRU paradigm. See chapter 3.
119 Chowdhury (2000).

4 'A Measure of Peace'? Monetary Policy in the 1990s

1   Grenville (2001: 41).
2   Macfarlane (1998: 14).
3   Interview, Sydney (November 2001).
4   Bernanke et al. (1999).
5   Mahadeva and Sterne (2000: 35–9).
6   http://www.rba.gov.au/Monetary Policy.
7   Fraser (1990b: 6).
8   Fraser (1993: 3).
9   Fraser (1990b: 7).
10 Interview, Sydney (November 2001).
11 Fraser (1993: 2).
12 Fraser (1994a: 21).
13 In testimony to the House of Representatives Standing Committee on Banking, Finance and Public Administration, 19 October.
14 Interview, Sydney (November 2001).

15 Macfarlane (1998: 15); Stevens (1999: 49).
16 Interview, Sydney (November 2001).
17 Written communication, 20 September 2003.
18 As related by Ross Gittins of the *Sydney Morning Herald*, who attended the meeting.
19 Interview, Sydney (November 2001).
20 Stevens (1999: 48).
21 Interview, Sydney (November 2001).
22 Though New Zealand later changed its target to 1–3 per cent.
23 Macfarlane (1998: 13).
24 Written communication, 20 September 2003, original emphasis.
25 Interview, Sydney (November 2001).
26 Macfarlane (1998: 14).
27 Grenville (1997: 147).
28 Macfarlane (1998: 12).
29 Interview, Sydney (November 2001).
30 Grenville (1997: 147).
31 Hughes (1997: 162).
32 Hall and Franzese (1998); Iverson (1999).
33 See Fraser (1994: 24).
34 Grenville (1997: 147).
35 Stevens (1999: 56).
36 Comments before House of Representatives Standing Committee on Economics, Finance and Public Administration, Melbourne, 22 May 2000, p. 47.
37 Fraser (1994a: 21).
38 The Bank announced this shift to a medium-term approach in its *Annual Reports* for 1991 and 1992.
39 Grenville (1997: 143).
40 Interview, Brisbane (October 2003).
41 Fraser (1994a: 23).
42 Stevens (1999: 57), my emphasis.
43 Stevens (2001: 25).
44 *Sydney Morning Herald* (3 June 1994). See also Eichbaum (1999: 186, 267).
45 Macfarlane (1998: 13).
46 See North (1990: 36). See also Gregory (1992: 16).
47 Eichbaum (1999: 267).
48 Macfarlane (1996: 36).
49 RBA (1996: 2), my emphasis.
50 Fraser (1996: 18).
51 Interview, Brisbane (October 2003).
52 Macfarlane (1998: 15).
53 Eichbaum (1999: 292).
54 Eichbaum (1999: 304, 290).
55 Grenville (1997: 146).
56 Fraser (1996: 17–18).
57 Macfarlane (1998: 17).
58 Grenville (2001: 41).
59 See, for example, Grenville (1999a; 1999b).

60 See Hartcher (2001).
61 Interview, Sydney (November 2001).
62 Commonwealth of Australia (1998: 5).
63 Quoted in Burrell (1999).
64 Interview, Sydney (August 2001).
65 In New Zealand monetary policy was framed for a period within a Monetary Conditions Index, which is an exchange rate and interest rate composite used to help guide policy.
66 Interview, Sydney (November 2001).
67 Macfarlane (2000: 2).
68 Fraser (1996: 17).
69 Interview, Canberra (January 1997).
70 Interview, Sydney (November 2001).
71 Stiglitz (1998).
72 Fortin, F. (1993, 2001); Akerlof, G. Dickens, W. and Perry, G. (1996); Bell (1999).
73 Stiglitz (1998: 215); see also Stiglitz (1997) and Galbraith (1997).
74 Solow (1998).
75 Bootle (1996); Grenville (1997); Thurow (1996: 189-90).
76 Grenville (1997: 153).
77 Interview, Sydney (August 2001).
78 Cleary (2000e).
79 *Reserve Bank of Australia Bulletin* (April 2000: 38).
80 *Reserve Bank of Australia Bulletin* (April 2000: 2).
81 Treasury (2000) *Budget Paper*, Part 3: 9–10.
82 Hendersen (2000).
83 Dodson (2000).
84 Wood (2000a).
85 Reserve Bank of Australia (2000: 38).
86 Commonwealth of Australia (2000: 83–5).
87 Colebatch, 'Reserve Must Exercise Restraint', *Age*, 16 March 2000.
88 Quoted in Grattan (2000).
89 Marris (2001).
90 Commonwealth of Australia (2003: 57).
91 Gittins, *Sydney Morning Herald*, 6 May 2002.
92 Commonwealth of Australia (2001: 57).
93 Press Conference, 29 July 2003.
94 Press Conference, 29 July 2003.
95 Former RBA Board member, R. G. Gregory (1992: 16) says: 'the present Bank Act and institutional framework can deliver whatever policy is wanted so it is a little difficult to understand why so much emphasis is placed on formal structures'. See Gregory (1992).
96 The single inflation target, over-zealously applied, led to a policy-induced recession in New Zealand in 1998.
97 The US Federal Reserve under Chairman Greenspan has also sought to test the limits of the NAIRU. For revisionist comments on central banking orthodoxy see Fischer (1995).
98 Interview, Sydney (August 2001).

5 Towards RBA Independence
1 Walsh (1989a).
2 MacLaury (1994: 79), original emphasis.
3 Goodhart (1995: 60).
4 Maxfield (1997: ch. 4). Data from the 1998 Bank of England survey is instructive (Mahadeva and Sterne 2000: Table 4.4). On the critical issue of who adjusts policy instruments, the results reveal that most central banks now wield operational independence.
5 McDonough (1994: 5).
6 Alesina (1989); De Long and Summers (1992); Grilli, Masciandero and Tabellini (1991); Cukierman (1992).
7 Fraser (1994b: 3).
8 Grilli et al. (1991: 369).
9 Reserve Bank of Australia (1993). John Phillips thinks this move was at least as significant as the float in the overall process of financial deregulation: Interview, Sydney (November 2001).
10 Grilli et al. (1991: 369). The German Bundesbank gets a score of 7.
11 Grilli et al. (1991: 368).
12 That is, a score of 3 out of a possible 8, with central banks in the United States and Germany, for example, scoring 5 and 6 respectively.
13 Interestingly, the views of the Treasurer are not canvassed at Bank Board meetings.
14 Cukierman (1992: 371–2); Fraser (1994b: 5); Kirchner (1997: 22–3).
15 Edwards (1996: 209).
16 Guttmann (2003: 99).
17 See Marr (1983: 13).
18 Memo entitled 'Housing Finance', supplied by the RBA.
19 Interview, Sydney (November 2001).
20 Interview, Sydney (October 2002).
21 Reserve Bank of Australia, *Annual Report* (1982: 7).
22 Written communication, 9 October 2002.
23 Interview, Sydney (November 2001).
24 Kelly (1992: 369).
25 Interview, Sydney (November 2001).
26 Interview, Sydney (August 2001).
27 Edwards (1996: 331); Maley (1994).
28 Quoted in Edwards (1985: 70).
29 Hewson (1980).
30 See, for example, *Commonwealth Parliamentary Debates*, 1 March 1989.
31 *Commonwealth Parliamentary Debates*, 28 September 1988.
32 Interview, Sydney (November 2001).
33 Gittins (1988).
34 Wood (1992: 65–6); Johnston, written communication, 4 November 2002.
35 Wood (1992: 65).
36 Written communication, 23 March 2003.
37 Johnston (1989: 17, 18),
38 Wallace (1993: 214–16).

39 Interview, Sydney (August 2001).
40 Interview, Sydney (August 2001).
41 Interview, Sydney (August 2001).
42 Keating (1989).
43 Interview, Sydney (August 2001).
44 Written communication, 4 November 2002.
45 Minutes of debrief, 11 November 1985 (RBA SD 85-0-35-16).
46 Minutes of debrief, 7 November 1984 (RBA SD 85-03424).
47 Minutes of debrief, 7 November 1984 (RBA SD 85-03424).
48 Edwards (1996: 291).
49 Kelly (1992: 383).
50 Edwards (1996: 291).
51 Written communication, 23 March 2003.
52 See, for example, Walsh (1989).
53 The 1989 comment was during a press conference on 16 February, while the 1990 comment was on 7 December, during a press gallery dinner. See *Sydney Morning Herald*, 22 September 1989.
54 Keating (1991).
55 Fraser (1996: 15).
56 Eichbaum (1999: 335).
57 Interview, Sydney (November 2001).
58 Tingle (1994: 107).
59 Written communication, 2 September 2003.
60 Macfarlane argues now: 'Debate! Yes, I know, but that didn't help because that really made him [Keating] stick to, defend the status quo.' Interview, Sydney (November 2001).
61 For arguments that politics has had little influence, see Tingle (1994: 322); Gregory (1992: 14); and Kelly (1992: 488).
62 Tingle (1991); Tingle (1994: 27, 141–3), and see also the discussion in Eichbaum (1999: 252–3).
63 Interview, Brisbane, 8 October 2003.
64 Asked why Treasury had urged him to take such a step, Kerin replied: 'Well I could never understand it. It was quite out of character, wasn't it? Unless they were trying to set me up?' Interview, Brisbane (August 2001).
65 Interview, Brisbane (August 2001).
66 Cleary (1991; 1991a).
67 Jonson (1990).
68 Cole (1990: 3, 4, 5).
69 Fraser (1989: 11).
70 Fraser (1989: 12).
71 Fraser (1996: 15).
72 Fraser (1993: 4).
73 Fraser (1993: 4), original emphasis. More recently, Edwards (1996: 209) has questioned this account of Bank independence. One problem with emphasising the debriefing sessions in this way is that it was usually the case that they were held *after* monetary policy had already been publicly announced.

74 Fraser (1996: 15).
75 Fraser (1994: 15). The *Australian* agreed: editorial, 10–11 October 1992.
76 Cole (1990: 8).
77 *Australian,* 22 May 1992.
78 Interview, Sydney (August 2001).
79 Edwards (1996: 379).
80 Written communication, 2 September 2003.
81 Interview, Sydney (August 2001).
82 Interview, Canberra (February 1997).
83 Keating (1991).
84 Keating (1991).
85 Interview, Canberra (February 1997).
86 Korporaal (1993).
87 Edwards (1996: 376).
88 Keating (1991).
89 Eichbaum (1999: 243).
90 Kelly (2000).
91 Written communication, 26 August 2003.
92 Interview, Sydney (February 1997).
93 Interview, Brisbane (8 October 2003).
94 Interview, Brisbane (August 2001).
95 Written communication, 26 August 2003.
96 Interview, Sydney (August 2001).
97 Interview, Brisbane (8 October 2003).
98 Interview, Brisbane (8 October 2003).
99 Burrell (1994). It was significant that Fraser did not mention the (rising) current account deficit in announcing the rate rise.
100 Treasurer, Press Release, 5 December 1995.
101 Interview, Sydney (August 2001).
102 Written communication, 3 September 2003.
103 Quoted in Wood (1995a).
104 Wood (1995).
105 Interview, Sydney (August 2001).
106 Eichbaum (1999: 333).
107 Interview, Brisbane (October 2003).
108 Macfarlane said: 'Of all the policy-makers in Australia, the one that Paul Keating had the most confidence in was Bernie. But see, that was a function of personalities. So in that sense it was not … it was independence that could be taken away very quickly if the personalities changed.' Interview, Sydney (August 2001).
109 Press conference, 14 August 1996.
110 See Wood (1996).
111 Kitney (1996).
112 Grenville (1997: 150).
113 Macfarlane (1996: 34).
114 Interview, Sydney (August 2001).

115 In December 2000 before the House of Representatives Economics Committee, Macfarlane said: 'The Treasurer has stayed out of that debate and that is okay with me. I certainly do not want him to come into that debate': Commonwealth of Australia (2000: 42).

116 *Australian Financial Review*, 5 May 2000.

117 Commonwealth of Australia (2000: 59).

118 Commonwealth of Australia (2000: 83–4).

119 The Labor members were Mark Latham, Anna Burke and Anthony Albanese. See Koukoulas (2000).

120 Commonwealth of Australia (2000a: 29).

121 Transcript of Q & A, Speech by Governor Macfarlane, Queensland University of Technology, 10 August 2000. See also Cleary (2000b; 2000c); Koukoulas (2000).

122 Reserve Bank, Press Release, 11 August 2000.

123 Marris (2001).

124 See Kane (1988).

125 Quoted in Grattan and Walker (1993).

126 Quoted in Kirchner (1997: 28).

127 Interview, Sydney (October 2002).

128 Interview, Sydney (November 2001).

129 Grenville (1997: 153).

130 Macfarlane (1992: 16).

131 Written communication, 3 September 2003.

6 RBA Independence – Why?

1 *The Economist* (10 February 1999: 10).

2 Capie, Goodhart and Schnadt (1994: 80).

3 Eichbaum (1999); King (2001).

4 Fraser (1994b: 3) was more generous, arguing that uncertainty regarding the timing and impacts of monetary policy may also influence politicians' preferences.

5 Political business cycles refer to manipulation of economic policy by governments at electorally opportune times. The 'time inconsistency problem' is the short-term incentive for governments to renege on long-term commitments to low inflation. See Kydland and Prescott (1977); Persson and Tabellini (1990).

6 Grilli et al. (1991: 375).

7 See Alesina (1989); De Long and Summers (1992); Alesina and Summers (1993). See also Eijffinger and De Haan 1996, ch. 5); Posen (1993); Hall and Franzese (1998); Banaian et al. (1986); Lohmann (1998); Cukierman (1994).

8 Hayo and Hefeker (2002); McCallum (1995); Drazen (2001); Leertouwer and Maier (2001).

9 Macfarlane (1998).

10 Grenville (1996: 34).

11 See for example, Cargill (1995); Forder (1998); Hayo (1998); Temple (1998).

12 Posen (1993; 1995).

13 See Maloney and Pickering (2000: 87).

14 Posen (1998).

15 Blinder (1998: 63).

16 See Eijffinger and De Haan (1996: 37-8); Baltensperger (2000).

17 Blinder (1999).
18 Hayo and Hefeker (2002).
19 On financial sector interests, see Posen (1993 and 1995); on low-inflation culture, see Hayo (1998). For a review see Hayo and Hefeker (2002).
20 Posen (1995); Forder (1998).
21 See, for example, Elgie and Thompson (1998), Appendix 1.
22 See Forder (1996); Kirchner (1997, ch. 4); Banaian, Burdekin and Willet (1998); Eijffinger and De Haan (1996).
23 Woolley (1994: 63); Mangano (1998); Posen (1998).
24 Forder (1998: 328; 1996: 50).
25 Eijffinger and De Haan (1996: 22).
26 Lohmann (1998: 443).
27 Blinder (1998: 56); see also Fuhrer (1997); Kirchner (1997: ch. 4).
28 Goodhart (1994: 112).
29 King (2001a).
30 Fraser (1994b: 8).
31 Keating (1989).
32 Fischer (1994: 293).
33 Although there is still no particular reason why a tougher monetary policy response might not have been worked out on a 'partnership' basis.
34 See Goodman (1991); Epstein (1992); Bowles and White (1994).
35 Macfarlane (1996: 32).
36 Epstein (1992: 3).
37 The evidence suggests that the profitability of banks and financial firms is more adversely affected by inflation than the profitability of non-financial firms: see Revell (1979); Boyd et al. (2001). See also Woolley (1985, 338–9); Maxfield (1991, 425); Weintraub (1978).
38 Kelty was on the Board from 1988 to 1996.
39 Hextall and Boyle (2000).
40 Hayo (1998).
41 Epstein (1992: 2).
42 See Bowles and White (1994: 251–2); Dyson, Featherstone and Michalopoulas (1998: 185); Chant and Acheson (1973); Goodfriend (1986).
43 Goodman (1991: 329)
44 On the British case, see Elgie and Thompson (1998: ch. 4).
45 Goodman (1991: 333).
46 Bernhard (2002).
47 Kelly (2000).
48 Elgie and Thompson (1998: 144) argue this was also the case in a comparative analysis of Britain and France.
49 Semler (1994: 50); see also Posen (1993).
50 Garrett (1999); Nevile (2000).
51 Maxfield (1997: 23).
52 Berman and McNamara (1999: 6).
53 Press conference, 14 August 1996.
54 Macfarlane (1996: 36).
55 Grenville (1997: 151).

7 Should the RBA Be Independent?
1 Kelly (2000).
2 *Australian Financial Review,* editorial, 23 May 2000.
3 Kenen (1995); Verdun (1999); Berman and McNamara (1999); Gormley and de Haan (1996); De Haan and Eijffinger (2000).
4 *Australian Financial Review*, editorial, 23 May 2000.
5 See, for example, Pierre and Peters (2000).
6 On the rationales here see Blinder (1996: 10).
7 Blinder (1996: 9).
8 Blinder (1996: 10).
9 Evans (2000: 1).
10 Peters (1996: 6) defines the problem: 'How to structure government in ways that recognize the reality, even the desirability, of a significant policy role for civil servants while simultaneously preserving the requirements of democratic accountability.'
11 The *Australian Financial Review* (23 May 2000) said: 'The RBA has more independence from government than a general.'
12 Verdun (1999: 114).
13 Mahadeva and Sterne (2000: Table 4.6).
14 Blinder (1996: 11–12). His six arguments are conflated to five here.
15 Chant and Acheson (1973); Goodfriend (1986). An earlier Bank of England Governor, Montagu Norman, used to wear a black hat and long cloak and travel under a pseudonym.
16 Carew (1991: 64).
17 Interview, Sydney (September 2001).
18 Coombs (1981: 141).
19 De Haan and Amtenbrink (2000).
20 Fraser (1996: 19).
21 Cf. Section 10 (1).
22 Jonson (1988: 41).
23 Jonson (1988: 41).
24 Blinder (1998: 73).
25 From 1997 the Bank released *Semi-Annual Statements* in May and November to accompany the Governor's appearances before the House Committee, and *The Economy and Financial Markets* in February and August. Since December 2000, *Statements on Monetary Policy* (up to 60 pages long) have been published in the *Reserve Bank of Australia Bulletin* in February, May, August and November.
26 Commonwealth of Australia (2001: 29).
27 *Australian Financial Review,* 9 January 2001.
28 Fraser (1995: 6; 1996: 17).
29 Fraser (1989: 12).
30 Cleary (2000d).
31 Cleary (2000d).
32 Commonwealth of Australia (2000a).
33 Havrilesky (1995).
34 Hendersen (2000a); Hudson (2000).
35 Hendersen (2000c); Hughes (2000). In its *ACCI Review* for December 2000, the Australian Chamber of Commerce and Industry argued: 'The RBA must explain the

basis for its decisions to raise rates, placing these decisions within a comprehensible framework.'

36 See the discussion in Commonwealth of Australia (1999: 43).
37 Cleary (2000); Hudson (2000).
38 Mitchell (2000).
39 Quoted in Hartcher (2001).
40 Mahadeva and Sterne (2000: Table 4.6).
41 *Australian Financial Review* (6 April 2000: 7).
42 Fraser (1993: 5).
43 Koukoulas (2000a).
44 House of Representatives, Standing Committee on Economics, Finance and Public Administration, 22 May 2000: 82.
45 House of Representatives, Standing Committee on Economics, Finance and Public Administration, 1 December 2000: 41.
46 House of Representatives, Standing Committee on Economics, Finance and Public Administration, 1 December 2000: 41.
47 Phone discussion, 14 May 2003.
48 *Australian Financial Review*, 9 January 2001.
49 Written communication, 3 September 2003.
50 House of Representatives, Standing Committee on Economics, Finance and Public Administration, 22 May 2000: 82.
51 Cleary (1999).
52 Stevens (2001).
53 House of Representatives, Standing Committee on Economics, Finance and Public Administration, 22 May 2000: 82–3.
54 Bassanese (2003).
55 House of Representatives, Standing Committee on Economics, Finance and Public Administration, 1 December 2000: 40.
56 House of Representatives, Standing Committee on Economics, Finance and Public Administration, 11 May 2000: 70.
57 Transcript of Press Conference, 29 July 2003.
58 Specifically, by removing the Treasury Secretary from the Bank's Board.
59 See Dryzek (2001).
60 Centeno (1993).
61 Havrilesky (1995a); Broz (2002).
62 Evans (2000: 2).
63 Hibbing and Thiess-Morse (2002); see also Freeman (2002).
64 Interview, Sydney (November 2001).
65 *Australian Financial Review*, 23 May 2000.
66 Commonwealth of Australia (2000a).
67 Havrilesky (1995a).
68 Stiglitz (1998: 200).
69 Blinder (1998: 59–60); Fraser (1996: 19).
70 Fraser (1996: 19, 20).
71 Quoted in Fraser (1989: 9).
72 Blinder (1998a); Business Council of Australia (1999); and for a critique, see Marsh (2002).

73 Commonwealth of Australia (1999: 22). See also Fraser (1999).
74 Macfarlane is quoted in Commonwealth of Australia (1999: 22); Kelly (2000).

8 Internal Governance and the Board

 1 Written communication, 7 July 2003.
 2 Until 2002, there was a 30-year moratorium.
 3 Stevens (2001).
 4 Meetings can be called at other times and Board members consulted by phone.
 5 Interview, Canberra (January 1997).
 6 Interview, Sydney (November 2001).
 7 The change to a nine-member Board came in 1998, following the implementation of certain Wallis enquiry recommendations and the splitting off of prudential responsibilities from the Bank to the Australian Prudential Regulation Authority (APRA).
 8 Interview, Canberra (January 1997).
 9 Interview, Canberra (January 1997).
10 Interview, Canberra (January 1997).
11 Commonwealth of Australia (2003: 59).
12 Interview, Canberra (January 1997).
13 Fraser (1996: 18).
14 Hartcher (2001).
15 Quoted in Wilenski (1986: 213).
16 Interview, Canberra (January 1997).
17 Interview, Sydney (February 1997).
18 Interview, Sydney (August 2001).
19 Interview, Sydney (August 2001).
20 Wood (1995).
21 Interview, Sydney (November 2001).
22 Interview, Sydney (August 2001).
23 Interview, Canberra (January 1997).
24 Fraser (1996: 18).
25 Coombs (1981: 112).
26 Fraser (1996: 18).
27 Quoted in Eichbaum (1999: 309).
28 Interview, Sydney (August 2001).
29 Fraser (1996: 18).
30 See also Eichbaum (1999: 310).
31 Interview, Sydney (February 1997).
32 Interview, Sydney (August 2001).
33 Interview, Canberra (January 1997), emphasis added.
34 See also Eichbaum (1993); Wood (1999).
35 Written communication, 7 July 2003.
36 McCrann (2000); Mellish (2003).
37 Cleary (2001).
38 Interview, Sydney (February 1997).
39 Cole (1990: 6).
40 Quoted in Cleary (1999).

41 Quoted in Cleary (2001).
42 Pagan (2001).
43 Quoted in Cleary (2001).
44 *Commonwealth Parliamentary Debates*, House of Representatives, 2001: 28429.
45 Quoted in Hudson (2000).
46 Interview, Sydney (November 2001).
47 Interview, Sydney (November 2001).
48 Evans (2000).
49 Interview, Sydney (August 2001).
50 Interview, Canberra (January 1997).
51 Interview. Rodney Maddock of the Business Council of Australia (2000) agrees.
52 See the discussion in Eichbaum (1999: 316–19).
53 Evidence before House of Representatives Economics Committee (22 May 2000: 78). For the Treasury Secretary's role on the Board see Eichbaum (1999: 319–25).
54 *Australian Financial Review*, editorial, 12 March 2001.
55 Commonwealth of Australia (2000: 74).
56 Marris (2003).
57 Commonwealth of Australia (2003: 49–50).
58 Commonwealth of Australia (2000a: 30).
59 Wood (2000).
60 Telephone interview, 7 May 2003.
61 Interview, Sydney (August 2001).
62 Interview, Sydney (August 2001).
63 Telephone interview, 7 May 2003.
64 Quoted in Eichbaum (1999: 324).
65 Quoted in Eichbaum (1999: 321).
66 The Secretary can discuss Board meetings with the Treasurer; the secrecy provisions declare only that Board members shall not make 'public' comments.
67 For a broader discussion of Australian perceptions of the New Zealand model, see Eichbaum (1999: 325–32).
68 Weller and Courtis (2000).
69 Quoted in Koutsoukis (2001).
70 Interview, Sydney (August 2001).
71 Campbell Committee (1981: 22).
72 Quoted in Cleary (2001).
73 Commonwealth of Australia (2001: 75).
74 Interview, Sydney (August 2001).

9 New Challenges in a World of Asset Inflation

 1 Interview, Sydney (November 2001).
 2 Goodhart (2000); Goodhart and Krueger (2001).
 3 Macfarlane (1999: Table 1).
 4 Borio and Lowe (2002).
 5 Borio and Lowe (2002); Goodhart (1995).
 6 Crockett (2001).
 7 See also Bell and Pain (2000); Eichengreen and Areta (2000).

 8 BIS (2001: 123).
 9 Borio and Lowe (2002: 11).
10 BIS (2001: 123).
11 BIS (2001: 131).
12 Minsky (1982; 1986).
13 See Schiller (2000).
14 Bell and Quiggin (2004).
15 Borio and Crockett (2000).
16 Brenner (2002).
17 Pollin and Dymski (1994: 373); Warburton (2000).
18 Quoted in *The Economist*, 25 September 1999.
19 Borio et al. (2003: 30).
20 Borio and Lowe (2002: 22).
21 Bean (2003: 2).
22 Alchian and Klein (1973); Goodhart (1999; 2001).
23 Filardo (2000).
24 Bernanke and Gertler (1999); Stevens (2003).
25 Greenspan (2002).
26 Greenspan (2002).
27 Borio et al. (2003: 31).
28 Borio and Lowe (2002).
29 See, for example, Bean (2003); Cecchetti (2003).
30 Stevens (2003: 26).
31 Crockett (2001: 5).
32 Interview, Sydney (November 2001).
33 Borio and Lowe (2002).
34 Borio and Lowe (2002: 24).
35 Borio et al. (2003: 21).
36 Carmichael and Esho (2001).
37 Schwartz (2002).
38 Carmichael and Esho (2001: 16).
39 Macfarlane (2003: 13).
40 Commonwealth of Australia (2003: 48).
41 Commonwealth of Australia (2003: 48, 49).
42 Australian Broadcasting Commission, 7.30 Report, transcript, 4 December 2003.
43 Reserve Bank of Australia (2003: 48).
44 Reserve Bank of Australia (2003: 3).
45 Mitchell (2003).
46 Carmichael and Esho (2001).
47 Borio and Lowe (2003).
48 Interview, Sydney (November 2001).

Conclusion
1   Bell (2002).

References

Akerlof, G., Dickens, W. and Perry, G. (1996) 'The Macroeconomics of Low Inflation', *Brookings Papers on Economic Activity*, No. 1: 1–76.

Alchian, A. and Klein, B. (1973) 'On a Correct Measure of Inflation', *Journal of Money, Credit and Banking*, 5: 173–99.

Alesina, A. (1989) 'Politics and Business Cycles in Industrial Democracies', *Economic Policy*, 8: 55–91.

Alesina, A. and Summers, L. H. (1993) 'Central Bank Independence and Macroeconomic Performance: Some Comparative Evidence', *Journal of Money, Credit and Banking*, 25: 151–62.

Aybar, S. and Harris, L. (1998) 'How Credible are Credibility Models of Central Banking', in Arestis, P. and Sawyer, M. (eds) *The Political Economy of Central Banking*, Edward Elgar, London.

Baltensperger, E. (2000) 'Central Bank Independence and Sacrifice Ratios: Some Further Considerations', *Open Economies Review*, 11: 111–25.

Banaian, K., Burdekin, R., and Willett, T. (1998) 'Reconsidering the Principal Components of Central Bank Independence: The more the merrier?', *Public Choice*, 97, pp. 1–12.

Banaian, K., et al. (1986) 'Central Bank Independence: An International Comparison', in Toma, E. F. and Toma, M. (eds) *Central Bankers, Bureaucratic Incentives, and Monetary Policy*, Academic Publishers, Boston.

Bank of International Settlements (BIS) (2001) *Annual Report*, June, Basle.

Bassanese, D. (2003) 'RBA's Prudent Reaction to Economy's Shifting Sands', *Australian Financial Review*, 3 July.

Battin, T. (1997) *Abandoning Keynes: Australia's Capital Mistake*, Macmillan, London.

Bean, C. (1999) 'Australian Monetary Policy: A Comparative Perspective', *Australian Economic Review*, 32: 64–73.

—— (2003) 'Asset Prices, Financial Imbalances and Monetary Policy: Are Inflation Targets Enough?', Paper to a conference on Asset Prices and Monetary Policy, Reserve Bank of Australia, Sydney, 18–19 August.

Beazley, K. (1963) 'The Labor Party and the Origin of the Commonwealth Bank', *Australian Journal of Politics and History*, IX: 27–38.

Bell, J. and Pain, D. (2000) 'Leading Indicator Models of Banking Crises: A Critical Review', *Financial Stability Review*, Bank of England, December: 113–29.

Bell, S. (1997) *Ungoverning the Economy: The Politics of Australian Economic Policy*, Oxford University Press, Melbourne.

—— (1999) 'The Scourge of Inflation? Unemployment and Orthodox Monetary Policy', *Australian Economic Review*, 32: 74–82.

—— (ed.) (2000) *The Unemployment Crisis in Australia: Which Way Out?*, Cambridge University Press, Melbourne.

—— (2002) 'The Contours and Dynamics of Unemployment', in Saunders, P. and Taylor, R. (eds) *The Price of Prosperity: The Economic and Social Costs of Unemployment*, UNSW Press, Sydney.

—— (2002a) 'The Limits of Rational Choice: New Institutionalism in the Test Bed of Central Banking Politics in Australia', *Political Studies*, 50: 477–96.

Bell, S. and Quiggin, J. (2004) 'Asset Bubbles, Financial Instability and Policy Responses: The Legacy of Liberalisation', mimeo.

Berman, S. and McNamara, K. R. (1999) 'Bank on Democracy: Why Central Banks Need Public Oversight', *Foreign Affairs*, 78: 2–8.

Bernanke, B. and Gertler, M. (1999) 'Monetary Policy and Asset-Price Volatility', Federal Reserve Bank of Kansas Symposium, August.

Bernanke, B., Laubach, F. and Posen, A. (1999) *Inflation Targeting: Lessons From the International Experience*, Princeton University Press, Princeton.

Bernhard, W. (2002) *Banking on Reform*, University of Michigan Press, Ann Arbor.

Blinder, A. (1996) 'Central Banking in a Democracy', Federal Reserve Bank of Richmond, *Economic Quarterly*, 82: 1–14.

—— (1998) *Central Banking in Theory and Practice*, MIT Press, Cambridge, Mass.

—— (1998a) 'Is Government Too Political?', *Foreign Affairs*, 76: 115–26.

—— (1999) 'Central Bank Credibility: Why do we Care? How do we Build it?', *American Economic Review*, 90: 1421–31.

Block, F. (1977) *The Origins of International Economic Disorder*, University of California Press, Berkeley.

—— (1977a) 'The Ruling Class Does Not Rule: Notes on the Marxist Theory of the State', *Socialist Revolution*, No. 7: 6–28.

Bootle, R. (1996) *The Death of Inflation: Surviving and Thriving in the Zero Era*, Nicholas Brealy, London.

Borio, C. and Crockett, A. D. (2000) 'In Search of Anchors for Financial and Monetary Stability', *Greek Economic Review*, 20: 1–14.

Borio, C., English, W. and Filardo, A. (2003) 'A Tale of Two Perspectives: Old or New Challenges for Monetary Policy', BIS Working Paper, No. 127, Bank of International Settlements, February.

Borio, C. and Lowe, P. (2002) 'Asset Prices, Financial and Monetary Stability: Exploring the Nexus', BIS Working Papers, No. 114, Bank of International Settlements.

—— (2003), 'Monetary Policy: A Subtle Paradigm Shift', *World Economics*, 4: 102–19.

Bowles, P. and White, G. (1994) 'Central Bank Independence: A Political Economy Approach', *Journal of Development Studies*, 31: 235–64.

Boyd, J. H., Levine, R. and Smith, B. S. (2001) 'The Impact of Inflation on Financial Sector Performance', *Journal of Monetary Economics*, 47: 221–48.

Brash, D. (1997) 'The New Inflation Target and New Zealanders' Expectations About Inflation and Growth', Address to Canterbury Employers' Chamber of Commerce, Christchurch, 23 January.

Brenner, R. (2002) *The Boom and the Bubble: The United States in the International Economy*, Verso, London.

Broz, J. L. (1998) 'The Origins of Central Banking: Solutions to the Free Rider Problem', *International Organisation*, 52: 231–68.

—— (2002) 'Political System Transparency and Monetary Commitment Regimes', *International Organisation*, 56: 861–87.

Burrell, S. (1990) 'Keating returns RBA's Serve', *Australian Financial Review*, 26 June.

—— (1994) 'Fraser Gets His Way This Time', *Australian Financial Review*, 25 October.

—— (1999) 'Yes, He's the Gov', *Sydney Morning Herald*, 27 November.

Business Council of Australia (1999) *Avoiding Boom/Bust: Macroeconomic Reform for a Globalised Economy*, BCA, Melbourne.

Butlin, S. J. (1983) 'Australian Central Banking 1945–59', *Australian Economic History Review*, 23: 95–192.

Button, J. (1998) *As it Happened*, Text Publishing, Melbourne.

Campbell Committee (1981) *Committee of Inquiry into the Australian Financial System*, Final Report, AGPS, Canberra.

Capie, F., Goodhart, C. and Schnadt, N. (1994) 'The Development of Central Banking', in Capie, F., Goodhart, C., Fischer, S. and Schnadt, N. *The Future of Central Banking*, Cambridge University Press, Cambridge.

Carew, E. (1991) *Fast Money 3*, Allen and Unwin, Sydney.

—— (1992) *Paul Keating: Prime Minister*, Allen and Unwin, Sydney.

Cargill, T. (1995) 'The Statistical Association Between Central Bank Independence and Inflation', *Banco Nazionale del Lavoro Quarterly Review*, 193: 159–72.

Carmichael, J. and Esho, N. (2001) 'Asset Price Bubbles and Prudential Regulation', Australian Prudential Regulation Authority, Working Paper No. 3.

Carroll, V. J. (1993) 'The Invasion of the Money Snatchers', *The Independent Monthly*, September: 26–8.

Cecchetti, S. G. (2003) 'What the FOMC Says and Does When the Stock Market Booms', Paper to a conference on Asset Prices and Monetary Policy, Reserve Bank of Australia, Sydney, 18–19 August.

Centeno, M. A. (1993) 'The New Leviathan: The Dynamics and Limits of Technocracy', *Theory and Society*, 22: 307–35.

Chant, J. and Acheson, K. (1973) 'Mythology and Central Banking', *Kyklos*, 26: 362–79.

Chapman, B. and Kapuscinski, C. A. (2000) 'Avoiding Recessions and Australian Long Term Unemployment', Paper to the CoFeE Conference, University of Newcastle, November 1999.

Chowdhury, A. (2000) 'Dealing With the Inflation Constraint to Growth', in Bell, S. (ed.) *The Unemployment Crisis in Australia: Which Way Out?*, Cambridge University Press, Melbourne.

Cleary, P. (1989) 'High Rates Damage the Economy, Say Leaders', *Sydney Morning Herald*, 17 February.

—— (1990) 'Tight Monetary Policy Under Fire', *Sydney Morning Herald*, 21 June.

—— (1991) 'Reserve has Influence on Interest Rates – PM', *Sydney Morning Herald*, 9 October.

—— (1991a) 'Kerin Defers to Reserve on Rates', *Sydney Morning Herald*, 10 October.

—— (1999) 'The Rise and Rise of the Reserve Bank of Australia', *Australian Financial Review Magazine*, December: 40–50.

—— (2000) 'Lots of Sun but Little Light on RBA Actions', *Australian Financial Review*, 4 February.

—— (2000a) 'RBA Model May Not be Perfect', *Australian Financial Review*, 23 May.
—— (2000b) 'Governor has KO Punch to Loose Fiscal Policy', *Australian Financial Review*, 11 August.
—— (2000c) 'Rates: RBA Warns Costello', *Australian Financial Review*, 11 August.
—— (2000d) '"Novice" Federal MPs Mix it With the RBA', *Australian Financial Review*, 22 May.
—— (2000e) 'MPs attack RBA on Rate Rise', *Australian Financial Review*, 19 May.
—— (2001) 'Rate Split Revealed', *Australian Financial Review*, 8 January.
Cockburn, M. (1990) 'Keating Rules out Fall in Rates', *Sydney Morning Herald*, 18 July.
Cole, W. (1990) 'A More Independent Reserve Bank?', *Economic Witness*, No. 45: 1–8.
Colebatch, T. (2003) 'Reserve Cautious on Raising Rates', *The Age*, 20 August.
Coleman, W. D. (1991) 'Monetary Policy, Accountability and Legitimacy', *Canadian Journal of Political Science*, 24: 711–34.
Coleman, W. (1999) 'A Brief History of the Australian Notes Issue Board, 1920–24', *Cato Journal*, 19: 161–70.
Commonwealth of Australia (1998) House of Representatives Standing Committee on Economics, Finance and Public Administration, Hansard, 15 December.
—— (1999) House of Representatives Standing Committee on Economics, Finance and Public Administration, Hansard, 29 November.
—— (2000) House of Representatives Standing Committee on Economics, Finance and Public Administration, Hansard, 22 May.
—— (2000a) *Review of the Reserve Bank of Australia Annual Report 1998–99*, House of Representatives Standing Committee on Economics, Finance and Public Administration, *Minority Report*, June.
—— (2001) House of Representatives Standing Committee on Economics, Finance and Public Administration, Hansard, 11 May.
—— (2003) House of Representatives Standing Committee on Economics, Finance and Public Administration, Hansard, 6 June.
Coombs, H. C. (1931) 'The Development of the Commonwealth Bank as a Central Bank', MA thesis, University of Western Australia.
—— (1981) *Trial Balance: Issues of My Working Life*, Sun Books, Melbourne.
Cornish, S. (1992) 'The Keynesian Revolution in Australia: Fact or Fiction?', *Working Papers in Economic History*, No. 170, September, Department of Economic History, Australian National University.
Crisp, L. F. (1977) *Ben Chifley: A Political Biography*, Angus and Robertson, Melbourne.
Crockett, A. D. (2001) 'Monetary Policy and Financial Stability', HKMA Distinguished Lecture, 13 February, Hong Kong.
Cukierman, A. (1992) *Central Bank Strategy, Credibility and Independence: Theory and Evidence*, MIT Press, London.
—— (1994) 'Commitment Through Delegation, Political Influence and Central Bank Independence', in de Baufort Winjhold J. A. H. et al. (eds) *A Framework for Monetary Stability*, Kluwer Publishers, Amsterdam.
De Haan, J. and Amtenbrink, F. (2000) 'Democratic Accountability and Central Bank Independence', *West European Politics*, 23; 179–90.
De Haan, J. and Eijffinger, S. (2000) 'The Democratic Accountability of the European Central Bank: A Comment on Two Fairy Tales', *Journal of Common Market Studies*, 38: 393–407.

De Kock, M. H. (1974) *Central Banking*, Crosby, Lockwood, Staples, London.

De Long, J. B. and Summers, L. H. (1992) 'Macroeconomic Policy and Long-Run Growth', *Economic Review (Kansas City)*, 77: 5–26.

Dodson, L. (2000) 'Politics Appears to Rate Above the National Interest', *Australian Financial Review*, 19 May.

Drazen, A. (2001) 'Political Business Cycles After 25 Years', *NBER Macroeconomics Annual* 2000.

Dryzek, J. (2001) 'Legitimacy and Economy in Deliberative Democracy', *Political Theory*, 29: 651–69.

Dyson, K., Featherstone, K. and Michalopoulas, G. (1998) 'Strapped to the Mast: EU Central Bankers Between Global Financial Markets and Regional Integration', in Coleman, W. D. and Underhill, G. R. D. (eds) *Regionalism and Global Economic Integration*, Routledge, London.

Economist (1997) 'Up the NAIRU Without a Paddle', 8 March.

—— (2003) 'Economics Focus: Still Bubbling', 18 January.

Edwards, J. (1985) 'The Secret World of Our New Economic Powerbrokers', *Bulletin*, 23 April, pp. 64–75.

—— (1996) *Keating: The Inside Story*, Penguin Books, Ringwood, Vic.

Eichbaum, C. (1993) 'Challenging the Intellectual Climate of the Times: Why the Reserve Bank of Australia is Too Independent', *Economic Papers*, 12: 1–17.

—— (1999) 'Reshaping the Reserve: The Political Economy of Central Banking in Australasia', PhD dissertation, Massey University, New Zealand.

Eichengreen, B. and Areta, C. (2000) 'Banking Crises in Emerging Markets: Presumptions and Evidence', Centre for International Economic Development Economics Research, Working Paper Coo-115, August.

Eichengreen, Barry, and Bordo, Michael D. (2002) 'Crises Now and Then: What Lessons from the Last Era of Financial Globalization', NBER Working Paper No. 8716.

Eijffinger, S. and De Haan, J. (1996) 'The Political Economy of Central Bank Independence', *Princeton Studies in International Economics*, No. 19, May.

Eisner, R. (1995) 'Our NAIRU Limit', *The American Prospect*, Spring: 58–63.

Elgie, R. and Thompson, H. (1998) *The Politics of Central Banks,* Routledge, London.

Epstein, G. (1992) 'Political Economy and Comparative Central Banking', *Review of Radical Political Economics*, 24: 1–30.

Evans, T. (2000) 'Some Aspects of Economic Governance', Address to the Sydney Institute, Sydney, 14 March.

Filardo, A. (2000) 'Monetary Policy and Asset Prices', *Economic Review*, Federal Reserve Bank of Kansas City, 85: 11–37.

Fischer, C. and Kent, C. (1999) 'Two Depressions, One Banking Collapse', *Research Discussion Paper*: 99–106, Reserve Bank of Australia.

Fischer, S. (1994) 'Modern Central Banking', in Capie, F., Goodhart, C. and Schadt, N. (eds) *The Future of Central Banking*, Cambridge University Press, Cambridge.

Fitzpatrick, B. (1969) *The British Empire in Australia: 1834–1939*, Macmillan, Melbourne.

Forder, J. (1996) 'On the Assessment and Implementation of "Institutional" Remedies', *Oxford Economic Papers*, 48: 39–51.

—— (1998) 'Central Bank Independence – Conceptual Clarifications and Interim Assessment', *Oxford Economic Papers*, 50: 307–34.

—— (1999) 'Central Bank Independence: Reassessing the Measurements', *Journal of Economic Issues*, 33: 23–40.

Fortin, F. (1993) 'The Unbearable Lightness of Zero-Inflation Optimism', *Canadian Business Economics*, 1: 3–18.

—— (2001) 'Inflation Targeting: The Three Percent Solution', *Policy Matters*, 2 (1).

Fraser, B. W. (1984) 'The Treasury Tendering Economic Advice', *Canberra Bulletin of Public Administration*, 11: 230–3.

—— (1989) 'Reserve Bank Independence and All That', *Reserve Bank of Australia Bulletin*, December: 8–13.

—— (1990) 'Understanding Australia's Foreign Debt and the Solutions', *Reserve Bank of Australia Bulletin*, August: 9–15.

—— (1990a) 'Inflation', *Reserve Bank of Australia Bulletin*, May: 18–26.

—— (1990b) 'A Proper Role for Monetary Policy', Address to the AGM Dinner of the Committee for Economic Development of Australia, Melbourne, 28 November.

—— (1991) 'Some Observations on the Role of the Reserve Bank', *Reserve Bank of Australia Bulletin*, December: 8–13.

—— (1992) 'Two Perspectives on Monetary Policy', *Reserve Bank of Australia Bulletin*, September: 1–8.

—— (1993) 'Some Aspects of Monetary Policy', *Reserve Bank of Australia Bulletin*, April: 1–7.

—— (1994) 'Managing the Recovery', *Reserve Bank of Australia Bulletin*, April: 20–8.

—— (1994a) 'The Art of Monetary Policy', *Reserve Bank of Australia Bulletin*, October: 17–25.

—— (1994b) 'Central Bank Independence: What Does it Mean?', *Reserve Bank of Australia Bulletin*, December: 1–8.

—— (1995) 'Governor's Statement to House of Representatives Standing Committee', *Reserve Bank of Australia Bulletin*, November: 6–8.

—— (1996) 'Reserve Bank Independence', *Reserve Bank of Australia Bulletin*, September: 14–20.

—— (1999) 'Restore Fiscal Policy Tool Kit', *Australian Financial Review*, 8 December.

Freeman, J. (2002) 'Competing Commitments: Technocracy and Democracy in the Design of Monetary Institutions', *International Organisation*, 56: 889–910.

Friedman, M. (1968) 'The Role of Monetary Policy', *American Economic Review*, 58: 1–17.

Fuhrer, J. (1997) 'Central Bank Independence and Inflation Targeting: Monetary Policy Paradigms for the Next Millennium', *New England Economic Review*, January–February: 19–36.

Galbraith, J. K. (1997) 'Time to Ditch the NAIRU', *Journal of Economic Perspectives*, 11: 93–108.

Garrett, G. (1999) 'Global Markets and National Politics: Collision Course or Virtuous Circle?' in Giblin, L. (1951) *The Growth of a Central Bank*, Melbourne University Press, Melbourne.

Giblin, L. (1951) *The Growth of a Central Bank*, Melbourne University Press, Melbourne.

Gittins, R. (1988) 'Reserved Bank Should be Less So', *Sydney Morning Herald*, 1 August.

—— (1990) 'Shock and Horror from the Reserve', *Sydney Morning Herald*, 25 June.

—— (1990a) 'Beating Inflation: The Reserve's Real Views', *Sydney Morning Herald*, 9 July.

Glynn, A. (1992) 'Exchange Controls and Policy Autonomy: The Case of Australia, 1983–1988', in Banuri, T. and Schor, J. B. (eds) *Financial Openness and National Autonomy*, Clarendon Press, Oxford.

Gollan, R. (1968) *The Commonwealth Bank of Australia: Origins and Early History*, ANU Press, Canberra.

Goodfriend, M. (1986) 'Monetary Mystique: Secrecy and Central Banking', *Journal of Monetary Economics*, 17: 63–92.

Goodhart, C. (1994) 'Game Theory for Central Bankers: A Report to the Governor of the Bank of England', *Journal of Economic Literature*, 32: 101–14.

—— (1999) 'Time, Inflation and Asset Prices', Eurostat Conference, August.

—— (2001) 'What Weight Should be Given to Asset Prices in the Measurement of Inflation?', DNB Staff Papers, No. 65.

Goodhart, C. A. E. (1990) *The Development of Central Banks*, MIT Press, London.

—— (1992) 'The Objectives for and Conduct of Monetary Policy in the 1990s', in Blundell-Wignall, A. (ed.) *Inflation, Disinflation and Monetary Policy*, Reserve Bank, Sydney.

—— (1995) *The Central Bank and the Financial System*, Macmillan, London.

—— (2000) 'Can Central Banking Survive the IT Revolution?', Financial Markets Group, Bank of England, Special Paper 125, August.

Goodhart, C. A. E. and Krueger, M. (2001) 'The Impact of Technology on Cash Usage', Financial Markets Group, Bank of England, Discussion Paper 374, April.

Goodman, J. (1991) 'The Politics of Central Bank Independence', *Comparative Politics*, 23: 329–49.

Gormley, L. and De Haan, J. (1996) 'The Democratic Deficit of the European Central Bank', *European Law Review*, April: 95–112.

Gowa, J. (1984) 'State Power, State Policy: Explaining the Decision to Close the Gold Window', *Politics and Society*, 13: 91–117.

Grattan, M. (2000) 'PM Anything But Reserved', *Sydney Morning Herald*, 19 May.

Grattan, M. and Walker, D. (1993) 'Keating Promises a More Open Reserve Bank', *The Age*, 12 March.

Greenspan, A. (2002) 'Economic Volatility', Remarks by Chairman Greenspan, Federal Reserve Bank of Kansas Symposium, Jackson Hole, Wyoming, 30 August.

Gregory, B. (1992) 'Comments on Professor Schedvin', *Economic Papers*, 11: 12–16.

Grenville, S. (1990) 'The Operation of Monetary Policy', *Australian Economic Review*, 2nd Quarter: 6–16.

—— (1996) 'Recent Development in Monetary Policy: Australia and Abroad,' *Australian Economic Review*, 1st Quarter: 29–39.

—— (1997) 'The Evolution of Monetary Policy: From Money Targets to Inflation Targets', in Lowe, P. (ed) *Monetary Policy and Inflation Targeting*, Reserve Bank, Sydney.

—— (1999a) 'Financial Crises and Globalisation', *Reserve Bank of Australia Bulletin*, August: 43–54.

—— (1999b) 'The International Reform Agenda: Unfinished Business', *Reserve Bank of Australia Bulletin*, December: 6–14.

—— (2001) 'Monetary Policy: The End of History?', *Central Banking*, 12: 38–42.

Grilli, V., Masciandero, D. and Tabellini, G. (1991) 'Political and Monetary Institutions and Public Financial Policies in the Industrialised Countries', *Economic Policy* 13: 342–92.

Guttmann, S. (2003) *The Rise and Fall of Monetary Targeting in Australia*, PhD thesis, Monash University, Victoria.

Hall, P. A. and Franzese, R. J. (1998) 'Mixed Signals: Central Bank Independence, Coordinated Wage Bargaining and European Monetary Union', *International Organisation*, 52: 505–35.

Harper, I. (1988) 'Monetary Policy in a Deregulated Financial System', *Australian Economic Review*, 4th Quarter: 58–63.

Hartcher, P. (2001) 'The Interesting Times of Ian Macfarlane', *Australian Financial Review Magazine*, 30 March.

Havrilesky, T. (1995) *The Pressures on American Monetary Policy*, Kluwer, Norwell, MA.

—— (1995a) 'Restructuring the Fed', *Journal of Economics and Business*, 47: 95–111.

Hayo, B. (1998) 'Inflation Culture, Central Bank Independence and Price Stability', *European Journal of Political Economy*, 14: 241–63.

Hayo, B. and Hefeker, C. (2002) 'Reconsidering Central Bank Independence', *European Journal of Political Economy*, 18: 653–74.

Heilbroner, R. L. (1979) 'Inflationary Capitalism', *New Yorker*, 8 October.

Hendersen, I. (2000) 'You Did it, You Explain it, Howard Urges Macfarlane', *The Australian*, 4 March.

—— (2000a) 'PM Passes the Buck to the RBA', *The Australian*, 24 March.

—— (2000b) 'RBA Blames Howard for Dollar's Fall', *The Australian*, 6–7 May.

—— (2000c) 'Economists Give PM Credit for TV Idea', *The Australian*, 25 March.

Hewson, J. (1980) 'How Much Independence for the Reserve Bank?', *Economic Papers*, No. 63.

Hextall, B. and Boyle, J. (2000) 'Manufacturers Lament Rate Rise', *Australian Financial Review*, 6 April.

Hibbing, J. R. and Thiess-Morse, E. (2002) *Stealth Democracy: Americans' Beliefs about How Democracy Should Work*, Cambridge University Press, New York.

Hirsch, F. (1978) 'The Ideological Underlay of Inflation', in Hirsch, F. and Goldthorpe, J. (eds) *The Political Economy of Inflation*, Martin Robertson, London.

Hudson, P. (2000) 'Face Music on Rates, RBA Chief Urged', *The Age*, 25 March.

Hughes, B. (1980) *Exit Full Employment*, Angus and Robertson, Sydney.

—— (1997) 'Discussion', in Lowe, P. (ed.) *Monetary Policy and Inflation Targeting*, Reserve Bank, Sydney.

Hughes, T. (2000) 'Would it Help if the Bank Wasn't So Secretive?', *Courier Mail*, 12 February.

Iverson, T. (1999) *Contested Economic Institutions: The Politics of Macroeconomics and Wage Bargaining in Advanced Democracies*, Cambridge University Press, Melbourne.

Johnston, R. A. (1987) 'Monetary Policy – The Lessons of History', *Reserve Bank Bulletin*, September: 1–10.

—— (1989) 'Doing it My Way: Some Reflections of a Retiring Governor', *Reserve Bank Bulletin*, August: 15–19.

Jones, E. (1983) 'Monetarism in Practice', *Australian Quarterly*, 44: 433–45.

—— (2001) 'The Industrial Finance Department: An Australian Experiment with Small Business Finance', *Australian Economic History Review*, 41: 176–97.

Jonson, P. D. (1988) 'Reflections on Central Banking', *Quadrant*, December: 36–44.

—— (1990) 'Inflation: Its Costs, Its Causes and Its Cure', *Policy*, Winter: 2–8.

Kaldor, N. (1982) *The Scourge of Monetarism*, Oxford University Press, Oxford.

Kahneman, D., Knetsch, J. L. and Thaler, R. H. (1990) 'Experimental tests of the Endowment Effect and the Coase Theorem', *Journal of Political Economy*, 98: 1325.

Kalecki, M. (1943) 'Political Aspects of Full Employment', *Political Quarterly*, 14: 322–31.

Kane, E. J. (1988) 'Fedbashing and the Role of Monetary Arrangements in Managing Political Stress', in Willet, T. D. (ed.) *Political Business Cycles: The Political Economy of Money, Inflation and Unemployment*, Duke University Press, Durham, NC.

Keating, M. and Dixon, P. (1989) *Making Economic Policy in Australia, 1983–88*, Longman, Melbourne.

Keating, P. (1989) 'The Reserve Bank: Let the Parliament Rule', *Sydney Morning Herald*, 22 September.

—— (1991) 'Rigid Monetary Control of Inflation Threatens a Backlash', *Sydney Morning Herald*, 13 August.

Kelly, P. (1992) *The End of Certainty*, Allen and Unwin, Sydney.

—— (2000) 'The Reserve Can Bank on Independence', *The Australian*, 16 August.

Kenen, P. (1995) *Economic and Monetary Union in Europe: Moving Beyond Maastricht*, Cambridge University Press, Cambridge.

King, M. (2001) 'Contrasting Approaches to Central Bank Independence: Australia and New Zealand', *Central Banking*, XII: 58–68.

—— (2001a) 'The Politics of Central Bank Independence', *Central Banking*, XI: 50–7.

Kirchner, S. (1997) *Reforming Central Banking*. Sydney: Centre for Independent Studies, Policy Monograph 36.

Kitney, G. (1996) 'Costello Gets a Lesson in Independence', *Sydney Morning Herald*, 1 August.

Korporaal, G. (1993) 'A Power Surge', *Australian Financial Review*, 10 August.

Koukoulas, S. (2000) 'Macfarlane's Chance to End RBA Silence', *Australian Financial Review*, 26 April.

—— (2000a) 'Room for RBA Improvements', *Australian Financial Review*, 17 July.

Koutsoukis, J. (2001) 'No Problems With RBA Board: Costello', *Australian Financial Review*, 9 January.

Kydland, F. and Prescott, E. (1977) 'Rules Rather than Discretion: The Inconsistency of Optimal Plans', *Journal of Political Economy*, 85: 473–91.

Leertouwer, E. and Maier, P. (2001) 'Who Creates Political Business Cycles: Should Central Banks be Blamed?', *European Journal of Political Economy*, 17: 443–63.

Lohmann, S. (1998) 'Federalism and Central Bank Independence: The Politics of German Monetary Policy, 1957–92', *World Politics*, 50: 401–46.

Love, D. (2001) *Straw Polls, Paper Money*, Viking, Melbourne.

Love, P. (1984) *Labor and the Money Power: Australian Labor Populism, 1890–1950*, Melbourne University Press, Melbourne.

Lowe, P. (1995) 'The Link Between the Cash Rate and Market Interest Rates', *Research Discussion Paper*, 9504, Reserve Bank of Australia, Sydney.

Macfarlane, I. (1999) 'The Stability of the Financial System', *Reserve Bank of Australia Bulletin*, August: 34–42.

Macfarlane, I. J. (1991) 'The Lessons for Monetary Policy', in Macfarlane, I. J. (ed.) *The Deregulation of Financial Intermediaries*, Reserve Bank of Australia, Sydney.

—— (1992) 'Making Monetary Policy in an Uncertain World', *Reserve Bank of Australia Bulletin*, September: 9–16.

—— (1992a) 'The Structural Adjustment to Low Inflation', *Reserve Bank of Australia Bulletin*, June: 1–5.

—— (1996) 'Making Monetary Policy: Perceptions and Reality', *Reserve Bank of Australia Bulletin*, October: 32–37.

—— (1997a) 'The Economics of Nostalgia', *Reserve Bank of Australia Bulletin*, March: 1–7.

—— (1998) 'Australian Monetary Policy in the Last Quarter of the Twentieth Century', *Reserve Bank of Australia Bulletin*, October: 6–17.

—— (1999) 'The Stability of the Financial System', *Reserve Bank of Australia Bulletin*, August: 34–42.

—— (2000) 'A Medium-term Perspective on Monetary Policy', *Reserve Bank of Australia Bulletin*, September: 1–3.

—— (2003) 'Do Australian Households Borrow too Much?', *Reserve Bank of Australia Bulletin*, April: 7–17.

MacLaury, B. K. (1994) 'The Fed: Reconciling Autonomy and Democracy', in Colander, D. C. and Daane, J. D. (eds) *The Art of Monetary Policy*, M. E. Sharpe, New York.

Mahadeva, L. and Sterne G. (2000) *Monetary Policy Frameworks in a Global Context*, Routledge, London.

Maley, K. (1994) 'Treasury Losing Ground to Reserve', *Sydney Morning Herald*, 17 September.

Malkiel, B. (2003) 'The Efficient Market Hypothesis and its Critics', *Journal of Economic Perspectives*, 17: 59.

Maloney, J. and Pickering, A. (2000) 'A Case of Wrongful Dismissal', *Central Banking*, XI: 86–9.

Mangano, G. (1998) 'Measuring Central Bank Independence: A Tale of Subjectivity and its Consequences', *Oxford Economic Papers*, 50: 468–92.

Marr, D. (1983) 'The Nation's Sock', *National Times*, 1 January.

Marris, S. (2001) 'PM Blames Bank Chiefs for Slump', *The Australian*, 8 March.

—— (2003) 'Interest Rate Cut Likely', *The Australian*, 5 August.

Marsh, I. (2002) 'Governance Beyond Government: Is There a Role for Independent Policy Institutions?' in Bell, S. (ed.) *The Institutional Dynamics of Australian Economic Governance*, Oxford University Press, Melbourne.

Maxfield, S. (1991) 'Bankers Alliances and Economic Policy Patterns: Evidence from Mexico and Brazil', *Comparative Political Studies*, 24: 419–58.

—— (1997) *Gatekeepers of Growth: The International Political Economy of Central Banking in Developing Countries*, Princeton University Press, Princeton.

May, A. L. (1968) *The Battle for the Banks*, Sydney University Press, Sydney.

McCallum, B. (1995) 'Two Fallacies Concerning Central Bank Independence', *American Economic Review*, 82: 273–86.

McCallum, B. T. (2000) 'The Present and Future of Monetary Policy Rules', *International Finance*, 3: 272–87.

McCrann, T. (2000) 'Interesting Times When Treasury and the Reserve Disagree', *The Australian*, 19–20 August.

Mellish, M. (2003) 'Board Games; Political Power versus the Public Interest', *The Australian Financial Review*, 4 August.

—— (2003a) 'Board Split on Cutting Rates, But That's Not Unusual', *Australian Financial Review*, 9 June.

Minsky, H. (1982) *Can 'It' Happen Again?*, M. E. Sharpe, New York.

—— (1986) *Stabilising an Unstable Economy*, Yale University Press, New Haven.

Mitchell, A. (2000) 'RBA Needs More Than a Minute's Thought', *Australian Financial Review*, 12 April.

—— (2003) 'Reserved Bubble-Blowing', *Australian Financial Review*, 20 August.

Mitchell, W. and Carlson, E. (eds) (2002) *Unemployment: The Tip of the Iceberg*, Centre for Applied Economic Research, University of New South Wales, Sydney.

Moore, D. (1992) 'Can Monetary Policy be Made to Work?', in Moore, D. (ed.) *Can Monetary Policy be Made to Work?*, Institute of Public Affairs, Melbourne.

Nevile, J. (2000) 'Can Keynesian Policy Stimulate Jobs and Growth?', in Bell, S. (ed.) *The Unemployment Crisis in Australia: Which Way Out?*, Cambridge University Press, Melbourne.

North, D. C. (1990) *Institutions, Institutional Change and Economic Performance*, Cambridge University Press, Cambridge.

Pagan, A. (2001) 'Bring on the Fresh Reserve', *Daily Telegraph*, 9 January.

Pauly, L. (1988) *Opening Financial Markets: Banking Politics on the Pacific Rim*, Cornell University Press, Ithaca.

Persson, T. and Tabellini, G. (1990) *Macroeconomic Policy, Credibility and Politics*, Harwood Academic Publishers, New York.

Peters, G. B. (1996) *The Future of Governing: Four Emerging Models*, University of Kansas Press, Lawrence.

Phillips, M. J. (1990) 'When the Music Stops', *Reserve Bank of Australia Bulletin*, July: 14–18.

—— (1992) 'Central Banking: A Parting View', *Reserve Bank of Australia Bulletin*, April: 14–19.

—— (1993) 'What Price Money?', *Collected Speeches*, Reserve Bank of Australia, Sydney.

Pierre, J. and Peters, G. (2000) *Governance, Politics and the State*, Macmillan, London.

Pitchford, J. (1989) 'A Sceptical View of Australia's Current Account and Debt Problem', *Australian Economic Review*, 2nd Quarter: 5–13.

Pollin, R. and Dymski, G. (1994) 'The Costs and Benefits of Financial Instability: Big Government Capitalism and the Minsky Paradox', in Dymski, G. and Pollin, R. (eds) *New Perspectives in Monetary Macroeconomics*, Michigan University Press, Ann Arbor.

Posen, A. (1993) 'Why Central Bank Independence Does Not Cause Low Inflation: There is No Institutional Fix for Politics', in O'Brien, R. (ed.) *Finance and the International Economy 7*, Oxford University Press, Oxford.

—— (1995) 'Declarations are not Enough: Financial Sector Sources of Central Bank Independence', *NBER Macroeconomics Annual*, Cambridge, Mass.

—— (1998) 'Central Bank Independence and Disinflationary Credibility: A Missing Link?', *Oxford Economic Papers*, 50: 335–59.

Quiggin, J. (1997) 'The Welfare Effects of Alternative Choices of Instruments and Targets for Macroeconomic Stabilisation', in Lowe, P. (ed.) *Monetary Policy and Inflation Targeting*, Reserve Bank, Sydney.

Reserve Bank of Australia (1979) 'Submission to the Committee of Inquiry into the Australian Financial System', RBA Occasional Paper, No. 7, Reserve Bank, Sydney.
—— (1993) 'The Separation of Debt Management and Monetary Management', *Reserve Bank Bulletin*, November: 1–5.
—— (1993a) *Towards Full Employment*, Occasional Paper No. 12, Reserve Bank of Australia, Sydney.
—— (1996) 'Statement on the Conduct of Monetary Policy', *Reserve Bank Bulletin*, September: 1–3.
—— (2000) 'Semi-Annual Statement on the Conduct of Monetary Policy', *Reserve Bank of Australia Bulletin*, May.
—— (2003) 'Statement on the Conduct of Monetary Policy', *Reserve Bank of Australia Bulletin*, November.
Revell, J. (1979) *Inflation and Financial Institutions*, Financial Times, London.
Rowse, T. (2002) *Nugget Coombs: A Reforming Life*, Cambridge University Press, Melbourne.
Schedvin, C. B. (1992) *In Reserve: Central Banking in Australia, 1945–75*, Allen & Unwin, St Leonards, NSW.
Schiller, R. (2000) *Irrational Exuberance*, Princeton University Press, Princeton.
—— (2003) 'From Efficient Markets Theory to Behavioural Finance', *Journal of Economic Perspectives*, 17: 59.
Schiller, R. J. (1989) *Market Volatility*, MIT Press, Cambridge, Mass., and London.
Schwartz, A. (2002) 'Asset Price Inflation and Monetary Policy', NBER Working Paper 9321.
Semler, D. (1994) 'Focus: The Politics of Central Banking', *East European Constitutional Review*, 3: 48–52.
Singleton, G. (1990) *The Accord and the Australian Labor Movement*, Melbourne University Press, Melbourne.
Solow, R. M. (1998) 'How Cautious Must the Fed Be?', in Freidman, B. (ed.) *Inflation, Unemployment and Monetary Policy*, MIT Press, Cambridge, Mass.
Stevens, G. (1999) 'Six Years of Inflation Targeting', *Reserve Bank Bulletin*, May: 46–61.
—— (2001) 'The Monetary Policy Process at the RBA', *Reserve Bank of Australia Bulletin*, October: 19–26.
—— (2003) 'Inflation Targeting: A Decade of Australian Experience', *Reserve Bank of Australia Bulletin*, April: 17–27.
Stiglitz, J. (1997) 'Reflections of the Natural Rate Hypothesis', *Journal of Economic Perspectives*, 11: 3–10.
—— (1998) 'Central Banking in a Democratic Society', *Economist*, 146: 199–226.
Stilwell, F. (1986) *The Accord and Beyond*, Pluto Press, Sydney.
Stutchbury, M. (1989) 'Economists Desert Tight Keating Policy', *Australian Financial Review*, 17 July.
—— (1989a) 'Bernie Fraser Straddles Credibility Gap in his Quest to Quell Inflation', *Australian Financial Review*, 19 July.
Suich, M. (1991) 'Bankrupted', *The Independent Monthly*, May: 15–17.
Temple, J. (1998) 'Central Bank Independence and Inflation: God News and Bad News', *Economics Letters*, 61: 215–19.
Thurow, L. C. (1996) *The Future of Capitalism*, Allen and Unwin, Sydney.

Tingle, L. (1991) 'Labor's Secret Battle Over Interest Rates', *The Australian*, 8 October.

—— (1994) *Chasing the Future: Recession, Recovery and the New Politics in Australia*, William Heinnemann, Melbourne.

Treasury (1981) Submission to the Committee of Inquiry into the Australian Financial System, Treasury Economic Paper, No. 9, AGPS, Canberra.

Verdun, A. (1999) 'The Institutional Design of the EMU: A Democratic Deficit', *Journal of Public Policy*, 18: 107–132.

Victoria Chamber of Manufactures (1977) '1977 – Crucial Time for Manufacturing', *VCM File*, 22, 28 January.

Wallace, C. (1993) *Hewson: A Portrait*, Macmillan, Melbourne.

Walsh, M. (1989) 'Nightmare of Free Central Bank', *Sydney Morning Herald*, 14 September.

—— (1989a) 'Fraser is Fine Fellow, But Not a Man to Bank On', *Sydney Morning Herald*, 29 June.

Warburton, P. (2000) *Debt and Delusion: Central Bank Follies That Threaten Economic Disaster*, London.

Watson, D. (2002) *Recollections of a Bleeding Heart: A Portrait of Paul Keating*, Random House, Sydney.

Weintraub, S. (1978) 'Wall Street's Mindless Affair with Tight Money', *Challenge* 20: 34–9.

Weller, B. and Courtis, N. (1999–2000) 'Governor's Power Diluted', *Central Banking*, 10: 29–33.

Weller, P. (1989) *Malcolm Fraser PM: A Study in Prime Ministerial Power*, Penguin Books, Ringwood, Vic.

White, G. (1992) 'Monetary Policy in the 1980s', in Moore, D. (ed.) *Can Monetary Policy be Made to Work?* Institute of Public Affairs, Melbourne.

Whitwell, G. (1986) *The Treasury Line*, Allen & Unwin, Sydney.

—— (1994) 'The Power of Economic Ideas: Keynesian Economic Policies in Post-War Australia', in Bell, S. and Head, B. (eds) *State, Economy and Public Policy in Australia*, Oxford University Press, Melbourne.

Wilenski, P (1986) *Public Power and Public Administration*, Hale & Iremonger, Sydney.

Wood, A. (1992) 'Commentary', in Moore, D. (ed.) *Can Monetary Policy be Made to Work?*, Institute of Public Affairs, Melbourne.

—— (1995) 'Fraser Draws his Sword as Massacred Ministers Attack Bank's Freedom', *The Australian*, 31 March.

—— (1995a) 'Why Interest Rates Should Not be Cut', *The Australian*, 10 October.

—— (1996) 'An Inflated Sense of Purpose', *The Australian*, 17–18 August.

—— (1999) 'Many Hands on the Purse Strings', *The Australian*, 23 November.

—— (2000) 'Row Taken on Board', *The Australian*, 30 May.

—— (2000a) 'Rate Rise is RBA's Declaration of Independence', *The Australian*, 5 February.

Woolley, J. T. (1985) 'Central Banks and Inflation', in Lindberg, L. and Maier, C. S. (eds) *The Politics of Inflation and Economic Stagnation*, Brookings Institution, Washington.

—— (1994) 'The Politics of Monetary Policy: A Critical Review', *Journal of Public Policy*, 14: 57–85.

Index

.